U.S. Military Involvement
In
Southern Africa

U.S. MILITARY INVOLVEMENT IN SOUTHERN AFRICA

Edited by
Western Massachusetts
Association of Concerned African Scholars

SOUTH END PRESS   BOSTON

Preface

This book is the result of the collective effort of a group of scholars who met together for a weekend in Amherst, Massachusetts in April 1978, to compile their individual researches on U.S. military involvement in southern Africa. The conference was jointly sponsored by the western Massachusetts Valley branch of the Association of Concerned African Scholars (ACAS)* and several students and faculty groups based in the five colleges in the Connecticut Valley.

The urgency of the project was underscored by the fact that the United States government had voted with the United Nations a few months earlier to impose a mandatory embargo on arms shipments to South Africa. Evidence of violations had already appeared, indicating that further measures were required to halt the on-going contribution of United States interests to South Africa's military-industrial build-up.

It is perhaps worth describing briefly the way the group worked together, for it may provide a model for similar future collective efforts of concerned scholars. The project was initiated by members of the ACAS research committee who were convinced that, although a number of individual scholars were pursuing important lines of research, it was essential to pull together the bits and pieces of evidence they were gathering to delineate the overall implications of United States military involvement in southern Africa. Individuals were therefore invited to present their findings to the group at the Amherst conference. Two students were assigned to work with each scholar. The students' task was to read extensively on the background of the topic covered by each scholar to whom they were assigned; to discuss the topic in depth with him or her; and to help incorporate the results of the general discussions of the conference into the appropriate chapters. This enabled the students to utilize their research for an immediately relevant project, deepening their understanding of the issues by working directly with experts in the field. At the same time, their contribution helped to bring the research results together in time for early publication. The scholars' discussions helped further the overall analysis of the relationship of United States military involvement in the southern African crisis to the overall international crisis confronting the major capitalist powers.

In short, the project provided a framework in which the participants, while remaining responsible for the integrity of their own work, could bring their disparate researches together into a cohesive whole.

The conference organizers wish to express sincere appreciation to all who participated in making the conference and the publication of this book possible. There is not space here to detail the contribution of all who took part. We wish, however, to thank the following in particular for their generous contributions to the expenses of the conference and publication:

Afro-American Association, University of Massachusetts
American Friends Service Committee, Northampton
The Association of African Scholars of Massachusetts
Committee for the Liberation of South Africa,
    University of Massachusetts

Five College Black Studies Executive Committee
Five College Faculty Lecture Series
Hampshire College
International Student Association, University
  of Massachusetts
Student Organizing Project, University of Massachusetts

Our thanks, too, to Francis Crowe and all those who provided
the hospitality which made the participants' stay in the Valley so
pleasant.

The Massachusetts ACAS Editorial Committee:

From University of Massachusetts-Amherst

Dovi Afesi	Garry Heiney
Ingrid Babbs	Tahir Iqbal(also of Sussex U.)
Timothy Belcher	Jim Jordan
David Brenner	Lisa Melilli
Ronald Corriveau	Timberly Otto
Kevin Crocker	Ann Seidman
Fred Curtis	Jane Vella
Ray Gutko	

From Harvard University:	From Clark University:
Neva Makgetla	Amy Novak
Cindy Ruskin	Philip O'Keefe
Gay Seidman	Nicholas Robbins(also of Sussex U.)

From Amherst College:	From Mt. Holyoke College:
Paul Klemperer	Thomasina Williams

* The Association of Concerned African Scholars (ACAS) was formed in 1978, under the co-chairmanship of Professors James Turner and Emmanuel Wallerstein. According to its statement of principles, it aims to bring together "scholars interested in Africa and concerned with moving U.S. policy toward Africa in directions more sympathetic to African interests."

Contents

Preface   v
List of Abbreviations   xi
List of Charts and Illustrations   xii

PART I   THE CRISIS IN SOUTHERN AFRICA   1
Chapter 1   The Crisis in Southern Africa   3
  by Western Mass. Editorial Collective
Chapter 2   The Roots of the Crisis   18
  by Dovi Afesi
PART II   WESTERN STRATEGY
IN SOUTHERN AFRICA   37
Chapter 4   Western Strategy in Southern Africa 39
  by Courtland Cox
Chapter 4   Sealanes, Western Strategy
and Southern Africa   58
  by John Prados
Chapter 5   Covert Operations
in Central and Southern Africa   82
  by James Dingeman
Chapter 6   Mercenarization   109
  by Cynthia Enloe

PART III   THE U.S. CONTRIBUTION TO
THE SOUTH AFRICAN MILITARY BUILD-UP   131

    Chapter 7   Breakdown of the U.S. Arms Embargo   133
      by Sean Gervasi

    Chapter 8   Evading the Embargo: How the U.S. Arms
    South Africa and Rhodesia   157
      by Michael Klare and Eric Prokosch

    Chapter 9   U.S. Policy and Nuclear Proliferation
    in South Africa   172
      by Ronald W. Walters

    Chapter 10   U.S. Transnational Corporations' Involvement
    in South Africa's Military-Industrial Complex   197
      by Neva Seidman Makgetla and Ann Seidman

    Chapter 11   Observation of the U.S. Arms Embargo   221
      by Robert Sylvester

    Chapter 12   Postscript: What Needs to be Done?   244

Appendices:
    A. An Outline for Further Research   249
    B. The U.N. Embargo Resolutions   253
    C. Letter from the Chairpersons of ACAS
    to President Carter   256
    D. General Motors South Africa
    Contingency Planning Report   259

Bibliography   263
Index   267
Contributors   275

List of Abbreviations

ANC (S.A.)	African National Congress of South Africa
BOSS	Bureau of State Security (South Africa)
CIA	Central Intelligence Agency (U.S.)
DGS	Directorate of General Security (Portugal before 1974)
ESCOM	Electricity Supply Commission (South Africa)
FNLA	Front for the Liberation of Angola
FRELIMO	Front for the Liberation of Mozambique
FRG	Federal Republic of Germany (West Germany)
G.E.	General Electric (U.S.)
G.M.	General Motors (U.S.)
GMSA	General Motors South African
IBM	International Business Machines (U S.)
IISS	International Institute for Strategic Studies (Britain)
ISCOR	Iron and Steel Corporation (South Africa)
ITT	International Telephone and Telegraph (U.S.)
MIDEASTFOR	Mid-East Force (U.S. Navy)
MPLA	People's Movement for the Liberation of Angola
NATO	North Atlantic Treaty Organization
NSSM	National Security Study Memorandum (U.S.)
OAU	Organization of African Unity
OTRAG	Orbital Transport and Rocket Co. (FRG)
PAC	Pan Africanist Congress (South Africa)
SAAF	South African Air Force
SACLANT	Supreme Allied Commander, Atlantic
SAGE	South African General Electric
SASOL	South African Oil, Gas and Chemicals Corp.
SATO	South Atlantic Treaty Organization (not yet in existence)
STOL	short takeoff and landing
SWAPO of Namibia	South West African People's Organization of Namibia
ZANU	Zimbabwe African National Union
ZAPU	Zimbabwe African People's Union

List of Charts and Illustrations

Map 1	The Economic Base of South Africa	19
Map 2	The Economic Base of Zimbabwe	25
Map 3	The Economic Base of Namibia	30
Table 1	Soviet Naval Ship-Days in the Indian Ocean	75
Table 2	Population of Zimbabwe/Rhodesia, 1970-'77	115
Table 3	The Armed Forces of S. Africa and Rhodesia, 1973-'77	115
Table 4	Major Weapons Systems in Use by South African Army and Air Force	143
Table 5	Deliveries of Weapons Systems Known to be in Service with the S. African Defence Forces	144
Table 6	Deliveries of Weapons Systems Not Generally Known to be in Service with the South African Defence Forces	146
Table 7	Arms Inventory for S. African Defence Forces	148
Table 8	Comparative Strength of Selected Armed Forces	150
Table 9	Major Weapons Systems in Service with the S. African Regular Army	152
Table 10	Schedule of Spending by S. Africa on the Koeburg Station, 1976-'84	177
Profile: South African Energy Board Expenditures		181
Table 11	Links Between S. African Public and Private Capital and Transnational Corporations	201
Table 12	U.S. Investment in S. Africa and Namibia, by Sector, 1976	205
Table 13	U.S. Transnational Banks and Affiliates with Major Commitments to S. Africa, 1974-'76	217

Part I
The Crisis in
Southern Africa

Chapter 1

The Crisis in Southern Africa

Southern Africa is torn by crisis.

Over the years, the United States and other Western interests—seeking to ensure the profitable flow of strategic materials and markets for their surplus manufactured goods—have helped South Africa build up an industrial-military complex which dominates the entire southern African region.

Today, African freedom fighters, spurred by the liberation of Mozambique and Angola, have stepped up their armed struggle. They seek, not merely to end racist rule, but to create conditions which would enable the peoples of the region to shape their own future.

The dangers of U.S. military involvement in southern Africa— as in Southeast Asia a few short years ago—have profound implications for the people of the United States.

The brutal murder of Steven Biko—detained without trial, tortured, driven hundreds of miles handcuffed and naked, and left to die alone in his cell—shocked the world. His death symbolized the brutal repression exercised daily by the racist South African regime against the majority black population.

Within a few weeks of Biko's death, the United States government voted with the overwhelming majority of United Nations member states to enforce a mandatory arms embargo on South Africa.* The U.N. aimed to end the flow of guns, planes, tanks and missiles which bolsters the white-minority regimes in southern Africa against increasingly militant demonstrations and mounting armed struggle. The U.S. government, however, successfully blocked the inclusion of nuclear technology transfers in the arms embargo, and joined the Western powers to veto sanctions on further investment in or trade with South Africa.

This book consists of papers presented at a conference held at the University of Massachusetts at Amherst in April 1978. They expose the extent of U.S. involvement in supporting the military build-up of the minority regimes in southern Africa. That support has a long history, despite the fact that the United States government announced, back in 1963, that it had imposed a voluntary embargo on U.S. sales of arms to South Africa.

The need for citizen understanding and action to halt further U.S. military involvement in southern Africa is crucial. The escalating crisis, the kinds of tactics and weaponry acquired by the minority regimes to perpetuate their repressive rule, have global implications. U.S. spokespeople are right—although for the wrong reasons—when they declare the crisis in southern Africa may threaten world peace. This book tries to explain why.

As the evidence presented below shows, South Africa, with the assistance of the Western powers, including the United States, has acquired an extensive, technically sophisticated military capability, including radar, missiles, jet-propelled aircraft, and possibly nuclear weapons. The racist regime has explicitly used its growing military strength to bargain with the West for increased political, economic and military support, as well as to threaten the liberation movements and independent African states.

What Is at Stake in Southern Africa?

The issue in southern Africa is not simply white minority rule,

*For the text of the mandatory U.N. embargo imposed in 1977, see Appendix B.

although that rule* is brutal and pervasive. What is at stake is the political-economic structure which condemns the black majority of the region to a life of grinding poverty. At the center of this regional repression is South Africa, dominated by a white state-capitalist regime: seven linked mining finance houses closely intertwined with the South African government and its parastatals,** as well as the transnational corporations and banks which own a fourth of the nation's invested capital. Over the years, white entrepreneurs in South Africa have manipulated state machinery to control the region's rich agricultural and industrial wealth, while coercing the black majority into a low-paid labor force. Elimination of discriminatory laws, alone, will not restore the region's mines, farms and factories to the people. The liberation movements call, not simply for the right to vote, but for the peoples' right to shape their own forms of social control over the region's wealth.

The Western powers, led by the United States, have proclaimed their desire to help create and maintain "moderate" governments throughout southern Africa. They seek to avoid a fundamental political-economic reconstruction—like that underway in Angola and Mozambique—which alone could give Africans meaningful access to the rich resources of their nations. U.S. policymakers explicitly seek to "reconcile the black desire for political power—which the blacks will get—with the white desire for economic control...—which they will retain."[1]

These conflicting views cannot be considered in isolation. They reflect a far larger international crisis, which arises from the (sometimes conflicting) efforts of Western industrial powers to perpetuate their profitable enterprise of extracting mineral and agricultural wealth and selling factory-made goods to Third World countries. When outright imperial rule collapsed under the demands of Third World peoples for liberation, they sought new forms to extend their global neo-colonial hegemony.

* See Chapter Two below for an historical overview of the imposition of white-minority rule in South Africa, Zimbabwe and Namibia.
** "Rhodesia" is the name given Zimbabwe by the white minority when it illegally seized control there in 1966. See below, Chapter Two.

On the surface, the first decades after World War II presaged an era of unprecedented prosperity for the United States, Europe and Japan. The United States, its industrial base intact after World War II, had established a seemingly impenetrable domination of the Western world in the '50s. The U.S. government had poured funds into the restoration of the economies of Europe and Japan to strengthen them as allies in the cold war. By the mid-'60s, U.S. corporate conglomerates had obtained control of entire sectors of industry, especially in Britain but also in France, the Federal Republic of Germany (FRG) and Japan. U.S. transnational corporations and banks used holdings in British and French corporations to gain access to markets and resources in the former colonies. The banks and other financial institutions shifted billions of dollars into the Eurodollar markets, contributing to the accumulation of vast sums of capital outside the control of national governments.

British and French industrial-financial strength, on the other hand, declined in the post-World War II era as their colonial empires crumbled under demands for national liberation. Their aging home industries, characterized by outmoded technologies long protected by colonial preference, required major state assistance merely to survive. In the '60s, many of the new, politically independent African states opened their doors to more aggressive transnational corporate investors. U.S. firms operated in the former colonies directly as well as through British and French affiliates, and increasingly overshadowed the former imperial powers.

Industrial and financial corporate giants from West Germany and Japan, aided by aggressive state intervention as well as infusions of U.S. capital and technology, had recovered from the ravages of World War II in the 1960s. They steadily expanded and strengthened their hold over markets and resources in the Third World. By the '70s, they were exporting basic manufactured machinery as well as capital, in sharp competition, not only with declining British and French interests, but also with U.S. firms.

The continued industrial expansion in the West began to give rise to contradictory trends. By the 1970s, these trends appeared to threaten cohesion and stability in the core industrial nations themselves. Transnational corporations, backed by their governments, entered into an ever-expanding, increasingly competitive scramble for new sources of raw materials, especially strategic ones like oil and uranium. Growing surpluses of manufactured goods required new markets, not just for light consumer goods, as in earlier years, but also for their vast output of heavy industrial equipment, incorporating the newest technologies. Continual accumulation of capital built up ever-greater pressure to open new, more profitable areas of investment, to seek and exploit new markets and deposits of strategic resources.

The gap between the "have" core nations and the "have nots" in the periphery, as indexed by international agencies, noticeably widened as the transnational corporations shipped home the immense profits obtained from their exploitation of raw materials and sales of manufactures in the Third World. The result was shrinking markets in the periphery as poverty and oppression spread. In country after country, liberation movements began to press for more fundamental political-economic structural change.

The intensified conflict among transnational corporations seeking to gain control of Third World markets and strategic resources led to rapidly increased investments in "safe" regional centers like South Africa, as well as Brazil, Israel and Iran. Transnationals have invested heavily in these sub-centers, trying to penetrate the neighboring regions, as they have in southern Africa. In most of these centers, oppressive state-capitalist regimes exercised police powers to force the populations into a low-wage labor force.

Spurred by transnational corporate investment, which provided almost half their total capital, South Africa's manufacturing industries expanded rapidly through the 1960s. Growth in these sectors strengthened South Africa's dominant position throughout the southern third of the continent. Hundreds of thousands of contract laborers were forced to migrate to work on South African mines and farms. At the same time, South African and transnational firms cooperated in mining the rich mineral wealth of neighboring countries—

Botswana, Swaziland, Namibia, Zambia, even Zaire—selling them, in return, surplus manufactured goods. The corporations drained the investible surpluses produced by this profitable business into their headquarters in South Africa and beyond, to Europe, Japan and the United States.

The illegal white Rhodesian regime*—representing less than 4 percent of the population—can only resist the liberation movement's armed struggle because of the constant flow of weapons, supplies, and even manpower from the regional imperialist sub-center in South Africa. Major sectors of Rhodesia's industries are owned outright by South African interests, together with transnational corporations.**

The particular features of the sub-center in each exploitative regional system varies. South Africa is the only nation in the world where the majority of the population is excluded by law, solely on the grounds of race, from any effective form of political participation, as well as from ownership of productive resources. Nevertheless, South Africa maintains extensive relationships with the other regional sub-centers, particularly Iran and Israel. Iran's government owns 18 percent of the South African government's oil refinery, Natref.[2] Together with the transnational oil companies (particularly the U.S. firms Mobil, Standard Oil of California, and Texaco) Iran continues to supply vitally needed oil for South Africa's modern military machine, despite OPEC's attempt to impose a boycott. Israel's Koor group has estalished a jointly-held agency with the South African parastatal, Iscor, to produce and market steel products. Israel is also reported to have sent material and personnel—at times with covert U.S. encouragement—to strengthen South Africa's military capability.[3]

---

* Parastatal corporations are partly owned by the government.
** U.S. firms such as Union Carbide have for years exploited Zimbabwe's wealth and labor. Union Carbide lobbied successfully to convince Congress to support the Byrd Amendment which permitted U.S. firms to import chrome from Zimbabwe (produced in Union Carbide's mines) for several years— although the United States government had signed the United Nations embargo which stopped all trade with the illegal Rhodesian regime. In 1978, Union Carbide began to finance lobbyists to persuade Congress to support a so-called "internal settlement" to install a few blacks, hand-picked by the white leader, Ian Smith, in a white-controlled regime.

By the 1970s, the United States had lost its pre-eminent position among Western nations. It had lost the Vietnam war. Military expenditures and overseas investments had over burdened its balance of payments, so that it was forced to devalue its currency, contributing to the emergence of the international monetary crisis. On top of this, the mobilization of the oil-producing nations in OPEC raised world oil prices sevenfold, further aggravating the balance of payments problem in core nations, as well as the periphery.*

The bubble of Western prosperity burst in the mid-'70s. First a severe recession and then economic stagnation, accompanied by mounting inflation, settled over the Western world.

A New Approach?

As poverty and oppression in the Third World increased with the growing crisis in the West, nationalist movements emerged. The peoples of countries such as Mozambique and Angola, as well as Cuba and Vietnam, began to demand liberation and the right to shape their own destinies. Their efforts have been increasingly characterized by open military conflict, as they have turned to armed struggle to win freedom.

The United States government's response to the crisis in southern Africa was profoundly influenced by the experience of Vietnam. U.S. military involvement there started with the shipment of equipment and "technicians" to boost a "moderate" South Vietnamese regime pledged to perpetuate the political-economic structures imposed by the departing French colonialists. But what President Kennedy originally characterized as a mere "brushfire war" ultimately involved hundreds of thousands of U.S. troops and cost billions of dollars to introduce increasingly capital-intensive anti-personnel weapons**—including long-range bombers, napalm and defoliants. The Vietnam war provided ample proof that even a

---

*The transnational oil companies were able to take advantage of the "energy crisis" to reap record profits and expand their oligopolistic control of the Western world's energy resources.[4]

**The major Western powers, led by the United States, have rejected the use of nuclear weapons to maintain their hegemony over the Third World. The potential for total destruction appears to be too all engulfing. The neutron

major industrial power, using equipment far in advance of that available to the white-minority regimes in southern Africa, cannot defeat an organized, determined people.

Even as the Vietnam war dragged on throughout the '60s, liberation movements began the armed struggle to free southern Africa. At the same time, transnational corporations based in the United States and other Western countries multiplied their investments in South Africa, to reach a total far higher than they had ever invested in Vietnam. Military strategists from the United States and other Western countries declared South Africa was critical to Western "defense" and to protection of Western interests throughout Africa. United States policymakers began to strengthen their ties to South African whites, whom they viewed as "there to stay."[5] They seemed prepared to make the same mistakes all over again.

But many Americans were more ready to learn from experience. The U.S. antiwar movement had eventually mobilized millions of white and black Americans who united to demand an end to U.S. military intervention in Vietnam. The lesson seemed clear: the people of the United States did not want ever again to send troops to support reactionary regimes in faraway Third World countries.

The newly formed Trilateral Commission* began to call for new "North-South" relations. Essentially, they proposed that the

bomb, however, with its more focused destructive capability for killing people within a narrow radius without destroying buildings, holds frightening prospects if the peoples of the world cannot prevent its production and use. The fact that France has announced that it, as well as the United States, can now produce neutron bombs augurs ill for southern Africa, since France has openly shipped armaments to South Africa and continues to sell nuclear technology there. Chapters Nine and Ten deal with nuclear power and South Africa in more detail.

* The Trilateral Commission, founded in the 1970s by Nelson Rockefeller, attempted to bring together intellectuals with corporate and labor leaders of the United States, Europe and Japan, to seek new ways to restructure the international system to overcome the international crisis. It included, initially, over 20 members who now hold high posts in the Carter Administration, including the president himself; his advisor on national security, Zbigniew Brzezinski, who originally headed the commission; U.N. Ambassador Andrew Young; and Secretary of Defense Harold Brown.

United States, Europe and Japan should work together to formulate new techniques for advancing their old goals. As one document declared, these core industrial nations "increasingly need the developing countries as sources of raw materials, as export markets, and most important of all, as constructive partners in the creation of a workable world order." The Trilateralists' support for oppressive regional sub-centers like South Africa at the same time may be explained by their complaint that Western nations suffer from an "excess of democracy."[6]

As the Amherst conference met in early 1978 to discuss the extent of U.S. involvement in the growing southern African crisis, elements in the United States administration, echoed widely in the press, were beginning to voice increasingly strenuous objections to Soviet and Cuban assistance in the form of training and weapons for the southern African liberation forces. They grossly exaggerated the Cuban and Soviet role in support of the new Angolan government. They painted with lurid strokes a picture of diabolical "communist" penetration which required dramatic Western intervention to "save" the African peoples.* These arguments were welcomed by the South African regime, which loudly insisted it truly represented the last and strongest bulwark of Western democracy against "communist" domination of the continent.[7]

United States and South African allegations of Cuban and Soviet "dominance" were an insult to the integrity of the national liberation forces. At the same time, they appeared manufactured to conceal the facts. For years, bilaterally and through NATO, the Western powers have directed extensive military support to the Portuguese and white-minority regimes of southern Africa. They repeatedly refused to provide military assistance to the liberation movements, except for small amounts of weapons to hand-picked, divisive splinter groups. Their call for "peaceful transition" ignored the ongoing, systemic violence against blacks, as well as the repressive tactics practiced by the white-minority regime. The liberation movements had, understandably,

---

* See Appendix C.

long welcomed military aid from the socialist countries, as they clearly could not expect help from the West.

The question raised at the Amherst conference was whether the United States and the Western powers were once again introducing the spectre of "communism" because they feared the spreading crisis would engulf southern Africa in a process of transformation which, while it might contribute to higher living standards for the people of the region, also threatened the survival of Western capitalist hegemony throughout the continent.

The Contents of This Book

The participants in the Amherst conference were engaged in a cooperative detective job. The bits and pieces of evidence each had culled from a range of sources combined to expose the real nature of the "new" international relationships the Western powers have sought to impose to contain the mounting southern African crisis. Each scholar was, of course, responsible only for that part of the overall puzzle that he or she individually authored. Nevertheless, the pieces presented a compelling and deeply disturbing picture of U.S. political, economic and military involvement in southern Africa, when brought together.

The conference exposed the way United States interests had made extensive use of the loopholes—or, more accurately, the full-scale breaches—permitted by the French, British and U.S. veto of United Nations efforts to end all trade and investment in South Africa. The South African military-industrial complex had become increasingly dependent on the advanced technology and financial aid provided by transnational corporations, backed by their governments. The white-minority regimes, faced by a manpower shortage as popular resistance grew, had no choice but to acquire ever more sophisticated, capital-intensive military technology: electronic devices to detect guerrilla attacks in urban townships and remote rural regions; tanks and armored cars to deliver troops safely and efficiently to strategic areas; long-range aircraft and missiles to threaten remote centers; nuclear weapons to enhance bargaining power by posing the ultimate threat.

The conference emphasized that United States military involvement in southern Africa could not be perceived narrowly as merely the shipment of conventional arms; nor could the growth of the white military machine be analyzed in isolation. These exist within the framework of, and assist in strengthening, the South African state-capitalist regime which seeks to dominate the entire region.

The participants made no effort to predict the outcome of the southern African crisis. Rather, they sought to explain what was happening, to give people in the United States a better understanding so they could exert pressure on their government to end United States involvement in a build-up which could culminate in another devastating military conflict.

This book of papers presented at the Amherst conference is divided into three parts. Part I contains, in addition to this introductory chapter, a chapter by Dovi Afesi which briefly reviews the development of the apartheid system in the southern African region. It shows the way racist ideology, introduced by the Europeans when they first arrived, has over the centuries become intertwined with and reinforced the coercion of the Africans into the low-paid, impoverished work force which made the colonial/capitalist system so profitable. Part II describes southern Africa's place in Western strategy. Part III analyzes some of the methods by which United States interests have been directly involved in building up the South African military-industrial complex, despite the voluntary (1963) and mandatory (1977) United Nations embargoes.

Chapter Three, by Courtland Cox, begins Part II by analyzing how the Western powers seek to re-stabilize southern Africa without fundamentally altering the *status quo*. It would be difficult for the United States, as circumstances now stand, to enter into open military intervention in the region in a replication of the Vietnam defeat. That possibility cannot be ruled out, however, if the necessary preconditions—in particular, the installation of so-called "moderate" black governments dedicated to leaving the present economic structure intact—are created. Cox lays out the emerging Western strategy in this situation.

Within the framework of overall Western strategy, John Prados outlines in Chapter Four the main features of the United States military presence in and planning for the Indian Ocean. The U.S. presence there is designed to facilitate rapid intervention anywhere on the African continent, including southern Africa, whenever and wherever desired. Prados analyzes the implications of the construction of a U.S. military base on the tiny island of Diego Garcia; the mobilization of a sizable, highly trained quick-strike force of airborne troops; and South Africa's moves to ally itself with the United States and NATO.

In Chapter Five, James Dingeman argues from known facts (including the existence of a secret agreement between the CIA and BOSS, South Africa's equivalent of the FBI) that covert actions form an element of Western strategy in southern Africa. This approach enables the governments involved to avoid taking public responsibility for their unpopular actions. Dingeman presents available evidence relating to recently revealed Western and South African secret actions designed to disorient and split liberation forces in Zaire, Mozambique and Angola, suggesting the probability of similar covert actions in other parts of southern Africa today.

Mercenarization is the systematization of the employment of paid private soldiers to fight for unpopular regimes. Cynthia Enloe emphasizes in Chapter Six that the issue in southern Africa is not the personal behavior of private U.S. or British adventurers who, with the implicit consent if not outright backing of their governments, are paid to fight for the white-minority regimes in Zimbabwe or South Africa. Rather, the increased employment of mercenaries must be understood as illuminating the contradictory and unstable nature of the larger system of which they are part.

Part III of the book focuses on the specific ways United States interests have contributed to South Africa's military-industrial growth. It begins with Sean Gervasi's description in Chapter Seven of the frequent and devious means by which the voluntary arms embargo was violated. The repeated and systematic nature of the violations indicates that the official United States rhetoric of opposition to continued white-minority rule camouflaged the reality of continued military and economic support for the South African regime.

A continuing supply of aircraft, parts and equipment are vital for the kind of capital-intensive military machine which the South African white minority must employ to patrol its lengthy borders, survey remote rural areas, and transport troops to critical trouble spots. In Chapter Eight, Eric Prokosch and Michael Klare report on the results of their investigation into the techniques which have furthered the flow of United States aircraft and spare parts into South African hands, despite the mandatory arms embargo imposed in 1977.

United States government representatives explicitly argued for the exclusion of the transfer of nuclear technology from the United Nations' mandatory arms embargo. In Chapter Nine, Ronald Walters, emphasizing that it is impossible to distinguish military from civilian nuclear technology, demonstrates that the continuing transfer of nuclear technology to South Africa has enabled the white-minority regime to achieve the capability to produce nuclear weapons. This capability, he holds, gives the racist South African government a powerful bargaining lever in its efforts to maintain the African population in conditions of near-slavery. Nor is it outside the realm of possibility that the regime could unleash the full destructive power of these weapons, in a last desperate attempt to preserve the exploitative system.

The basic economic infrastructure underpinning the South African military-industrial complex, as Neva Makgetla and Ann Seidman show in Chapter Ten, has been and is still being provided by transnational corporations through affiliates in that country. Their investments escalated through the 1960s and early '70s. United States transnationals brought in capital-intensive and increasingly automated technologies which rendered the South African economy more self-sufficient and eased the shortage of white skilled labor, increasing unemployment among blacks. The new technologies built up the industrial base required for domestic production of weapons, enabling the regime to avoid the full impact of the U.N. embargoes. Loans worth billions of dollars, made by transnational banks in the '70s, enabled South Africa to continue to import oil and essential equipment for its strategic industrial program, and to buy more weapons.

Chapter 11, by Robert Sylvester, analyzes the inadequacies of the machinery which the United States has set up to enforce the arms embargo, and makes specific proposals for eliminating them.

Most of the conference participants agreed, however, that enforcement of a complete embargo on all trade and investment is essential to ensure an effective halt to further U.S. involvement in the South African military build-up. This was originally proposed by the majority of United Nations members, but was vetoed by the United States and its allies in 1977.

In the course of discussion, the conference participants noted several areas in which further research needs to be conducted. These are outlined in Appendix A, in hopes that concerned individuals and groups will pursue them further. The suggested areas include:

●Further analysis of the international crisis and how the shifting international division of labor and emerging regional sub-imperialist centers have contributed to South Africa's military-industrial growth;

●Study of the specific ways United States public and private involvement facilitates South Africa's military-industrial build-up, including an analysis of the regime's military capability and the role of the capital-intensive technologies contributed by transnational corporations;

●Examination of the way regions in the United States itself are affected by transnational industrial, financial and military involvement in southern Africa; and how they might benefit from the reconstruction of the southern African economy to meet the needs of its inhabitants, resulting in expanding, mutually beneficial trade, and the creation of more jobs and higher living standards on both sides of the Atlantic.

The conference participants agreed that, wherever possible, it would be useful to conduct this type of research in cooperation with the liberation movements of southern Africa. They emphatically rejected, however, any inference that this might argue for research concerning the liberation movements, unless requested by the movements themselves. No matter how well intentioned, such research often aids elements seeking to divide and weaken those struggling for their freedom. At the same time, the participants underscored the fact that the need for further research should not be permitted to hinder citizen action *now* to end the current dangerous course which permits increased United States military involvement to buttress the exploitative systems of southern Africa.

The Massachusetts ACAS Editorial Collective

References

1. *The New York Times*, April 18, 1978
2. See below, Chapter Ten.
3. See, *The New York Times*, June 1, 1976, and February 10, 1978; see also Chapter Ten.
4. See annual reports of the major U.S. oil companies, 1973-'77
5. El-Khawas, Mohammed, and Cohen, Barry, *The Kissinger Study of Southern Africa* (Westport, Conn.: Lawrence Hill and Co., 1976), p. 105
6. See Gardner, R.N., Kito, S., and Jdink, B.J., *A Turning Point in North-South Economic Relations*, Trilateral Commission Report, No. 3, 1974; and Crozier, R.J., Huntington, Samuel P., and Watanuki, J., *The Crisis of Democracy, Report on the Governability of Democracies to the Trilateral Commission* (New York: New York University Press, 1975)
7. See for example, South African Ministry of Information, *South African Digest* (Pretoria), June 9, 1978

Chapter 2

The Roots of Conflict
in Southern Africa

Dovi Afesi

Racist ideologies, evolved over centuries, have provided the rationale for the conquest and exploitation of the peoples of South Africa, Zimbabwe and Namibia. Liberation requires, not merely an end to white-minority rule, but political-economic reconstruction to give the blacks, the vast majority of the people, access to the region's rich productive resources.

Knowledge of southern African history is essential to an understanding of the full implications of U.S. military involvement in southern Africa. It sheds light on the reasons why African nations, especially the five Frontline States—Tanzania, Mozambique, Botswana, Zambia and Angola—are adamant in their support of the national liberation movements and reject outright the spurious arguments of those who object to Soviet and Cuban assistance.

This chapter provides a brief historical review of the trickery and brute military force employed by the Western colonial powers to impose white-minority rule in the three southern African countries whose people are, today, still waging armed struggle for their freedom.

18

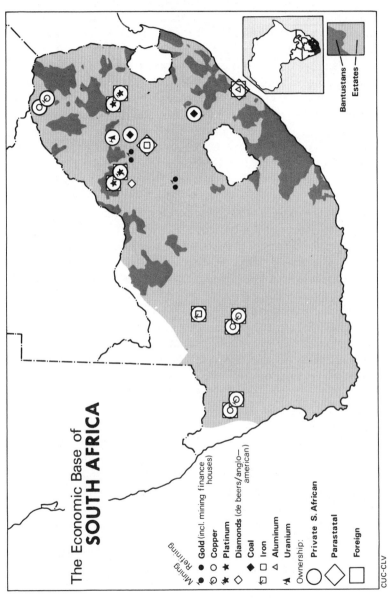

The Economic Base of
SOUTH AFRICA

Mining
Refining

● ○ **Gold** (incl. mining finance houses)
ᗄ ○ **Copper**
✦ ★ **Platinum**
◇ ◆ **Diamonds** (de beers/anglo—american)
     ◆ **Coal**
◻ ◻ **Iron**
     △ **Aluminum**
ᐱ   **Uranium**

Ownership:

○ **Private S. African**

◇ **Parastatal**

◻ **Foreign**

Bantustans
Estates

CUC-CLV

The Roots of Apartheid

The Dutch East Indian Company planted the first European colony on the Cape of Good Hope in South Africa in 1652, primarily as a victualling station for ships sailing to its East Asian possessions. At the very outset, the hostile character of this intrusion was revealed by repeated attacks on the Khoi Khoi and San people who inhabited the region. As the colony expanded, the Dutch settlers confiscated the Africans' cattle and grazing lands. Thinly spread out across vast areas, the Khoi Khoi and San—sneeringly labelled "Hottentots" and "Bushmen" by the Dutch—were unable to offer well organized, concerted resistance in the face of the guns of the European invaders. In the course of numerous clashes and skirmishes, they were conquered, exterminated or enslaved.

From the first, racist assumptions rationalized the settlers' brutal treatment of the Africans. Echoing the general attitudes of 17th century Europe, the Afrikaners or Boers—as they came to be called—viewed Africans as savages in need of redemption and civilization, who might, in the meantime, be enslaved. Adherents of a form of Calvinism, the Boers preached the inferiority of blacks as Biblical truth.

From 1652 to the British conquest in the 19th century, the Boers, joined by the French Huguenots, waged brutal wars on the local inhabitants, added Africans' cattle to their own, reduced the survivors to serfdom or outright slavery, and everywhere practiced segregationist policies against Africans. It became abundantly evident that the mutually reinforcing relationship between the economic needs of the settlers (land and cheap labor) and fundamentalist religious values (black heathenism and inferiority) combined to shape a policy of white domination, exclusionism, segregation and subjugation of blacks. Defending apartheid in the 20th century, Prime Minister D.F. Malan could truthfully invoke history and tradition:

> It must be appreciated from the outset that Apartheid, separation, segregation or differentiation...whatever the name...is part and parcel of the South African tradition as practiced since the first Dutch settlement at the Cape in 1652.[1]

The British, seizing the Dutch colonies between 1795 and 1806, sought to win African support by limited intervention on their behalf. The resentful Boers, considering the British intrusion into their domain intolerable, embarked on the so-called "Great Trek" into the fertile plains of the Transvaal. In their large-scale northward migration, the Dutch encountered and conquered hitherto independent African peoples, whom they sought to enslave in their newly created republics. The constitution of the Transvaal Republic explicitly proclaimed, "There shall be no equality between black and white, either in State or Church."

The Boer dream of independence from British rule was shattered with the discovery of gold and diamonds in the 1860s. The British imperialists, led by the ruthless and ambitious Cecil Rhodes, fomented a series of crises in their efforts to monopolize the newly discovered mineral wealth. After decades of bickering, the Anglo-Boer War broke out in 1899, and dragged on for three years. The British emerged victorious. They had won an opportunity to stem the tide of racist expansion in South Africa. But clearly the British did not fight the war to secure African rights. Cecil Rhodes, the British empire builder, sounded much like his Boer counterparts insofar as treatment of the Africans was concerned:

> My idea is that the natives should be kept in these native
> reserves and not mixed with the white men at all.[2]

In 1910, the British compromised with the defeated Boers to establish the Union of South Africa. At this critical juncture, the British again had the opportunity to insist on guarantees for African rights. But British capitalists, secure in their domination over South Africa's rich mineral wealth, shared with the Boer farmers the desire to coerce the African majority into a low-cost labor force. The resulting union left the future welfare and destiny of millions of Africans in the hands of avowed racists.

> The price of unity and conciliation was the institutionalization
> of white supremacy.[3]

Between 1910 and 1948, South African whites continued to legislate themselves into permanent domination of the black majority. During the entire period, every South African government, whether Boer or British oriented, endorsed and advocated white supremacy. All generously contributed to the creation of ever more widely encompassing discriminatory laws shaping their avowed "Master-Servant" system, a system which guaranteed to the entrenched white capitalist class control over the mineral and agricultural wealth of the nation. When the Nationalist Party installed apartheid as national policy in 1948, it was essentially consolidating, refining and formalizing white supremacist tendencies, policies and practices which had evolved over the centuries since the arrival of the Europeans.

White South Africans have been very explicit about the aims of apartheid.

> Our policy is that Europeans must remain masters in South Africa...Our view is that in every sphere the Europeans must retain the right to rule and keep it a whiteman's country.
>
> *J.G. Strijdom, in the 1950s[4]*
>
> Reduced to its simplest form, the problem is nothing else than this, we want to keep South Africa white—keeping it white can only mean one thing, namely white domination.
>
> *H.F. Verwoerd, Prime Minister, in the 1960s[5]*
>
> The fact of the matter is that we need them [Africans] because they work for us...But the fact that they work for us can never entitle them to claim political rights. Not now, not in the future, under no circumstances...South African nationhood is for the Whites only...
>
> *B.J. Vorster, Prime Minister, in the 1970s[6]*

The apartheid system is designed to reduce the masses of Africans to a permanent pool of cheap labor. Education is compulsory and free for white children. The impoverished Africans must pay for what little schooling they get. While Christiandom preaches "love thy neighbor," the injunction is nullified if thy neighbor is of a different skin pigmentation. In all things essential—except work—the races are totally segregated.

Dispossessed of their land, the 20 million blacks—almost 80 percent of the population—are restricted by apartheid law to the Bantustans, so-called "homelands." The Bantustans form scattered, fragmented splinters of marginal land, carefully delineated to exclude the nation's rich mines and farms. They comprise less than 13 percent of the national land area, and are barely the size of the state of Kansas. The 87 percent of South

Africa's land allocated for the four million whites, equals in contrast, the size of the combined area of all the New England states plus Delaware, Maryland, New Jersey, Pennsylvania, New York, Illinois, Indiana, Ohio and Michigan.

Absolute poverty, starvation and disease are common in the barren confines of the Bantustans. There, over half the children die before they reach six years of age. But under apartheid, Africans have rights only in the Bantustans. Even if they have lived all their lives in a "white" area, they may "legally" be deported to a "homeland" they have never seen.

Apartheid is enforced through the pass laws, which require every adult African to carry a reference book, or pass. To obtain a job in "white" areas, this pass must be signed by a white employer. Africans must carry it with them 24 hours a day. If found without it, they face arrest and jail or deportation to the Bantustans. It does not matter if they forgot it while visiting neighbors or going to the store. Over a thousand Africans are prosecuted every day under these laws.

Yet to support their families, Africans must migrate to work in the "white" areas where over half the African population of South Africa lives. They may not vote or own land there, and must live in segregated townships outside the main cities like Soweto. Often their families are not allowed to stay with them. But lack of jobs and starvation in the Bantustans means they must accept almost any wage offered by their white employers. Their position is further weakened by laws which prevent them from striking or bargaining collectively through officially recognized unions.

The Africans have never submitted docilely to this brutal system, in which the worst features of colonial/capitalist exploitation are exacerbated and envenomed by a racist ideology which freezes millions into impoverished bondage. They fought back over the centuries with whatever weapons they could obtain; but the whites, backed by European industrial might, were able to defeat and subjugate them militarily. In 1912, just after the Union of South Africa was formed, the African National Congress—the first African political party in sub-Saharan Africa—called on all Africans to unite politically to demand their rights. Non-violent demonstrations, strikes, boycotts—the African population tried them all, only to be met with increasingly vicious repression culminating in the shooting of 69 unarmed men, women and children who gathered at Sharpeville in 1961 to protest the pass laws. It was then that the liberation movement turned once more to armed struggle. Thousands of young men and women have escaped across the borders to training camps abroad, to learn to use guns and hand grenades. Thousands more have begun to seek ways to organize guerrilla warfare against the growing industrial-military might of the white-minority regime. In 1975, the Soweto uprising symbolized a new stage of their struggle.

It is against this background that South Africa's white minority regime is spending billions to build up its military might. Imbued with the "laager" mentality* that led the Boers to trek into the wilderness of the Transvaal rather than grant even minimal rights to Africans, the regime aims to buy the most destructive weaponry available to perpetuate what it perceives as its God-given place. It seeks once again to crush the Africans' struggle to win the right to shape their own destinies.

The Illegal Rhodesian Regime

In neighboring Zimbabwe,** the oppressed African population is nearing victory in its armed struggle against the tiny white minority that still illegally rules the country. The seeds of their current revolutionary struggle were planted 90 years ago, when that arch imperialist, Cecil Rhodes, seeking gold in the general "scramble" for Africa, decided to grab what he claimed were "large tracts of valuable land, ruled by savage native chiefs in the interior of Africa."[7] In 1888, Rhodes and his men thrust northward from their base in South Africa and eventually succeeded in enticing Lobengula, king of the large Ndebele

---

* The "laager" was the circle of wagons the Boers made during the Great Trek to protect them from attack.

** Zimbabwe is the African name for Southern Rhodesia, which the illegal white-minority regime calls "Rhodesia." It is derived from an ancient Central African state.

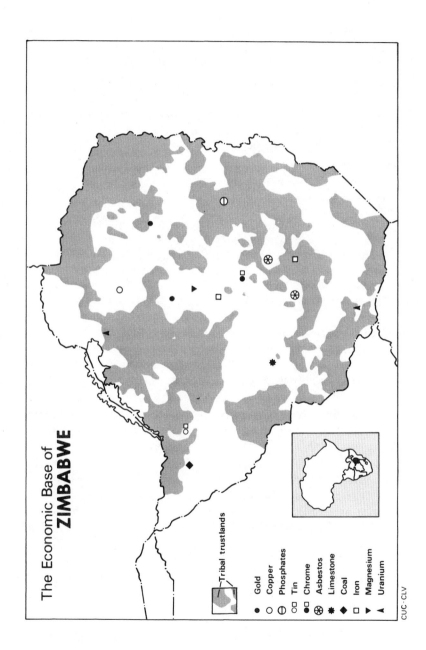

The Economic Base of
ZIMBABWE

Tribal trustlands

- ● Gold
- ○ Copper
- ◐ Phosphates
- ○□ Tin
- ●□ Chrome
- ⊛ Asbestos
- ✳ Limestone
- ◆ Coal
- □ Iron
- ▶ Magnesium
- ◀ Uranium

CUC - CLV

kingdom, into signing a commerce/friendship treaty, commonly known as the Rudd Concession.

Before the ink was fully dry on the parchment, Lobengula realized he had been fooled. He was told that, according to the document, he had in fact relinquished his sovereignty and the independence of his people to the Europeans. He was shocked, incredulous. Still, trusting in the supposed decency and integrity of the white man, Lobengula set out to correct the situation by appealing to the queen of England. In his letter, the king summed up his understanding of the Rudd Concession:

> A document was written and presented to me for signature. I asked what it contained, and was told that in it were my words and the words of these men. I put my hand to it.
>
> About three months afterwards I heard from other sources that I had given by that document the right of all the minerals of my country...I have since had a meeting of my Indunas and they will not recognize the paper, as it contained neither my words nor the words of those who got it...
>
> I write to you that you may know the truth about this, and may not be deceived.[8]

But as repeatedly happened in Euro-African relations, Lobengula's efforts and appeals fell on unsympathetic ears. The fate of Lobengula and the Ndebele nation was sealed and doomed at the birth of Rhodes's chartered British South Africa Company. African colonial history is replete with such acts of fraud, duplicity and coercion. In this case, to the calamitous end, the Europeans continued to abuse trust, friendship, and sincerity. In 1890, when a restive Lobengula wanted to know the true intentions and reasons for the pending march of the pioneer column into his kingdom, Sir Henry Loch assured him in writing that "the men assembled by the British South Africa Company are not assembled for the purpose of attacking him, but on the contrary are assembled for a peaceful object, namely searching for gold..."[9] No mention was made of the fact that the men assembled were not only armed to the teeth, but were also promised and guaranteed land—a minimum of 3000 acres each on successful completion of their mission.

By 1896, Rhodes, a self-paraded super-imperialist, who once willed all his fortune to the British Colonial Office to be used "for the extension of British rule throughout the world," had created through perfidious and military means a vast personal empire, Northern and Southern "Rhodesia." But Rhodes was more than the image of a British entrepreneur-imperialist. He was also a racist, whose views played a major role in establishing the character and pattern of the relationship between the white settlers and Africans, not only in Rhodesia, but also in South Africa proper. The southern Africa of 1978 closely resembled that prescribed by Cecil Rhodes some 90 years ago:

> I will lay down my own policy on this native question. Either you have to receive them on an equal footing as citizens, or to call them a subject race. I have made up my mind that there must be Pass Laws and Peace Preservation Acts, and that we have to treat natives, where they are in a state of barbarism, in a different way to ourselves. We are to be lords over them...The native is to be treated as a child denied the franchise... We must adopt a system of despotism in our relations with the Barbarians...[10]

Even Christiandom and its emisaries, the missionaries, argued that the introduction of Christianity, Commerce and Civilization could best be done by the Cross and the sword, "the former converting and the latter chastising..."[11]

Under the rule of Rhodes's British South Africa Company, from 1896 to 1923, the settlers confiscated from the Africans untold thousands of cattle and other livestock, delimited and arrogated the best farming and grazing land for themselves, and created "reserves" to which dispossessed Africans were removed and confined. Rhodes had recommended that,

> We take away their power of making war and at present we give them nothing to do, therefore, we want to get hold of these young men *and make them go out to work, and the only way to do this is to compel them to pay a certain labour tax.*[12]

The company and the settlers, together, imposed an inflexibly cruel system of forced labor, described by Sir Richard Martin, the first Resident Commissioner and an avid colonialist himself, as being "synonymous with slavery." Thus by 1923, the ruthless exploitation of Africans and their land, rendered feasible, justifiable and secure through racist legislation and force, had seemingly become permanent.

The British government "bought out" the company and

annexed the colony to the crown in 1923, thereby inheriting the wealth as well as problems of Rhodes' empire. Once again, the British government had the opportunity and responsibility to intervene on behalf of the Africans. Instead, the government handed all effective power in Southern Rhodesia to the settler whites, granting them "self-government." Not a single African opinion was solicited.

For the settler whites, self government meant license. They accelerated their efforts to entrench themselves as the masters and owners of Rhodesia. "Separate development" became the war cry, the standard crowd pleaser among the whites. Clearly, dividing the country into "black" and "white" areas meant decided economic and security advantages: more of the best lands for the whites; larger numbers of dispossessed, landless Africans to swell the supply of cheap labor. Racism provided the justification. The Lands Commission of 1926 recommended that, "until the native has advanced very much further on the paths of civilization, it is better that [native] landholding should be reduced..."[13]

By 1931, the Europeans had allotted about half of the entire land area of Southern Rhodesia to themselves. They continue to hold it to this day, although they make up less than 4 percent of the population. The Africans, 96 percent of the population, have been forced to resettle on poor, infertile land in areas devoid of known mineral deposits.

But, as in South Africa, "separate development" was never meant to imply the total exclusion of blacks from white areas. Who would work in the gold and chrome mines, clean and sweep the cities, and tend the large tobacco farms—all in white areas? Blacks were tolerated in the white area as temporary workers and transients, with no permanent rights at all. The Land Apportionment Act (1931) was followed by a series of others: the Industrial Conciliation Act (1934), the Native Registration Act (1936) and the Native Passes Act (1937). Together, these laws provided the white minority with the tools necessary for controlling and exploiting the African majority. The Industrial Act and the pass laws, in Rhodesia as in South Africa, froze the African workers into semi-slavery. By excluding them from the status of "employee," they effectively barred Africans from unionism and the benefits of legal collective bargaining. The Registration Act made African participation in the political process virtually impossible by imposing tax, income and literacy requirements which almost no Africans could meet. All these were passed although Britain had reserved the power to veto "any legislation detrimental to the rights of the Natives."[14]

With white domination seemingly assured, and with cheap land and labor available, white immigration to Rhodesia increased. The white population multiplied from 40,000 in 1930 to 200,000 in 1960, and 250,000 in 1976. But the overwhelming majority of the population today—over six million people—is still black.

In 1963, the settler-dominated Central African Federation which bound Northern Rhodesia and Nyasaland to Southern Rhodesia, collapsed, largely because of African opposition. Northern Rhodesia became independent Zambia, and Nyasaland became Malawi. In 1965, the white minority in Southern Rhodesia, led by Ian Smith, rejected the legitimate demands of the African majority for equality and justice, and illegally declared independence from Britain, with the stated aim of protecting white power, wealth and privilege. Once again, Britain abdicated its responsibility. As the colonial power, it had the constitutional power to insist upon majority rule and to bring Smith down by force if necessary. It did neither. An angry Zambian diplomat compared Britain to a "toothless bulldog."[15]

From 1966 until today, the illegal white minority regime has played constitutional shenanigans with African national demands. Those who called for justice, freedom, independence and majority rule were suppressed through force and packed into jails. By 1969, despite worldwide pressure, the Smith regime had created so many new protective and oppressive devices that the then Minister of Law, L. Burke, could taunt the world and African nationalists with the claim that "African majority rule as an aim is no longer constitutionally attainable."[16]

The African liberation movement, naming their land Zimbabwe, chose the only alternative remaining to win freedom: armed struggle.

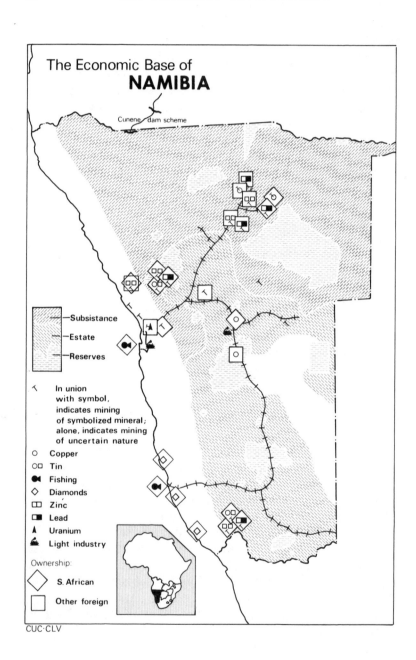

The Economic Base of
NAMIBIA

Cunene dam scheme

Subsistance
Estate
Reserves

⊀   In union
      with symbol,
      indicates mining
      of symbolized mineral;
      alone, indicates mining
      of uncertain nature
○   Copper
○□   Tin
◖●   Fishing
◇   Diamonds
▥   Zinc
◧   Lead
▲   Uranium
♠   Light industry

Ownership:

◇   S. African

▢   Other foreign

CUC·CLV

The Struggle for Namibia

Namibia—which is the internationally accepted name for the former U.N. protectorate South West Africa—remains, like Zimbabwe and South Africa, a white-ruled settler colony. All economic, as well as socio-political privilege, power and advantage is controlled by a white settler minority, tied by an umbilical cord to South Africa.

Namibia is a large country, the size of France and Britain put together. Its wealth in diamonds, copper, lead, zinc and other precious minerals is vast. The land, although largely desert, also contains extensive grazing pastures and fertile farming areas. But the Africans have virtually no share in the nation's wealth. They have no voice in the political process. They have been forced, in their own land, to endure pervasive racist policies of segregation, dehumanization and exploitation.

As in Zimbabwe and South Africa, the roots of the Namibians' struggle for liberation lie in the history of the colonizing process. In the "scramble for Africa" in the late 19th century, Bismark's Germany annexed four African countries: Togoland, the Cameroons, German East Africa (Tanzania) and South West Africa (Namibia). The German settlers, like the British, used widespread fraud and force to induce unwilling African chiefs to grant vast land concessions. In 1888, a Nama chief, Witboois, prophetically warned the Herero people that "this giving yourself into the hands of the white man will become to you a burden as if you were carrying the sun on your back."[17] Witboois himself was defeated by a rapacious German army some years later. Like trickery, force was also used to take land from the Africans. The Herero and Nama, pastoralists of long tradition, were herded into designated areas so as to open up more land for German settlement. By 1900, the settlers had stolen, through raids and outright theft, half the Herero cattle.

African protests and resistance were ruthlessly suppressed. "Punitive military operations" were carried out against chiefs who sought to protect their land and the freedom of their peoples. These "operations" against "recalcitrant" chiefs were brutal and frequent. In one instance, in 1893, well equipped soldiers slipped into an African village in the dead of night and fired 16,000 bullets into the sleeping huts.[18]

By 1900, as African resistance continued, the Germans' policy of conquest was escalated into large-scale extermination. General von Trotha minced no words in announcing their policy:

> I know these African tribes. They are all the same. They respect nothing but force. To exercise this force with brute terror and even ferocity is my policy. I wipe out rebellious tribes with streams of blood.[19]

When the Herero and Nama revolted against German atrocities, von Trotha unleashed such violence that, by 1907, the African population was decimated. Von Trotha's determination to "pacify" the colony once and for all was particularly aimed at the Herero. "The Herero nation must disappear...if not through shooting then through death by thirst," he declared.[20] In practice this meant, he said, the unmitigated "exercise of terror against every Herero who is sighted."[21]

Armed African resistance was broken, but not before von Trotha and the German soldiers virtually committed genocide. Out of an African population of 100,000, a total of 80,000 men and women, old and young, perished. Germany's annexation of Namibia in 1883 had taken some 20 years of concentrated butality, wars and untold violence. Although African resistance was tenacious, superior guns in the hands of men with an unrestrained enthusiam to "wipe out rebellious tribes" gave the Germans victory.

The outline of German colonial policy was clear: the settlement of German farmers and capitalists meant the expropriation of land from the surviving Africans, who in turn were reduced to suppliers of cheap labor. Sharing the Eurocentric assumptions of African backwardness and European superiority, the German settlers also instituted policies of racial segregation, discrimination and exploitation.

But German rule in Namibia was short lived. After losing the First World War, Germany was stripped of its African colonies. In 1920, the League of Nations transferred the administration of Namibia to South Africa under a mandate system. That anyone with any knowledge of the racist trends in South Africa could entrust the destiny of the Namibians to South Africa raises serious questions about the motives of the League's decision-makers.*

Although the League of Nations took Namibia away from Germany, it is important to remember that it left the German settlers there and made no effort to alter the already established institutions, ideologies and practices of white supremacy, racism and segregation. The German settlers and white South Africans, sharing similar historical experiences and racist ideas, became natural allies, dedicated to perpetuating white supremacy and African exploitation, in Namibia as in South Africa.

In the years since the South African government took control over Namibia, it steadily introduced, extended or reinforced racially oppressive policies parallel to those practiced in South Africa itself. In 1966, when pressures mounted in the United Nations for liberation of the Namibian people, the South African government responded by incorporating the entire territory as a province of South Africa.

To this day, only 10 percent of the population, some 80,000 whites, own Namibia's resources. A handful of settler ranches and estates spread over the vast farmlands. South African and transnational corporations still own the rich copper, diamond and uranium mines. The 800,000 Namibians are forced to live on arid, infertile so-called "tribal" lands, from which they must migrate to work as contract laborers on white-owned farms and mines at wages even below those in South Africa.

Faced with South African intransigence, the South West African People's Organization (SWAPO) of Namibia has been fighting for years, mobilizing the people to regain their national heritage through armed struggle. They are backed by United Nations Security Council Resolution 385 which calls for withdrawal of the South African presence, and affirms the right of the Namibian people to self-determination.

In recent years, five Western Powers—the United States, Britain, Canada, West Germany and France—have moved

---

* Especially as the African National Congress of South Africa had sent a delegation to urge the League not to make such a decision.

outside the United Nations to propose a negotiated agreement which may subvert the principles of the U.N. resolution and undercut SWAPO's position. The Western powers have not insisted on total withdrawal of the South African police and army from Namibia, although the continued presence of these colonizing forces destroys the possibility of a free and fair election even if held under United Nations auspices. The Western governments' proposals would, instead, permit South Africa to maintain total control over the transition to "independence." This strategy raises the question as to whether, once again, the Western powers seek to use the proposals as a new technique to divide and weaken the united African opposition to the perpetuation of South African domination of Namibia.

Conclusion

The roots of the southern African crisis in which the United States is becoming increasingly embroiled, not only politically but also militarily, stretch back into the history of brutal colonial-settler conquest. The racist white-minority governments of South Africa, Zimbabwe and Namibia have always ruled by trickery backed by military might. Today, the people of southern Africa are determined to win the struggle, through war if need be, to shape their own future.

References

1. Quoted in Rich and Wallerstein, *Africa: Tradition and Change* (New York: Random House, 1972) p. 346. For the full text of Malan's argument, see Kuper, L., *Passive Resistance in South Africa* (New Haven: Yale University Press, 1957)

2. Quoted in Gibson, Richard, *African Liberation Movements* (New York: Oxford University Press, 1972), p. 25

3. Thompson, Leonard, "The Compromise of Union," in Wilson and Thompson, eds., *The Oxford History of South Africa*, Vol. II (London: Oxford University Press, 1971), p. 364

4. Quoted in Akinye, S.A., *Emergent African States* (London: Longman Group Ltd., 1976), p. 59

5. *Ibid.,* p. 58; also see, Belzer, A.N., ed., *Verwoerd Speaks, 1948-1966* (Johannesburg, 1966)

6. Quoted in Wiley and Wiley, *Africa* (West Haven: Pendulum, 1973), p. 139

7. Quoted in Nkrumah, Kwame, *Neo-Colonialism: The Last Stage of Imperialism* (New York: International Publishers, 1969), p. 153

8. Quoted in Kange, Sam, *Origins of Rhodesia* (London: Heineman, 1968), p. 115

9. Mason, Philip, *The Birth of a Dilemma* (London: Oxford University Press, 1958), p. 140

10. Fisher, John, *The Afrikaners* (London: Cassell Press, 1969), p. 127; also see Vindex, *Cecil Rhodes—His Political Life and Speeches, 1890-1900* (London: 1958)

11. Mason, *op. cit.,* p. 147

12. *Ibid.,* p. 149

13. Wills, A.J., *Introduction to the History of Central Africa* (London: Oxford University Press, 1973), p. 255

14. *Ibid,* p. 247

15. Gibson, *op.cit.,* p. 149

16. *Ibid.,* p. 148

17. Hallet, Robin, *Africa Since 1875* (Ann Arbor: University of Michigan Press, 1974), p. 622

18. For a fuller account, see Bley, H., *South West Africa Under German Rule,* translated by Ridley, G.H. (London: 1971)

19. *Ibid.*

20. Davidson, Basil, *Africa in History* (New York: Collier Books, 1974), p. 253

21. *Ibid.,* p. 254

Part II
Western Strategy
in Southern Africa

Chapter 3

Western Strategy
in Southern Africa

Courtland Cox

United States policies for southern Africa appear to reflect the conflicting views of successive presidential administrations, and even the relative strengths of different elements within each. These differences are, however, more apparent than real. Underneath, the basic aim is to avoid fundamental reconstruction of the regional political economies.

Events in Angola encouraged radicals to press for a military solution in Rhodesia. With radical influence on the rise, and with immense outside military strength apparently behind the radicals, even moderate and responsible African leaders—firm proponents of peaceful change—began to conclude that there was no alternative but to embrace the cause of violence...We were concerned about a continent politically embittered and economically estranged from the West; and we saw ahead a process of radicalizations which would place severe strains on our allies in Europe and Japan. There was no prospect of successfully shaping events in the absence of a positive political, moral and economic program of our own in Africa.
  —*Former Secretary of State, Henry Kissinger*[1]

Since the decolonization of the Portuguese colonies in Africa, the United States and its Western allies have been involved in a number of strategies designed to protect Western political and economic hegemony in southern Africa. Although liberation struggles in southern Africa are on the surface nationalist in their objectives, these struggles also represent a continuing African challenge to a political and economic order that was established nearly a century ago. During the 19th century, the European powers, and to a lesser extent the United States, had established a political and economic system in Africa which gave the Western European states sole access to the African continent's commodities, labor and markets.

Much of the political and economic system established by the Western powers remains intact today. Africa is still a vast storehouse of commodities for the West, and a dumping ground for its products. The European political and economic dominance of Africa is, however, constantly under assault by the people of the African continent. Nowhere on the continent of Africa is this challenge more pronounced than in southern Africa.

In less than five years, the political-military relationships in southern Africa have changed dramatically. Angola and Mozambique are no longer under Portuguese rule. The Zimbabwean Patriotic Front conducts military operations anywhere it pleases inside Rhodesia, while the staunch defender of white supremacy, Ian Smith, is forced to scurry around preaching his brand of so-called "majority rule." The South Africans have 50,000 troops in Namibia, but SWAPO is still effective militarily within the country. The political will of the majority of Africa supports the military struggles in southern Africa. Nigeria, the most powerful African country, gives substantial financial support to the liberation movements.

In 1974, major blows to Western political and economic power in southern Africa caught the United States government by surprise. The Nixon Administration believed the white-minority regimes invincible to any military threats from the African liberation movements. It was wrong.

The Nixon Administration had built its entire southern Africa policy on the premise that the whites of southern Africa were there to stay,

...and the only way constructive change can come about is through them. There is no hope for the blacks to gain the political rights they seek through violence, which will only lead to chaos and increased opportunities for the communists.[2]

In 1969, Henry Kissinger, then Nixon's national security advisor, commissioned a study of United States policy in southern Africa. The final study was entitled National Security Study Memorandum (NSSM) No. 39. The study outlined five premises and strategies that the Nixon Administration could follow. Kissinger recommended and the administration adopted Option Two—whose premise is stated above.

The strategy of Option Two of NSSM 39 called for the Nixon Administration to continue the rhetoric of the Kennedy and Johnson Administrations and "maintain public opposition to racial repression but relax political isolation and economic restrictions on the white states."[3] (The white states were Rhodesia, South Africa and Namibia, and Mozambique and Angola under Portuguese colonial rule.) The Nixon Administration strategy also called for "diplomatic steps to convince the black states of the area that their current liberation and majority rule aspiration in the south are not attainable by violence and that hope for a peaceful and prosperous future lies in closer relations with the white-dominated states."[4] The Nixon Administration would deny the existence of the liberation movements.

Beginning in the 1970s, the Nixon-Ford Administrations put into place programs necessary to the strategies outlined in Option Two of NSSM 39. The United States increased its military support to the Portuguese colonial regime, South Africa and Rhodesia. While the U.S. arms embargo against South Africa was kept on the books, the Nixon and Ford Administrations liberalized the treatment of equipment which could serve either military or civilian purposes.[5] Military goods such as light aircraft, C-130s, helicopters, communications equipment, jeeps and trucks were sent to the white-minority regimes of southern Africa.* The United States shipped quantities of herbicidal ingredients 2, 4-d, and 2, 4, 5-t to Mozambique and Angola to be

* See Chapters Ten and Eleven below.

used against Africans in the colonial wars. (The use of these herbicides in Vietnam was stopped in 1971 because they were considered too lethal.) The United States also trained hundreds of Portuguese military personnel in psychological operations, intelligence gathering, precision photography, mine warfare and biological and chemical warfare. Many of the personnel trained in the United States were used in the colonial wars in Angola and Mozambique. Like their predecessor, the Nixon-Ford Administrations gave the Portuguese tanks, armored cars, long-range guns and all the materials of war, under the guise of selling equipment for NATO purposes. The Portuguese General Paiva wrote in 1969,

> ...our contribution to NATO is rather small due to our great efforts in our overseas territories...Portugal is becoming more of a burden on NATO than an asset. And it is only the U.S. that has apparently failed to even take note of this fact.[6]

The United States trained, and still trains, South Africans in nuclear technology. It also gave the South African government enriched uranium and other nuclear materials (see Chapter Nine). In addition, the Portuguese colonial government received $1 million in educational assistance from the Pentagon and a waiver of Portuguese support payments for the United States military advisory assistance group in Lisbon.[7]

The Nixon Administration, following the economic scenario outlined by Option Two of NSSM 39, liberalized or entirely removed external constraints on the white-minority regimes in southern Africa. Probably the most dramatic reversal of former United States policy was the Byrd Amendment. This amendment allowed the importation of chrome from Rhodesia to the United States, in official violation of United Nations sanctions. While the importation of chrome was a source of foreign exchange for the white-minority regime, it was, still more importantly, interpreted by the Ian Smith regime as an act of U.S. political solidarity.

The Portuguese colonial regime also received a political boost from the Nixon Administration with the signing of the Azores agreement in 1971. Congressman Charles Diggs said of the agreement that,

...the United States in effect turned its back on its support for self-determination in Africa, it gave the Portuguese the comfort of a political alliance with the United States.[8]

The Portuguese made good economic use of their excellent political relations with the Nixon Administration. On June 21, 1973, the United States Export-Import Bank (Ex-Im Bank) announced the sale of 22 General Electric locomotives to Mozambique at a cost of $9.5 million. On July 19, 1973, $4 million was used to finance the sale of tire production facilities in Mozambique. On October 5, 1973, $6 million was used to help finance the sale of one Boeing 737, jet aircraft spare parts and related ground equipment to the Mozambique Harbors, Railways and Transport Administration.[9]

For South Africa, NSSM 39 suggested that the United States "remove constraints on Ex-Im Bank facilities for South Africa; actively encourage U.S. export and facilitate U.S. investment consistent with the Foreign Direct Investment Program."[10] United States investment in South Africa, under the Nixon-Ford Administrations, doubled between 1970 and 1975. In 1970, United States investment in South Africa totalled $778 million. In 1975, United States investment had reached $1.57 billion.[11] During the same period, United States trade with South Africa increased greatly. U.S. exports to South Africa rose from $288 million in 1970 to $1.27 billion in 1977. United States imports from South Africa rose from $568 million to $1.54 billion.[12] The level of authorization from the Ex-Im Bank for loan guarantees and insurance to South Africa quadrupled from 1971 to 1975. In 1971, the Ex-Im Bank was authorized to make up to $43 million available to South Africa; the level of authorization was $162 million in 1975.[13]

During the years 1970 through 1974, the United States government followed a political, economic and military policy of normalcy when dealing with the white-minority regimes of southern Africa, and a policy of benign neglect toward the independent African states. Toward the liberation movements, the government displayed a policy of callous disregard. Former Secretary of State William Rogers is reported to have testified to the Senate Foreign Relations Committee on March 20, 1973, that

"There are no wars in Africa."

The military victory of the African nationalist forces over the Portuguese colonial regime forced a total reassessment of United States premises, strategies and programs for southern Africa. By May 1974 it was clear, even to Henry Kissinger, that there was hope for blacks to gain the political rights they sought through armed struggle. Because the Nixon Administration failed to appreciate the strength and determination of the African nationalist forces, some of the former Portuguese colonies were able to become independent without much interference from the United States government.

In Angola, however, it was quite different. Kissinger was determined to make sure that the FNLA, the Angolan faction most sympathetic to the United States and Zaire's President Mobutu Sese Seko, would come to power.* The political leadership of Angola could effect both the military situation in southern Africa and the economic welfare of the central African states of Zambia and Zaire.

In July 1974, the CIA made covert payments to the FNLA. "These payments of $15,000 and $25,000 were...intended to buy the CIA a favored position with Holden Roberto, the head of the FNLA."[14] In January 1975, the CIA gave $300,000 to the FNLA for "bicycles, desks and paperclips."[15] With the encouragement of the CIA and President Mobutu of Zaire, the FNLA armies moved in Angola. In February 1975, they attacked the MPLA forces repeatedly, and the fate of Angola was sealed in blood. In reaction to the United States escalation of arms to the FNLA troops, the Soviet Union sent arms to the MPLA in Angola. The hostilities in Angola escalated until, in June 1975, the MPLA evicted the FNLA and UNITA from the capitol, Luanda. Then,

> In July 1975, the National Security Council responded to the CIA option paper and approved a $14 million covert paramilitary operation in Angola. [16]

The Ford-Kissinger team wanted a military confrontation with the Soviet Union in Angola. Kissinger needed to stop the

* See also Chapter Five.

unravelling of the political-economic order that had been disrupted by the demise of the Portuguese colonial empire. He also wanted to nip in the bud any future challenges to Western interests that radical Africans could make with the support of the Soviet Union.

The Ford-Kissinger-Zairian attempt to install the FNLA in power failed because Holden Roberto of the FNLA tried to take by arms what he could not win by political means and because the Zairian army, a necessary ally, was corrupt and inefficient. The U.S.-inspired offensive failed because there was no political will in the United States to support intervention in Angola (even officials within the State Department and CIA opposed U.S. intervention); and because the United States underestimated "the decisive negative reaction of key African leaders to the presence of South African military on the side of FNLA and UNITA."[17]

The Kissinger-Ford offensive failed because they also did not foresee the Cuban and Soviet response. Cuba introduced 15,000 regular army troops into Angola to stem the tide of the South African invasion of Angola. The Kissinger-Ford offensive "underestimated the political scope of the Soviet-Angola program. The CIA option paper of July 6, 1975, stated that the Soviet response would not likely exceed $45 million. By February 1976, the Soviet program had topped $400 million."[18] Finally, the Ford-Kissinger offensive failed because the United States Congress, remembering Vietnam, ran leary of covert operations that would commit the government in unpredictable ways. It blocked further escalation of United States involvement in Angola with the Clark Amendment to the 1976 Defense Appropriations Bill.

After the failure of the Angola offensive, Kissinger made a trip to Africa in April 1976, "to present proposals aimed at bringing about moderate, negotiated solutions to the urgent political problems of southern Africa."[19] In testimony before the Senate Subcommittee on Africa, Kissinger outlined why his African trip was so important. He stated:

> Africa is a continent of vast resources. We depend on Africa for many key products: cobalt, chrome, oil, cocoa, manganese, platinum, diamonds, aluminum, and others. In many of those

commodities Africa supplies from 30 to 60 percent of our total imports...Africa's importance to us as a commercial partner—as producer of energy and commodities and as a market for our own products—is substantial...the reliance of Europe and Japan on Africa for key raw materials is even greater than our own...the continent [Africa] provides a growing area of investment for our allies, and is an important trading partner as well. Western Europe and Japan's combined trade with Africa now exceeds $30 billion a year.[20]

Kissinger travelled to Kenya, Tanzania, Zambia, Zaire, Liberia and Senegal. (He was refused entry into Nigeria.) The centerpiece of his trip was his speech in Lusaka, Zambia, on April 27, 1976. This speach dealt primarily with majority rule in Rhodesia. Kissinger declared, "The United States is totally dedicated to seeing to it that the majority becomes the ruling power in Rhodesia. We do not recognize the Rhodesian minority regime."[21] Kissinger then read a ten-point program. Some elements of the program were:

a.   independence must be preceded by majority rule, which, in turn, must be achieved in two years;

b.   the Ian Smith regime cannot expect support from the United States in its fight against the African liberation movements;

c.   repeal of the Byrd Amendment;

d.   the United States would be willing to give economic assistance to Mozambique to compensate for the hardships encountered by closing its borders with Rhodesia;

e.   humanitarian assistance to refugees;

f.   a post-independence Zimbabwe Development Fund;

g.   a constitutional structure to protect minority rights.

Kissinger was trying to ride the horns of the southern Africa dilemma: how could he appear to acceded to insistent demands for African majority rule without loosening the Western grip on the economic, political and military future of Namibia, South Africa and Rhodesia?

Kissinger's strategy in southern Africa called for:

1.   increasing the possibility that moderate African leaders take the lead away from the "men with guns;"

2. initiating a dialogue between the African states and South Africa;

3. discussing the problems of southern Africa on a step-by-step basis: first Rhodesia, then Namibia and, sometime in the future, South Africa;

4. the United States to serve as an intermediary between South Africa and the African states;

5. the United States to use a series of carrot-and-stick measures on South Africa to encourage it to bring Ian Smith into line, if the Africans stopped the liberation movements from fighting;

6. the United States to raise up to $1.5 billion internationally for Zimbabwe development; and

7. the Frontline States to get economic assistance from the United States.

Kissinger's shuttle diplomacy filled the air, and he succeeded in creating a dialogue between the African states and white-ruled southern Africa. The results of the dialogue, however, were not impressive. This was predictable. The premise of Option Two, NSSM 39 remained at the heart of all the Kissinger proposals: "whites are here to stay and the only way that constructive change can come about is through them."

The Carter Administration Approach to Southern Africa

With the election of Jimmy Carter to the presidency, the tone of United States policy in southern Africa changed. The new administration wanted to put a clear distance between itself and the Kissinger-Ford formulations on southern Africa. Ambassador Andrew Young, President Carter's point person on a still *unconcretized* administration policy on southern Africa, criticized the previous administration for looking at southern Africa through the eyes of European cold warriors. Instead of Kissinger's cold war view, Young advocated to the Carter Administration a policy that would seriously try to accomodate, at a minimal cost to the Western capitalist system, the African demand for majority rule.

Young drew upon his civil rights experiences to suggest a strategy for the Carter Administration's early southern African policy. Dr. Martin Luther King, Jr. had been able to enlist the support of Roger Blough, chairman of United States Steel, in putting an end to racial segregation in Birmingham, Alabama. As Young is fond of recalling, it just took a phone call from Blough in New York to his plant manager in Birmingham to start the process of dismantling segregationist policies and putting an end to the brutality of Birmingham Police Chief Bull Connors. A part of the new Carter Administration's early strategy therefore involved putting pressure on the illegal white-minority regimes through the United States and South African business community. In an interview with the South African *Financial Mail* of November 5, 1976, Carter stated,

> I think our American businessmen can be a constructive force in achieving racial justice within South Africa. I think the weight of our investment there, the value the South Africans place on access to American capital and technology can be used as a positive force in settling regional problems.

Young also maintained that, to avoid political and economic chaos in southern Africa, the Carter Administration had to recognize the present leadership in Angola and Mozambique. In testimony before the House International Relations Committee, he stated that, regardless of their political belief in socialism or Marxism-Leninism, Samora Machel and Agostinho Neto—the presidents of Mozambique and Angola—were men schooled in Western and Christian traditions. But, Young warned, if the United States did not deal with Neto and Machel, there were young Africans in the wings who were not schooled in these traditions. If they came to power, it would most likely mean chaos for U.S. economic interests. In a departure from previous policy, Young advocated that the Carter Administration not only talk with the independent African states and white-supremacist regimes, but also start a direct dialogue with the nationalist forces in the region.

Although there was some skepticism about the Carter Administration's civil rights approach to southern Africa, many African nations responded favorably to its new style. The African leaders were especially pleased by Carter's devaluing of the Kissinger-Ford position that communism and the Soviet Union were the only threats in southern Africa. For the early Carter Administration, economic chaos caused by warfare in southern Africa, with its consequences for the Western world, was a more overwhelming threat. Although the Carter Administration was concerned about Soviet involvement in southern Africa, it appeared to feel the best way to contain the Soviets would be an orderly, non-violent transfer of political power from the white-minority regimes to a democratically elected government. The Carter Administration reasons that an orderly transfer to majority rule favored the West, and the escalating warfare by the liberation movements favored the Soviets.

The new administration did not seem disturbed by pleas from the illegal white-minority regimes of Ian Smith and John Vorster that an ordered transfer to majority rule without guarantees of a moderate and controlled African leadership equalled a Soviet takeover of the natural resources of the region. In an interview with *Africa*, Ambassador Young gave little weight to the economic threat that radical African leadership could cause to the Western economies. He stated:

> I think we crossed that hurdle to some extent in Angola, when we came to realize that any government in southern Africa will not remain Communist for long...the economic interest of southern Africa, of Black Africa, requires markets for their resources...I mean, Zaire has to sell its copper and so does Zambia to survive. Angola needs to sell its oil. Now the Russians and Chinese are not importing any natural resources, because they've got all the resources they can utilize and they don't have enough capital and technology to develop their own resources in the Soviet Union. So if the resources of Africa are going to be developed even in conditions of a socialist state, Africa has got to sell its resources to the West.[22]

Young used Angola as a practical example. He pointed out that the Soviets gave approximately $400 million in military assistance to the MPLA, but the United States firm, Gulf Oil, takes the crude oil from Cabinda.

Zimbabwe/Rhodesia

The escalating conflict in Rhodesia presented the first practical test for the new administration. The Kissinger proposal had not taken root. There was no dialogue between the nationalist forces and Ian Smith's illegal white-minority regime, and the nationalist forces, although divided, had become increasingly effective.

The first action of the Carter Administration on southern Africa was to send Secretary of State Cyrus Vance to Congress to testify for the repeal of the Byrd Amendment. The administration argued that repeal, although largely symbolic, would signal a shift in United States policy on Rhodesia and establish the *bona fides* of the United States with the independent African states. The Carter Administration then moved to convince the British that they should take a leading role in finding a solution to the Rhodesia conflict. After all, Rhodesia was still legally a colony of Britain. Finally, the Carter Administration committed the economic strength and influence of the United States to guarantee the economic interest of both the local whites and the multinational corporations under majority-rule government. The Carter Administration proposed to press for these economic guarantees through the $1.5 billion Zimbabwe Development Fund initiated by Kissinger.

In September 1977, the British government, with the full agreement of the United States government,[23] drew up certain proposals for "the restoration of legality in Rhodesia and the settlement of the Rhodesian problem."[24] The Anglo-American proposals, as they became known, centered around seven points:

1.   The surrender of power by the illegal regime to Britain;
2.   Transition to independence in the course of 1978;
3.   Elections based on universal suffrage;
4.   The establishment of a British transitional administration to conduct the elections;
5.   A United nations force to keep the peace during the transitional period;
6.   An independent constitution providing for a democratically elected government, individual human rights and the independence of the judiciary; and
7.   A development fund to revive the Rhodesian economy.[25]

The political thrust of the Anglo-American proposals was to give each party just enough to make it worthwhile for them to come to the negotiating table. The bait for the Africans of

Rhodesia, who constitute 96 percent of the population, was the promise of an independent Zimbabwe and a government based on universal adult suffrage. Additionally, the new Zimbabwean army would incorporate troops from the liberation forces. For the local white population, who make up 4 percent of the population, the constitution would be drawn up to protect them from deprivation of property; guarantee them the right to conduct their own schools, and "ensure that pensions...can be freely remitted abroad" by all civil servants; provide amnesty for all acts committed under the illegal Smith regime; and encourage skilled workers and personnel to remain after independence. For the multinational corporate interests in Rhodesia, the plan proposed the lifting of sanctions, and the development fund to "encourage commercial flows, especially in the extractive, processing and manufacturing industries."[26]

After presenting the Anglo-American proposals to all sides, the Carter Administration hoped to bring them together in a two-stage process. The first step would be to get the African Frontline States and the nationalist leaders to agree to the Anglo-American accord. The United States would then use a series of carrot-and-stick measures to get Ian Smith to relinquish power.

To date, the Carter Administration, like its predecessor, has made little headway in bringing about a transition to majority rule in Rhodesia. It now appears that Smith has outflanked the Anglo-American accord by involving two prominent national-ists—Ndabaningi Sithole and Bishop Abel Muzorewa—in a so-called "internal settlement." This "settlement" allows for some increased black participation in the Rhodesian government, but the key positions of power would remain in the hands of Ian Smith's party. Nonetheless, the Carter Administration has responded by calling the agreement a "significant step." President Carter has stressed its congruence with the Anglo-American accords.

Namibia

Following the Carter Administration's strategy for southern Africa, the United States government took the lead in trying to bring a peaceful transition to majority rule in Namibia. The

United States, along with four other Western governments,[27] made proposals to SWAPO and South Africa that the Western powers hoped would bring an end to the fighting in Namibia. The Western proposals called for:

1.   a special representative of the United Nations secretary-general to satisfy himself as to the fairness and appropriateness of the political process leading to "free elections" for a constitutional assembly. Control of the electoral process and administration, however, would rest with the South African Administrator General;

2.   a phased withdrawal of South African troops over a 12-week period, except for 1500 who would stay in two northern bases until after the elections;

3.   a finesse of the question of who owns Walvis Bay.

The Western plan was vague on a number of key points, including the strength of the proposed U.N. forces.[28]

The Western plan for Namibia narrowed the gap between SWAPO and South Africa considerably. The Carter Administration's plan for a peaceful transition to majority rule in Namibia seemed well on the way until South Africa launched an invasion of Angola and attacked a SWAPO camp 150 miles inside that country. According to SWAPO, the South Africans killed over a thousand people in the attack, about 300 of them children. SWAPO then rejected the Western proposals, and was only persuaded to reopen negotiations by the Frontline States.

The Carter Administration's Current Policy

In late 1977 and early '78, a decided shift became apparent in the Carter Administration's approach to southern Africa. The initial focus on peaceful transition to majority rule in Southern Africa swung back to a revival of East *vs.* West confrontation politics in Africa. Instead of concentrating on putting an end to minority rule in the region, the Carter Administration began to orchestrate a steady drumbeat of anti-Soviet and anti-Cuban statements.

As a direct consequence of the new cold war approach of the United States, it became unclear whether any of the administration's previous southern African policies and strategies remained operative. It was no longer certain that the Carter Administration would continue to support the Anglo-American accords. It seemed increasingly possible that Carter would accept some version of Ian Smith's so-called "internal settlement," especially if Joshua Nkomo, leader of the ZAPU party in the Patriotic Front, could be persuaded to join the settlement.* Much of the attraction for the United States of an internal settlement plus Nkomo appeared to lie in the assumption that this would block Robert Mugabe (the leader of ZANU in the Patriotic Front, who is perceived as more of a Marxist) and the fighting forces of the Patriotic Front from coming to power through an armed struggle which would lead to a thorough-going restructuring of the Rhodesian political economy. This maneuver, the administration seemed to believe, would bring to power in Zimbabwe the "moderate" type of African leadership acceptable to the West, but with enough legitimacy to be accepted by the African states.

Elements in the Carter Administration's strategy also began to indicate a more explicit desire to destabilize and destroy the MPLA-led Angola government, which it considered hostile to Western interests in southern Africa. The French, Saudis and the United States had already provided $20 to $40 million to forces working against the MPLA government.**

The new cold warriors of the Carter Administration appeared anxious for opportunities to do battle with the Soviets and Cubans in Africa. The United States eagerly joined France and Belgium to intervene militarily in the conflict in Zaire's Shaba Province between Katangese rebels and President Mobutu. The fighting for the rich province had been going on for some 15 years, as the Katangese soldiers fought for control of Shaba (formerly Katanga) Province with the aid of the Belgians, Portuguese, and now the Angolans. Nevertheless, the "new Christopher Columbuses" of the Carter Administration claimed to "have discovered in this conflict the grand design of the Soviet

*Nkomo, on a trip to the United States, explicitly denied this possibility and condemned the growing anti-Soviet and anti-Cuban campaign of the United States administration on June 18, 1978.
**See Chapter Five.

Union and Cuba to take over Africa."[29] The Carter Administration sought to justify its rush to involve the United States in Zaire with the following reasons:*

1.   The lives of Europeans were threatened or were rumored to be threatened.

2.   The corporate property of Belgium, France, West Germany and the United States was in danger of being damaged or destroyed. (Most of the mineral wealth of Zaire is located in Shaba Province. A West German company also has a missile research program located there.)

3.   The Soviets had allegedly given arms and munitions to the Katangese.

4.   The Cubans were reported to have trained the nationalist forces.

5.   Africans involved in the fighting were suspected of being Marxist.

6.   President Mobutu of Zaire is a moderate, Western-allied leader, supportive of the "free world's" economic interest.

7.   The Katangese crossed international borders to wage their war against Mobutu.

The increasingly anti-communist mind-set within the Carter Administration, and continued application of these criteria for intervention in southern Africa appeared to justify the conclusion that the United States could conceivably intervene militarily on the side of the white-minority regimes of Rhodesia, Namibia and South Africa. During the war between Ethiopia and Somalia over the Ogaden region,** Zbigniew Brzezinski, Carter's national security advisor, according to a Congressional staffer, said: "The problem isn't the war, the problem is the Soviet and Cuban presence."[30] The Congressional source remarked that Brzezinski seemed never to have considered that the war was what led to the Soviet and Cuban presence. Brzezinski's attitude now pervades every Carter Administration policy, strategy and program for Africa, southern Africa included. Brzezinski could

* See Appendix D
**The war started when Somalia invaded Ethiopia. Ethiopia in turn asked for Soviet and Cuban help to defend its territorial integrity.

just as easily say that the problem in southern Africa is not apartheid or white-minority rule, but the Cuban and Soviet presence in Angola, Soviet assistance to SWAPO or ZAPU, or the alleged Cuban presence in Zambia, Tanzania, and Mozambique.

The logic of the Carter Administration's new cold war stance brings South Africa and the Western nations, led by the United States, into close military cooperation with each other. Despite the United States vote for the United Nations arms embargo in 1977, it began to appear increasingly probable that the apartheid regime would be looked upon by the Western nations as a strong ally in their fight against Soviet and Cuban influence in southern Africa. Brzezinski's predecessor, Henry Kissinger, had, after all, used the same arguments to involve the United States in an unholy alliance with South Africa during the Angolan civil war. By mid-1978, the Carter Administration seemed more and more to view South Africa as a Western outpost and not, as they had previously argued, a Western outcast. The logical outcome of Brzezinski's cold war view would be increased support for a militarily strong South Africa.

There are other consequences of the Carter Administration's cold war strategies. The administration has seemed prepared to spend millions on arms to tie down the Cubans in Ethiopia and Angola—apparently so that the Cuban troops could not be used against Rhodesia. Monies and arms were distributed to the Eritrean nationalists and Somalia to tie down the Cubans in Ethiopia, and to UNITA and Zaire to tie down the Cubans in Angola. Apparently, the idea has been that increasing the strength of the Eritrean, UNITA and Somali forces would make the Cuban presence in Africa as costly as possible by killing or wounding as many Cubans as possible. In the process, the Carter Administration will certainly ensure that many Africans are killed.

Conclusion

The events of April, May and June of 1978 have made it clear that although the Western nations had dutifully accepted the inevitably of the legal independence of African states, they still viewed the entire continent of Africa through the lens of relationships developed more than a century ago. The habit of "regarding Africa as an appendage of Western Europe has not been broken."[31]

In a reaction to the so-called new threats to African freedom from outside forces, the Carter Administration met with the former colonial powers in Washington, Paris and Brussels to map new strategies for Africa. In characterizing these meetings, President Julius Nyerere of Tanzania said:

> Whatever the official agenda, the Paris and Brussels meetings are not discussing the freedom of Africa. They are discussing the continued domination of Africa, and the continued use of Africa by Western powers. They are intended to be taken together [as] a second Berlin Conference.
>
> The real agenda, inside and outside the formal sessions of these meetings, will be concerned with two things. It will be concerned with neo-colonialism in Africa for economic purposes—the real control of Africa and African states. That will be led by the French. It will be concerned also with the use of Africa in the East-West conflict. That will be led by the Americans. These two purposes will be coordinated so that they are mutually supportive, and the apportionment of the expected benefits—and costs—will be worked out. It is at that point—the division of the spoils—that disputes are most likely to occur.[32]

References

1. Testimony of former Secretary of State Henry Kissinger before the Senate Subcommittee on Africa, May 13, 1976.
2. See Option Two of NSSM 39, presented in full in, El-Khawas, M.A., and Cohen, Barry, *The Kissinger Study of Southern Africa* (Westport, Conn.: Lawrence Hill, 1976), p. 106.
3. *Ibid.*, p. 106
4. *Ibid.*
5. The U.S. arms embargo on South Africa was initiated voluntarily under the Kennedy Administration in 1963. See Chapters Seven and Eleven.
6. Rogers, Barbara, Testimony before the House Subcommittee on Africa, on "The Complex of United States-Portuguese Relations: Before and After the Coup," March 14, 1974

7.   Rep. Charles Diggs, introductory statement to hearings on "The Complex of United States-Portuguese Relations," March 14, 1974
8.   *Ibid.*
9.   *Ibid.*
10. El-Khawas and Cohen, *op.cit.*, p. 106
11. U.S. Department of Commerce, Bureau of Data Analysis.
12. Department of State, Southern Africa desk.
13. Washington Office on Africa.
14. Stockwell, John, "Roots of the Shaba Crisis in Past CIA Covert Operations," testimony before the House Subcommittee on Africa, May 25, 1978 1978
15. Statement of Henry Kissinger before the Senate Subcommittee on Africa
16. Stockwell, *op.cit.*
17. *Ibid.*
18. Stockwell, *ibid.*, p. 6
19. Kissinger, Henry, Testimony before Senate Subcommittee on Africa, May 13, 1976.
20. *Ibid.*, p. 182
21. Kissinger, Henry, speech given in Lusaka, Zambia, April 27, 1976, p. 3
22. Interview with U.S. Ambassador to the United Nations, Andrew Young, in *Africa* (London), July 1977
23. Rhodesia—Proposals for Settlement. Presented to Parliament by the Secretary of State for Foreign and Commonwealth Affairs.
24. *Ibid.*
25. *Ibid.*
26. *Ibid.*
27. Britain, France, West Germany and Canada.
28. *Washington Notes on Africa*, Spring 1978; produced by the Washington Office on Africa (Washington, D.C.)
29. Statement of David Callaghan, British representative to NATO summit in Washington, D.C., May 1977
30. *The Washington Post*, "The Change in Carter's Foreign Policy," June 3, 1978
31. Special message by the President of the United Republic of Tanzania, His Excellency Julius K. Nyerere, delivered on June 8, 1978, to foreign envoys accredited to Tanzania.
32. *Ibid.*

Chapter 4

Sealanes, Western Strategy and South Africa

John Prados*

United States military strategists have frequently complained about Soviet ships in the Indian Ocean. In fact, the Soviet presence there has been grossly exaggerated. Currently it is overshadowed by the strength of NATO and allied forces in the region. Nonetheless, the United States military has continued to increase its power in the South Atlantic/Indian Ocean area, using the Soviet presence as pretext. In the process, the United States has established a quick-strike force capable of intervening anywhere in Africa.

On May 17, 1978, after fighting broke out in Zaire's Shaba province, the United States alerted the "ready" battalion of its 82nd Airborne Division and aircraft of the Military Airlift Command for possible commitment in Zaire. No combat forces were actually dispatched by the United States. Instead, on the following day, the French and Belgian governments sent paratroops, with U.S. airlift support. It is interesting that the

* The author wishes to thank Paul Klemperer for his assistance in the preparation of this chapter.

possibility of intervention in Zaire formed part of a Defense Department contribution on force-planning to a National Security staff study known as PRM-10, which was prepared in early 1977. Zaire probably served as an illustration because of the Shaba incident of that year; and the United States abstained from overt military involvement there in 1978. Nonetheless, the fact that the United States came so close to an open use of force merits further examination in view of the unstable political conditions in southern Africa and the alleged threat to adjacent ocean areas.

This paper focuses on the environs of Africa, the South Atlantic Indian Ocean, and how the security concerns of Western countries over the viability of sealanes has contributed to a disposition to intervention in Africa. It also discusses the dimensions of the posited threat, principally in the Indian Ocean region, and the strategic rationale underlying the supposition of threat. The response of the Western alliance is a further subject of analysis. Finally, the paper will examine efforts to limit naval armaments in the area.

It is clearly impossible to give an exhaustive treatment to the myriad factors contributing to this situation in one chapter. In particular, economic, social and political trends in Africa are reserved for treatment elsewhere in this book. The emphasis here is rather on the history of Western preparations to ensure the military security of adjoining ocean areas, and on the strategic justifications that have evolved.

Notions of Intervention

Military interventions in foreign areas are not new phenomena, although they have not previously been the subject of such detailed examination as at present.[1] In part such interest reflects the heightened awareness of the dangers to which intervention can lead. The increasing cost of maintaining special military forces has led governments, in particular, to re-examine rationales for intervention.

In July 1969, President Nixon elaborated the doctrine that bears his name, maintaining the United States would help local forces through military aid and air and naval support. Since the late '60s, the United States has also shown a decided preference for selling armaments rather than supplying direct military assistance. This latter trend has resulted in United States cooperation with a core of regional powers capable of supplying local forces.[2] Apparently, however, the United States has not been completely satisfied with dealing through regional powers. Action through allies is less reliable and less controllable. Moreover, allies may exact high prices for their support.

Besides political difficulties, simple factors of military capability stand in the way of an attempted military intervention. Disposable force must exist and be able to arrive in time to be of use. The speeds of aircraft and ships impose finite upper limits to a contemplated use of force. In five major international crises since 1968,* disposable military forces have either been inadequate or of the wrong type for intervention. In particular, in the United States, discussions of military intervention in the Persian Gulf as a result of the Arab oil embargo served to highlight the paucity of forces for intervention.[3]

Such perceptions have periodically led to the creation of conventional military forces suited to rapid intervention.[4] The most recent effort has been to organize what Secretary of Defense Harold Brown has termed a "Rapid Reaction Strike Force."[5] The force is built around "light" divisions, which use relatively little of the heavy equipment considered necessary for combat in Europe. This organization facilitates transport of the divisions by the Military Airlift Command, which would do most of the troop-moving in an urgent situation.[6]

The Rapid Reaction Strike Force currently consists of three divisions: the 82d Airborne, the 101st Air Assault, and a Marine Division. Altogether, it is reported to number some 100,000 men.[7] One battalion of the 82d, with attachments, is forward-deployed in Italy. It has been estimated that a total of 27 battalions (essentially three divisions) could be deployed 5000 miles from the east coast of the United States within two weeks.[8] A battalion of the 82d Airborne Division was alerted in the Zaire incident in May. Planning for contingencies was already clearly

---

* The *Pueblo* crisis, the Indo-Pakistani War (1971), Black September (1970), the October War (1973), and the Ogaden fighting (1976-'77).

in hand. Defense Department planners believe such contingencies could arise in the Indian Ocean region or along Africa's western coast.

United States Planning for the Indian Ocean Region

United States military interest in the Indian Ocean has increased gradually since the end of World War II. At that time, the decision was made to place a Middle East Force (MIDEASTFOR) of two destroyers in the area, to be based at Bahrein in the Persian Gulf. This force has remained the core of United States naval strength in the region ever since. In addition, U.S. Navy units periodically travel from the Atlantic to the Pacific by way of the Indian Ocean.

In the early '60s, Defense Department planners began to look seriously at strategic possibilities in the Indian Ocean. With the establishment of a world-wide communications net to keep in contact with United States Polaris missile submarines, completed by stations in Australia and Ethiopia, the Indian Ocean began to look like an advantageous location for ballistic missile submarines.[9] While there is no evidence that such submarines (SLBMs) were ever stationed there, Soviet leaders could not discount the possibility. Ultimately, they also stationed fleet warships in the Indian Ocean. In the meantime, the United States Joint Chiefs of Staff (JCS) had accepted a proposal from the British to develop a network of staging bases together, mostly on islands off East Africa and the Near East. The JCS favored one atoll, Diego Garcia in the Chagos Archipelago, as an alternate communications link to those in Australia and Ethiopia.[10]

Total combatant tonnage in the U.S. Navy dropped after 1967, and the MIDEASTFOR was reduced. In July of that year, the British announced their withdrawal from east of Suez.[11] Thus the first appearance of Soviet warships in the Indian Ocean, in 1968, occurred at a time of decreasing Western capabilities in the region. In the United States, the Soviet presence attracted attention and became increasingly controversial.[12]

In 1968, the Navy presented a study of Indian Ocean bases. It recommended a communications study at Diego Garcia. After some initial wariness, the Defense and State Departments approved. A request for obligational authority for $26 million passed Congress in 1968. The first funds were appropriated in 1969.[13]

Under the Nixon Administration, the question of protection of sealanes was brought into high relief, making the Indian Ocean a prime candidate as an area of confrontation. In 1970 the Chief of Naval Operations, Admiral Elmo Zumwalt, ordered a new Indian Ocean study by the Naval War College.[14] That November, the National Security Council (NSC) issued terms of reference for National Security Study Memorandum (NSSM) 104:

> an assessment of possible Soviet naval threats to U.S. interests in the Indian Ocean area and the development of friendly naval force and basing alternatives consistent with varying judgments about possible threats and interests over the 1974-75 period.[15]

Then Secretary of Defense Melvin Laird stated publicly that the United States would maintain a "fleet" in the Indian Ocean.

The following November, in the context of the Indo-Pakistani War, the Soviets sent additional warships to the Indian Ocean, increasing their overall force level in the manner known as "surging" naval forces into an area.[16] The United States also "surged" its naval force, with an aircraft carrier task force. Carrier task forces were also "surged" into the Indian Ocean, in succession, in the wake of the 1973 October War betwen Israel and the Arab states.

This latter experience was decisive for subsequent United States policy in three respects. First, there were difficulties associated with operating the MIDEASTFOR from a base in an Arab nation. Second, the "surge" of carrier task forces tied down almost the entire seaborne logistics force of the U.S. Pacific Fleet,[17] underlining the value of a permanent operating base in the Indian Ocean. Third, the Arab oil embargo made the Western developed countries more sensitive about the supply of natural resources and the protection of resource shipments. Significantly, in the United States international affairs analysts who claimed to be serious raised the question of invading the Persian Gulf to take over the oil wells there.[18] Kissinger himself hinted at this in a January 1975 press conference, ultimately leading to a feasibility study by the Congressional Research Service that summer.[19]

United States capabilities in the Indian Ocean were totally inadequate for any such use.

Thus, 1974 was a turning point in United States strategic policy in the region. Administration rhetoric became even more strident. On March 12, 1974, Deputy Secretary of Defense William Clements told a Senate committee:

> [We] feel that the circumstances that prevailed during the [October War] are of sufficient importance to have us restudy this entire situation and bring it to your attention. The Suez Canal will be open shortly, the Soviet presence within this area will be enhanced without any question, and the lines of supply both to ourselves and to our allies in Europe and Japan will certainly be threatened to a degree that they have not been heretofore. Under these circumstances, we feel that [the Diego Garcia] program should be put on a priority basis.[20]

Together with Admiral Thomas Moorer, Chairman of the Joint Chiefs of staff, Clements proposed transforming Diego Garcia into a base capable of servicing major naval and air forces. The cost was five times the original 1968 request for a communications site on the island. In addition, the Navy made a show of force in the Indian Ocean with a huge multilateral naval exercise there. The United States, within the NATO framework encouraged other national efforts in the Indian Ocean. It also studied the feasibility of alliance efforts in the sealanes of the South Atlantic—a point that will be taken up again later in this narrative.

In 1974-'75, however, the Navy did not obtain funding for expansion on Diego Garcia. Senator Mike Mansfield sponsored a Congressional measure to disapprove the project.[21] The Navy claimed the Soviet presence made larger United States forces in the Indian Ocean imperative. In June 1975, however, it emerged that a National Intelligence Estimate coordinated by the CIA had concluded that "surges" in the Soviet presence had always *followed* increases in the United States presence there.[22] The Navy was supported by both the Secretary of Defense, James Schlesinger, and President Ford. Eventually, the decision to improve the facilities at Diego Garcia was confirmed.[23] Congress, however, provided that the president would have to certify the need for the base before appropriations would be made. Need was certified on May 12, 1975. Construction has continued on Diego Garcia, despite some efforts to limit naval forces in the Indian Ocean. The facilities should be fully operational by 1979. A Navy SeaBee battalion is working around the clock on the island.[24]

A familiar pattern of naval operations has evolved. In 1976, a carrier task force "surged" into the Indian Ocean for almost a month, with anti-submarine patrol aircraft operating from Nairobi, Kenya. Another carrier task force sailed into the Indian Ocean in January 1977. Long-range air patrols reportedly operate from Israeli airfields in the Sinai.[25] Thus the United States appears to be asserting a much greater presence in the Indian Ocean region.

Arms Control: A Path Fitfully Taken

In December 1964, the Soviets tabled a resolution in the United Nations to declare both the eastern Mediterranean and the Indian Ocean "nuclear-free zones." While nothing came of that initiative, the concept of an Indian Ocean arrangement was supported by the Group of Non-Aligned Nations meeting at Lusaka in 1969, which called for a "zone of peace" in the Indian Ocean. Subsequent conferences of littoral and non-aligned countries have repeated these calls every year since 1971. The African, Arab and Indian nations, with few exceptions, backed a United Nations General Assembly resolution declaring the Indian Ocean a "zone of peace." On June 11, 1971, Soviet leader Leonid Brezhnev stated a willingness to resolve the problem of military forces in the Indian Ocean on an "equal footing."[26]

For some years, however, United States policymakers refused to grapple with the problem of resource shipment protection by means of arms control.[27] In the authorization hearings for Diego Garcia's expansion, in March 1974, the chairman of the Joint Chiefs of Staff was unaware of any efforts at naval arms limitations in the Indian Ocean. Opinion inside the government was divided. In 1970, NSSM-104 revealed that the State Department and the Arms Control and Disarmament Agency (ACDA) saw little threat to United States interests in the Indian Ocean. They recommended a policy of mutual negotiated reduction between the United States and the Soviet Union. The military vehemently opposed this approach, and advocated a continued and increased United States presence. As Nixon was reportedly unable or unwilling to choose between these views,[28] no response was made to Soviet overtures.

The arms control possibilities were pressed simultaneously with the Navy's request to expand Diego Garcia. On March 19, 1974, Senators Edward Kennedy, Frank Church and Hubert Humphrey, among others, presented a Senate concurrent resolution calling on the president to seek negotiations on "limiting deployment" of military forces in and around the Indian Ocean. After the effort to stop expansion of Diego Garcia failed, a second Senate resolution passed, and funds were held up for several months while the State Department evaluated the possibilities of an Indian Ocean agreement. The State Department rejected this proposal on April 15, 1976, asserting that,

> an arms limitation initiative at this time in a region immediately contiguous to the African continent might convey the mistaken impression to the Soviets and our friends and allies that we were willing to acquiesce in this type of Soviet behavior.[29]

The 1976 election brought the Carter Administration into office. The new Secretaries of Defense and State, and the head of ACDA, reportedly favored the idea of an Indian Ocean pact. President Carter himself said repeatedly in early 1977 that he hoped the Indian Ocean could be demilitarized. He expanded on this view on March 24, 1977:

> We're going to try to move toward demilitarizing the Indian Ocean...and we're going to express our concern about the future of Africa and ask the Soviet Union to join us in removing from that troubled continent outside influence.[30]

When Secretary of State Cyrus Vance visited Moscow at the end of March 1977, almost the only aspect of United States-Soviet talks which made progress was the agreement to form a working group for negotiation of an Indian Ocean treaty.

Bilateral negotiations began when Paul Warnke, head of ACDA, led a delegation to Moscow in June 1977. Initial expectations were optimistic.[31] Warnke told reporters he felt there was no basis for substantial competition between the United States and the Soviet Union in the Indian Ocean, and he would like to keep it that way. Both sides were careful to be non-polemical in the talks, although the Soviet news agency, Tass, released a statement criticizing the base at Diego Garcia. The main issues appear to have been the form of the treaty, restraints on specific types of warships (such as ballistic missiles submarines or aircraft carriers), and constraints on base structures. In a return round in September 1977, the United States proposed to "stabilize" naval activity on both sides at present levels and consider reductions in subsequent negotiations. The Soviet position was favorable, although they were concerned about the vagueness of the United States formula. In addition, the Soviets were widely reported to be interested in banning "nuclear-armed" ships (essentially missile submarines and perhaps aircraft carriers) and in strict constraints on base improvements.[32] Further rounds of negotiations in December 1977 and February 1978 failed to bridge all outstanding differences. The issue was further complicated by the Soviet expulsion from a facility at Berbera, Somalia, in November 1978, after which the United States refused to forego the use of Diego Garcia to quiet Soviet concerns.[33]

Most recently, negotiations have been clouded by the United States campaign against Soviet and Cuban involvement in Africa. Concerns expressed by the National Security Council and at the White House have led to an even more cautious United State attitude toward any Indian Ocean agreement.[34] The military takes the view that an accord restricting United States strength in the Indian Ocean, given the Soviet presence in the Horn of Africa, would be "inconsistent." President Carter has taken a tough rhetorical line. This suggests that the United States will come to rely more upon the second component of the strategy followed since 1974, that is, military activities within an alliance framework.

Sealanes in an Alliance Framework

In his Wake Forest speech of March 17, 1978, President Carter remarked that the United States and its allies have had to take measures to provide for short-term vulnerabilities and long-term threats. One of the more portentous elements of Carter's statement is its hint of multilateral initiatives. The Zaire incursion of May 1978 shows how Western powers can act in concert.

Significantly, the efforts involve a broadening of the traditional
NATO alliance, and a degree of cooperation with the white-
minority regime in South Africa.

Despite the relatively small Soviet presence in the Indian
Ocean, the NATO nations have become increasingly concerned
about the security of resource shipments,[35] many of which need
to transit both the east and west coasts of Africa to reach Europe
or America. Oil is central to the resource question. As the
Secretary of Defense put it in the 1979 Defense Posture Statement:

> Soviet control of the vital oil producing regions of the Persian
> Gulf, in particular, could destroy the cohesion of NATO and
> perhaps NATO's ability to defend itself.[36]

Thus, although Article Six of the 1949 North Atlantic Treaty
confines NATO to activities essentially north of the Tropic of
Cancer, pressures have risen to extend its range.

In November 1972, the NATO Assembly voted to recommend
to the North Atlantic Council that the Supreme Allied Commander, Atlantic (SACLANT) be authorized to plan for defense
operations, surveillance and communications in the Indian
Ocean and the South Atlantic.[37] Orders to this effect were given
by the Defense Planning Committee during June 1973, following
adoption of a resolution by the North Atlantic Council on May
26, 1973.[38] The following year, NATO echelons began to show
interest in using communications and tracking facilities maintained by South Africa at Silvermine, and under improvement
since 1973. In October 1974, the NATO ministerial conference at
Ottawa issued a declaration extending NATO's range to "where-
ever mutual interests arise."[39] During November, a British
admiral suggested that several of the NATO partners combine
outside the alliance to monitor the Indian Ocean. Subsequently,
the United States launched feelers in 1975 about the use of the
South African naval base at Simonstown. In 1976, there was
discussion of a multilateral naval force in the South Atlantic
involving Latin American nations and South Africa (see the
appendix to this chapter).[40] SACLANT was once again authorized by NATO to engage in contingency planning for the South
Atlantic in mid-1977. In addition, NATO's SHAPEX-77 com-

mand post exercises, held shortly thereafter, reportedly covered scenarios dealing with Djibouti, Ethiopia and the Horn of Africa.[41]

The most graphic demonstration of Western multilateral efforts was a 1974 naval exercise named Midlink 1974. The maneuvers involved British and United States flotillas; the United States contributed a carrier group, and the British a 14-ship task force. About 50 warships and 150 aircraft were involved, including some from Iran, that staged into Diego Garcia. Midlink-74 was a display of naval force far superior to anything the Soviets might have in the Indian Ocean.[42]

Great Britain appears to be forming an informal alliance extension alongside the United States in the Indian and South Atlantic Oceans. After 1967, the British rapidly reduced their force levels in the Indian Ocean. The number of British ships dropped by 80 percent between 1960 and '70. By 1973, the British were down to ten vessels in the area.[43] Nevertheless, the British have been willing to raise their force levels, as in the 1974 deployment. Indeed, a British squadron engaged in joint maneuvers with the South African Navy in October 1974.[44] Despite the efforts of conservative M.P.s, who have been pushing for NATO to extend its range of operations to the South Atlantic and Indian Oceans,[45] British naval forces in the Indian Ocean were minimal by 1976.

In contrast, the French have followed a much more active policy in the Indian Ocean region and Africa. They have maintained interests in former colonial areas and have never entirely withdrawn their military forces from Africa. French troops have intervened militarily in many instances, notably in Senegal, Chad and Zaire. In 1977, President Valery Giscard d'Estaing convened a conference of 22 African states, most of them former French colonies. He offered French help to resist any invasion of a "friendly" country. The conference considered a Senegalese proposal for a joint military force. Such a force was again proposed by Belgium after Mobutu had to be saved again in May 1978. A force actually was deployed in that year, largely as a facade for Moroccan troops, which had also intervened in Zaire, in cooperation with France, the year before.[46]

French concern has basically paralleled the predominant fears of the United States administration, but France has acted more forcefully in Africa. The French military presence has been increased to roughly double its 1965 level. In recent months, the French forces in Senegal have been reinforced and new forces sent into Chad.[47] Estimates of French troops in Djibouti range from 4500 to 8000. French strength peaked during the Zaire intervention at 12,000 to 15,000 men in Africa and the Indian Ocean islands.[48] The strength of the French *corps d'intervention* is believed to total perhaps 25,000. France is thus maintaining an almost maximal forward deployment of its intervention forces in Africa.

The French Navy has also been active in the Indian Ocean, along the east coast of Africa, and in the Mozambique Channel. The number of French warships based at Djibouti and Reunion has risen steadily since 1969. In September 1973, the French created an independent naval command for the Indian ocean. A task group with the helicopter carrier *Jeanne d'Arc* sailed the Indian Ocean in March 1974, and two additional French destroyers were sent in 1974. Since then, it has been French standard-operating practice to deploy aircraft carriers in the Indian Ocean. The *Jeanne d'Arc* was deployed in 1974 and 1976, and the larger carrier *Clemenceau* has been in the Indian Ocean in 1975 and '78. Two attack submarines were added in 1976. In that year, the most recent for which statistics are available, French military ship-days in the Indian Ocean outnumbered the Soviet figure by three to one.[49] Like the British, the French Navy has held joint exercises with the South Africans.[50]

Sitting squarely astride the Cape of Good Hope shipping routes, South Africa itself is in a good position to monitor shipping traffic. Since 1969, its extensive military communications and intelligence installation at Silvermine has located shipping traffic from the Bay of Bengal to the South American coast. In 1973, it was linked to NATO communications channels.[51] Near Silvermine, on the Cape, is a major naval base at Simonstown. The base was formerly slated for British use in case of war, but is now available to any NATO country.[52] These two facilities form a good infrastructure, but South Africa does not have comparable operating forces. Its navy has 5500 men and a core of only three submarines and four large escore ships.[53] Reportedly, South Africa was also to procure several missile patrol boats from Israel.

South Africa is highly interested in multilateral initiatives to safeguard South Atlantic and Indian Ocean shipping lanes. These suggestions assume close cooperation between NATO nations and South Africa, and provide Pretoria with leverage to use in African conflicts. Pretoria feels that closer integration with NATO would encourage NATO members to ensure the continued existence of the white-minority government in order to maintain the "stability" of the alliance. Thus the South Africans have been among the strongest supporters of conservative British efforts to encourage multilateral initiatives.

Both the United States and France possess naval capabilities that are considerable. In addition, some littoral countries—notably Iran and Pakistan—possess significant naval capabilities. South Africa has excellent infrastructure, and has encouraged a belief in the "Russian threat" in the Indian Ocean and South Atlantic. To the extent the military ties have been demonstrated by combined naval exercises, port calls by the French and British, etc., the South Africans have benefited from NATO concern about sealanes and supply. It is interesting, in this light, to assess the real dimension of Soviet naval operations in the Indian Ocean and South Atlantic.

Is There a Threat?

Soviet warships first appeared in the Indian Ocean in March 1968, on a cruise which included port calls in India, Pakistan, Iraq and Somalia. This squadron returned to the Pacific in July. That November, a second Soviet squadron entered the Indian Ocean, which has since then never been without a Soviet presence. Until 1974 the Soviet flotilla increased steadily in size and combat capability. Examination of the composition and activities of this flotilla is necessary to understand the issues involved in the Indian Ocean and, more generally, the question of the security of resource shipments.

Currently, the Soviet flotilla in the Indian Ocean aggregates perhaps 20 ships.[54] Of these, only seven or eight are surface warships; one is a submarine. The fleet probably includes one or two cruisers or missile-armed destroyers; a minesweeper; an amphibious ship; several space-event support ships; and various auxiliary and service vessels. This level of deployment has been fairly constant since 1974 (see Table 1).[55] It is a small but balanced force with some capability for almost every activity except air operations.

After 1970, Soviet auxiliary vessels which support the combat ships accounted for about 60 percent of total Soviet shipdays in-ocean. Auxiliaries include oilers, stores ships, oceanography vessels, intelligence trawlers and several ships which form part of the Soviet orbital tracking system. Such auxiliaries have an important indirect military value, although their direct combat capabilities are minimal. The ship-days measurement, however, takes no account of the capabilities of a ship. Even minesweepers and amphibious-lift vessels are usually counted as warships, although they possess marginal military value. The presence of one of each of these types of vessels for a year would generate over 700 ship-days.

But the core of any military threat resides in the force's four or five major surface combat ships and the submarine. This force, while larger than the MIDEASTFOR, does not even outnumber the Iranian Navy, to say nothing of French and other Western naval forces present in the Indian Ocean. Even in 1974, the peak year of Soviet deployment, French-American ship-days totalled more than Soviet. The total displacement of a Soviet naval force of this size is less than that of one United States aircraft carrier. Also, such detached naval squadrons have been tracked down and sunk in both major naval wars of this century. The occurrence of a secret war at sea is highly unlikely under modern conditions.[56] The Soviets could threaten to intervene against shipping routes, but the credibility of such a threat is open to question. A massive increase in Soviet deployed forces would be necessary to raise their naval capabilities in the Indian Ocean from marginal to significant.

Under modern conditions, missile-equipped ships and submarines pose the main threat, which means that the Indian Ocean threat amounts to two or three Soviet warships. The effective force of the flotilla is consequently much less than its apparent size suggests. The Soviet Navy has been greatly modernized in recent years. Several new classes of ships have been introduced, and missile armament increased. Nevertheless, the aggregate tonnage of the Soviet fleet should decline in the 1980s due to the retirement of a large number of older vessels.[57] This block obsolescence problem must at some point affect Soviet naval strength. The strategic priorities to which the Soviets respond in planning deployments give greater weight to needs in the Mediterranean, Pacific and Arctic Oceans than to southern seas like the South Atlantic and Indian Ocean. Probably, the most the Soviets will do is maintain roughly their current force levels in these areas.

The Soviet aim in deploying warships may be political—to show the flag and threaten military force in crisis situations. There have been cases where the Soviets have used naval forces in latter-day gunboat diplomacy in Africa.[58] But recent research on host country press coverage of Soviet naval visits shows interest drops after initial visits.[59] Most Soviet port calls are for operational rather than state purposes.*

A final constraint on Soviet naval power in the Indian Ocean is the availability of bases. Reports have credited the Soviets with "bases" almost everywhere they have any dealings at all.** It turns out that most of the reports are totally unfounded. An Indian naval officer who visited Socotra in 1970, for instance, disclaimed the reports of a full-scale base, replete with airfield and amphibious force staging areas.[60] In reality, the Soviets have mooring buoys near that island. Other reports derive from Soviet efforts to clear a port for Bangladesh and to help develop a sub-

---

* Specifically, it has been claimed that the Soviets possess bases at Adan, Port Sudan (Sudan), Hodeida (Yemen), Berbera and Mogadishu (Somalia), Umm Qasr (Iraq), Visakhaptatnam (India), Chittagong (Bangladesh), Port Blair (Andaman Islands), Socotra, Mauritius, Luanda (Angola), and Conakry (Guinea).

**Merely comparing the number of United States and Soviet "port calls" does not take into account the United States base at Bahrein in the Persian Gulf, which decreased U.S. need for operational port calls.

marine base for the Indian Navy, or simply list harbors to which the Soviets have made port calls.

The closest the Soviets have come to a full-fledged naval base was at Berbera, in Somalia. Here a start was made toward providing extensive facilities, but the efforts were not entirely successful. A wide difference between the U.S. Navy and CIA analyses of the Berbera "base" emerged during Congressional hearings in 1975.[61] In particular, it is not certain that an airfield or repair facilities were ever completed. The number of Soviet personnel at Berbera is thought to have peaked at 2600 in 1976, but the size of the contingent dropped after talks that year between the Soviet naval chief of staff and Somali officials.[62] Subsequently, the Soviet Union elected to support Somalia's opponents in the Ogaden fighting. On November 12, 1977, Somalia ordered the Soviets to vacate Berbera.[63] In the absence of bases, one may expect a diminution of the Soviet squadron, and an increase in the proportion of auxiliary vessels in the force. The absence of a base also militates against the Soviets' use of their most modern and capable warships in this area.[64] These ships, with their complex electronic gear, are most in need of secure base facilities.

A number of factors, then, combine to limit Soviet naval strength in the Indian Ocean and South Atlantic. In addition, logistic difficulties increase as the distance from home bases to deployment areas lengthens. Any Soviet planner seriously interested in interdicting the flow of oil to Western ports must realize it is easier to attack incoming tankers near those ports. Areas close to those ports would also be filled with other types of shipments, including, in a war situation, NATO reinforcements. Soviet submarines working the traditional approaches to European ports would contribute more directly to a battle situation in Europe, with shorter transit times and easier coordination with air and surface elements of the Soviet fleet. A future Soviet anti-shipping war would probably be fought out along the same lines as the two World Wars. The South Atlantic and Indian Oceans, then, would be very much peripheral theaters.

Conclusions

Militarily, those who would be secure against *any* threat can never be satisfied. They are not pleased with a situation in which a Soviet flotilla has even a marginal capability to affect trade routes. But the amount of Western naval power needed to ensure no Soviet force could be present in the Indian Ocean would be enormous. Even then, supertankers could still be sunk by aircraft based in the Soviet Union or even by solitary guerrillas with lucky hits at strategic choke points. Defense against the single submarine scenario is analogous to the problem of the single terrorist with a nuclear weapon. It is simply not feasible to maintain such naval forces in the Indian Ocean or South Atlantic.

The "threat" to oil routes in the Indian Ocean has been much exaggerated. Present Soviet forces in the area are not able to "threaten the industrial life of the West," as some have argued. The Soviet flotilla is simply not strong enough. Moreover, if they were, the "threat" would be so serious that its materialization would probably precipitate a major confrontation between the United States and the Soviet Union. The more one pursues it, the less sense the argument makes.

Why, then, is the argument repeated so insistently these days? First, the NATO powers, increasingly concerned about the erosion of their influence in Africa, need a rationale for building a naval presence which will enable them to project power onto the continent. Second, they know that the expansion of their naval capacities in the Indian Ocean will, for a variety of reasons, create closer links with South Africa. That country has the only modern repair, bunkering, provisioning and communications facilities in the western Indian Ocean. Expansion of the Western naval presence thus serves to create interdependence and ties which the military now see as important if the West is to "stabilize" the region.

The Carter Administration is reacting strongly to the African situation. A fully manned Rapid Reaction Strike Force will soon be available to lend weight to such responses. But military intervention is an exceedingly blunt instrument which cannot be applied with the precision that limited war theorists would like. Had such a strike force existed, with a 12,000-foot runway at Diego Garcia, at the time of the oil embargo furor, the consequences could have been disastrous. Meanwhile, the temptation to use forces in being may prove insuperable, whether in Africa or in the Persian Gulf. Administration statements notwithstanding, there is some question as to whether the United States needs such military capabilities.

In many respects, the statements heard today about sealanes, Soviet threats and Cubans are similar to those made in bygone days about upholding the SEATO treaty. Diego Garcia by itself may not have been a "large" decision; nor, for that matter, is the "linkage" to Indian Ocean talks, or the decision to form a strike force. But by degrees, the United States seems to be painting itself into a corner, once again, by means of incremental misdirections in which seemingly small, reversible steps lead to a rigidly structured situation used to justify intervention. As John F. Kennedy once observed, the escalation process is like taking a drink: when the affect wears off, it is necessary to have another. One wonders whether the "threat" in the Indian Ocean and South Atlantic may not lead to the countries of southern Africa.

Table 1: Soviet Naval Ship-Days* in the Indian Ocean

year	total	Combatant shipping	Auxiliary shipping
1968	1,200	530	650
1969	4,100	1,138	2,928
1970	4,900	1,670	3,256
1971	4,000	1,500	2,500
1972	8,900	3,500	5,400
1973	9,000	3,500	5,500
1974	10,500	4,100[1]	6,400[1]
1975	7,100	2,800[1]	4,300[1]
1976	7,300	2,800	4,500

*A ship-day represents the presence of one ship for one day.
[1]estimated

Source: Information supplied by the Department of Defense to the Senate Armed Forces Committee, hearings on "Disapprove Construction Projects on the Island of Diego Garcia (S. 160)," 94th Congress, 1st Session (Washington, D.C.: Government Printing Office, 1975), and hearings on "Authorization for Military Procurement, R&D and Personnel, Fiscal Year 1978," Part I (Washington, D.C.: Goverment Printing Office, 1977).

References

1. Useful studies include, Stern, E.P., ed., *The Limits of Military Intervention* (Beverly Hills: SAGE Publications, 1977); Blechman, B.M., and Kaplan, Stephan S., *The Use of the Armed Forces as a Political Instrument* (Washington, D.C.: Brookings, 1977); George, Alexander, ed., *The Limits of Coerceive Diplomacy* (Boston: Little Brown, 1971); and Barnet, Richard J., *Intervention and Revolution* (New York: Signet edition, 1968)

2. Department of Defense, Security Assistance Agency, *Foreign Military Sales and Military Assistance Facts*, December 1976

3. See for example Tucker, Robert W., "Oil: The Issue of American Intervention," in *Commentary*, March 1975; and Ignatius, Miles, "Seizing Arab Oil," in *Harper's Magazine*, March 1975

4. Eg., the build-ups associated with NSC-68 in 1950 and with Kennedy's "flexible response" doctrine a decade later. See Osgood, R., *Limited War* (Chicago: University of Chicago Press, 1957); Kaufmann, William, *The McNamara Strategy* (New York: Harper, 1964); and Klare, M., *War Without End* (New York: Knopf, 1972)

5. See, *U.S. News and World Report*, February 27, 1978, pp. 24-5; *The Washington Post*, February 24, 1978, p. A21, and March 11, 1978, p. A10.

6. Pickett, J.R., "Airlift and Military Intervention," pp. 137-150, in Stern, *op. cit.*

7. *U.S. News and World Report*, February 27, 1978

8. Ware, Col. Fletcher K. (U.S. Army), "The Airborne Division and a Presence in the Indian Ocean," in *Naval War College Review*, October 1970.

9. Jukes, Geoffrey, *The Indian Ocean in Soviet Naval Policy* (London: International Institute for Strategic Studies, Adelphi Paper No. 87, May 1972), p. 7. Also see Bezborua, M., *U.S. Strategy in the Indian Ocean: The International Response* (Praeger: 1977), p. 137

10. *The Times* (London), August 10, 1964

11. Darby, Phillip, *British Defense Policy East of Suez, 1947-1968* (London: Oxford University Press), pp. 316-321

12. See, for example, Georgetown University, Center for Strategic and International Studies, *The Gulf: Implications of British Withdrawal*, Special Report No. 8 (Washington, D.C.), p. 13; and U.S. Senate, Committee on Appropriations, Subcommittee on Defense Appropriations, hearings on "Department of Defense Appropriation for Fiscal Year 1970," 91st Congress, 1st Session, Part I, p. 940

13. Bezboruah, *op. cit*, pp. 63-66

14. The study group's finding were published in "An Evaluation of U.S. Naval Presence in the Indian Ocean," in *Naval War College Review*, October 1970.

15. Terms of reference cited in Zumwalt, Admiral Elmo (USN-ret.), *On Watch: A Memoir* (New York: Quadrangle Books, 1976), p. 362

16. The Soviet "surge" during the Indo-Pakistani War may have been related to the transformation of a routine rotation of deployed units in the Indian Ocean. See, McConnel, J.M., and Kelly, Anne M., "Superpower Naval Diplomacy: Lessons of the Indo-Pakistani War," in *Survival* (London: IISS), XV.6 (November-December 1973)

17. Zumwalt, *op. cit.*, p. 455

18. Academics' comments are listed in note 4. In addition, see: *Newsweek*, (New York) October 7, 1974; Tobias, Andrew, "War—The Ultimate Anti-Trust Action," in *New York*, October 14, 1974; and McCarthy, Terence, "Will We Go to War?" in *Ramparts*, March 1975. Views like Tucker's have not disappeared yet, as witnessed by a 1978 RAND analysis (Pauker, G.J., "Military Implications of a Possible World Order Crisis in the 1980s")

19. House International Relations Committee, *Staff Report: Oil Fields As Military Objectives,* 94th Congress, 1st Session (Washington, D.C.: U.S. Government Printing Office, 1975)

20. Senate Armed Services Committee, hearings on "Fiscal Year 1974 Supplemental Military Procurement," 93rd Congress, 2nd Session (Washington, D.C.: U.S. Government Printing Office, 1974). Hereafter as FY1974 Supplemental.

21. Senate Armed Services Committee, hearings on "Disapprove Construction Projects on the Island of Diego Garcia (S. 160)," 94th Congress, 1st Session (Washington, D.C.: Government Printing Office,1975). Hereafter cited as Disapprove.

22. Colby, W.E., and Forbath, P., *Honorable Men: My Life in the CIA* (New York: Simon and Schuster, 1978), pp. 358-9

23. Bezboruah, *op. cit*, pp. 110-111

23. See Jack Fuller, "Dateline Diego Garcia: Paved Over Paradise," in *Foreign Policy*, 28 (Fall 1977); *The New York Times*, April 7, 1977 and April 10, 1977; *The Washington Post*, April 7, 1977; and *Commander's Digest*, March 1978 (photo feature)

25. Senate Armed Services Committee, hearings on "Authorization for Military Procurement, R&D and Personnel, Fiscal Year 1978," 95th Congress, 1st Session, Part I (Washington, D.C.: Government Printing Office, 1977), p. 580 (hereafter cited as FY1978, Pt. 1) gives ship-day figures. Other operational details from *Baltimore Sun*, July 30, 1976; *The New York Times*, January 30, 1977 and March 15, 1978; *The Washington Post*, January 31, 1978; *The New York Times,* March 26, 1978

26. *Current Digest of the Soviet Press,* March 15, 1972, p. 2

27. See Moorer testimony in "FY1974 Supplemental," *op. cit*

28. Zumwalt, *op. cit*, pp. 362-3

29. Senate Concurrent Resolution 76, March 19, 1974, p. 2

30. See, for example, *The New York Times*, April 22, 1976, and March 25, 1977

31. See, *The New York Times,* June 22, 1977

32. *The New York Times,* September 25, November 20, December 14 and 18, 1977; Haass, R., "Naval Arms Limitation in the Indian Ocean," in *Survival* (London: IISS), XX.2 (March-April 1978); Hanks, Rear-Admiral R.D. (USN-ret), "The Indian Ocean Negotiations," in *Strategic Review* (London: IISS), VI.1 (Winter 1978)

33. *The New York Times,* February 10, 1978

34. See *The New York Times,* February 10, 1978

35. U.S. Department of Commerce forecasts are presented in Kelly, David J., "African Oceans," in *Defense and Foreign Affairs*, 4 (1977), p. 43; cf. Van

Rensburg, W.C.J., "Africa and Western Lifelines," in *Strategic Review*, VI.1 (Winter 1977); and *The New York Times,* July 21, 1974

36. Brown, Harold, *Department of Defense Annual Report: Fiscal Year 1979,* February 2, 1978, p. 8

37. *The Observer* (London), May 19, 1974

38. Peck, Winslow, "Silvermine," in *Counterspy*, III.1 (Spring, 1976), p. 59

39. Manning, R.A., "A South Atlantic Pact in the Making," in *Southern Africa*, X.3 (April 1977), p. 6

40. *Ibid.*

41. *The New York Times,* May 12 and 16, 1977

42. Hanks, *op. cit.* Also, *Battle Magazine,* "Briefing: Exercise Midlink-74," February 1975, pp. 45-7

43. "FY1974 Supplemental," *op. cit.*, p. 52

44. *The Observer* (London), September 1, 1974; *The Times* (London), August 29, 1974; *Sunday Telegraph* (London), September 1, 1974

45. Notably Mr. Patrick Wall, M.P. See Wall, Patrick, ed., *The Indian Ocean and the Threat to the West* (London: Stacy International, 1975). In the United States, retired Army general Daniel Graham has expressed similar views.

46. Morocco used 1500 troops in 1977, and provided 1000 in 1978 for a 2000-man force not yet fully assembled at the time of writing.

47. *The New York Times*, November 3, 1977, April 21 and May 12 1978

48. Talbot, Steve, "France's new Foreign Legions," in *Inquiry*, March 20, 1978, pp. 19-22, gives a good overview, as does Crocker, C.A., "The African Dimension of Indian Ocean Policy," in *Obis*, XX.3 (Fall 1976), pp. 637-667. French strength figures given are derived from Talbot's figures, the technical literature and press reports.

49. "FY 1978 Appropriations," *op. cit.*, Part I, p. 580

50. *The New York Times,* November 9, 1977

51. Peck, *op. cit*

52. Dudd, Col. N., "Simonstown," *Defense*, March 1975; *Defense*, "Twelve Months After," June 1976; Hessman, J.D., "South Africa, Simonstown, Soweto, Shaka, Silvermine and Separate Development" in *Seapower*, November 1975; Ramamurthi, R.G., "Southern Africa and the Indian Ocean," in *India Quarterly* October-December 1972; and Nathan, A.J., "The South African Navy," in *Sea Classics*, January 1976

53. IISS, *The Military Balance 1977-'78,* p. 47

54. *The New York Times,* September 25, 1977

55. See Hanks, *op. cit.*, p. 26; SIPRI Yearbook 1975, pp. 70-71

56. The paradigm case is the Italian "pirate" submarine campaign against merchant shipping during the Spanish Civil War. Even at that time, there was little question of whose submarines were active.

57. Dismukes, B., "Soviet Employment of Naval Power for Political Purposes, 1967-1975," In McGwire, M., and McDonnell, James M., ed., *Soviet Naval Influence* (New York: Praeger, 1977)

58. Phillips, Heidi S., "Host Press Coverage of Soviet Naval Visits to Islamic Countries, 1968-1973," Center for Naval Analysis Paper CRC-283, June 1976

59. Although the Defense Intelligence Agency (DIA) disputes the contention about Soviet "block obsolescence," first made when James Schlesinger was Secretary of Defense, that agency has been criticized for frequent overestimation of Soviet shipbuilding efforts. See *The New York Times*, July 18, 1977

60. Bindra, Capt. A.P.S. (Indian Navy), "The Indian Ocean as Seen by an Indian," in U.S. Naval Institute, *Proceedings*, May 1970, pp. 178-203

61. "Disapprove," *op. cit*

62. Talks recorded in Manthorpe, Capt. William H.J. Jr., (USN), "The Soviet Navy in 1976," in U.S. Naval Institute *Proceedings*, May 1977, p. 207

63. *The New York Times*, November 13, 1977

64. See Weinland, R.G., "Land Support for Soviet Naval Forces: Egypt and the Soviet Escadra, 1962-1976," in *Survival* (London: IISS), XX.2 (March-April 1978), pp. 73-9, for a discussion of these factors with reference to the Mediterranean.

Appendix*

Since the late 1960s, the South African regime has waged a nonstop campaign to form military alliances with other states, in particular NATO and the countries of South America. The most recent feature in this campaign has been the recurrent proposal to form a South Atlantic Treaty Organization (SATO), based in South Africa.[1] In pushing for this alliance, the South African regime has been able to offer potential participants first crude, and later enriched, uranium. This has been especially important in the regime's relations with other repressive states, such as Iran and Brazil,[2] which are also developing nuclear power.

Since the Soweto uprising in 1976, the United States and other NATO powers have apparently been less willing or able to further a treaty involving South Africa. Observers from Britain and two other NATO countries were, however, present at South African military maneuvrers in spring 1978 as observers.[3]

*South African Naval Maneuvers, Meetings and Military Exercises with Other Countries, 1967-'76**

1957: the South African Navy takes over Simonstown Naval Base from Britain; continue joint defense operations with Britain until 1964

---

*Information supplied by Ronald Corriveau, mainly from South African Ministry of Information, *South African Digest* (Pretoria).

December 1967: South Africa held maneuvers off the coast of Argentina with the Argentine Navy.

July 1970: South African naval and air forces participated in joint maneuvers with the British in the South Atlantic. Two South African ships and four British vessels took part in the exercise.

March 1971: a contingent of South African marines stopped in Lisbon to meet with Portuguese naval officials. Meetings were held betwen Portuguese Navy Minister Manuel Crespo, and South African Ambassador Barerd van der Walt.

July 1971: Dr. C.P. Mulder, the South African Minister of Information and the Interior, met Vice President Spiro Agnew and other United States leaders to discuss "the dangers of Russian infiltration in the Indian Ocean and the importance of the Cape Sea Route."

October-November 1971: Naval maneuvers held between South African naval and air forces and the British Navy. Exercises were commanded by W.D. Hogg, South African Senior Ocean Naval Officer.

July 1972: Iranian Navy visits facilities at Simonstown. Chief of the Imperial Iranian Navy Admiral Faiajollah Rassai stays for two weeks of talks that are keyed to establish "close ties between Iran and South Africa," and "chiefly on naval matters."

December 1972: Netherland's Counsel General Dr. J. Weldema was given a tour of South African naval vessels and their operation at sea. There was a joint visit with the British to inspect facilities at Simonstown.

March 1973: Dr. Rui Patrica, Foreign Minister of Portugal, met with Prime Minister J.B. Vorster and Connie Mulder to discuss the "danger of Communist-inspired activities and subversion," and "constructive and fruitful cooperation between South Africa and Portugal."

May 1973: Dr. H. Mulder and an unspecified delegation of South African representatives go to Buenos Aires, Argentina, to attend the inauguration of President (General) Campora.

July 1973: the British Navy and the South African naval and air forces take part in joint naval maneuvers under the Simonstown agreement. Six English vessels participated, including a nuclear submarine, the *Dreadnought*. Several South African ships and aircraft took part in the exercises, in which over 2000 men participated.

November 1973: The British navy and the South African Navy took part in the largest joint exercise held at the Cape to that date. The maneuvers, called Operation Capex, involved a month-long joint exercise that involved the South African and British Air Forces, over ten military vessels, and two submarines.

Early 1974: British held maneuvers with South Africa, which later developed into the multilateral maneuvers, "Midlink-74."

March 1975: The French aircraft carrier *Clemenceau* came to Simonstown for a three-day operational visit with the South African Navy.

May 1975: Defense Minister Botha announced plans to double the size and capacity of the Simonstown naval facilities over the next few years. Botha stressed the fact that the base was available to any power in the "free world" that was interested in protecting the sea route around the Cape.

June 1975: Britain and South Africa formally end the Simonstown agreement, but hasten to remark that this action does not preclude future joint military maneuvers.

1976: South American and United States officials hold conference in Buenos Aires to discuss South Atlantic Treaty Organization (SATO) proposals. Shortly thereafter, South African Navy officials visit Washington, D.C., to discuss the outcome of the conference.

References:

1. For original formulation, see *Background,* "Defense of South Africa," (Johannesburg), May/June, 1969
2. South African Ministry of Information, *South Africa Scope* (Pretoria), July 1975
3. Minty, Abdul S., Statement to United Nations Special Committee Against Apartheid, December 22, 1977 and May 30, 1978

Chapter 5

Covert Operations in Central and Southern Africa

James Dingeman

Previous behind-the-scenes destabilizing and military activities of United States agents have been exposed in the Congo (now Zaire), Ghana and Angola. The kinds of covert activities reported in this chapter are undoubtedly being conducted today in southern Africa.

As marines deployed around the United States Embassy in Saigon to protect the hasty evacuation, the United States had already begun to intervene seriously in southern Africa. In Angola, a country most Americans did not even know existed, the United States Central Intelligence Agency (CIA) was expanding its covert activities. As the longest imperial war of the United States was ending in ignominious defeat in Asia, another was brewing in Africa.

Vietnam had made the United States public cynical and weary of the usual cant recited to endorse interventions abroad. Domestically, the United States was living through the trauma of Watergate. These events fueled unprecedented scrutiny of the CIA, following the exposure of its domestic operations against anti-war activists in 1974.[1]

A systematic study of the CIA's activities in Vietnam has revealed that covert operations are a decisive first step in military intervention.[2] General Lansdale's team helped sabotage the Geneva Accords in 1954, and contributed to the establishment of the regime of Ngo Dinh Diem. Nine years later, events leading to Diem's overthrow also pointed strongly to CIA involvement. The Gulf of Tonkin incident was precipitated by covert CIA operations. Throughout the war, the CIA waged a "secret war" in Laos, hidden from the eyes of the United States public. As a result of its cooperation with Meo allies in Laos, the CIA became deeply involved in the world-wide marketing of heroin.[3] The devastating war in Cambodia was initiated by CIA machinations.[4]

Covert activities are among the most carefully concealed of intelligence activities. Generally, hard information about them comes to light only after months or even years have elapsed. But extensive evidence now exists which reveals that the focus of CIA efforts is now moving to Africa, especially southern Africa. In 1975 and '76, the CIA's role in Angola was "blown." In 1978, John Stockwell, head of the CIA's Angola Task Force, published his book, *In Search of Enemies*, which provides an in-depth picture of the CIA's intervention in Angola, despite Congressional passage of the Clark Amendment, which prohibited funding for covert activities in Angola and Zaire.

Although the Carter Administration pledged to follow a different path in Africa, the *Washington Post* reported in May 1978 that,

> White House strategists for at least two months have attempted to funnel sophisticated arms and funds clandestinely to African guerrilla forces fighting Soviet-backed Cuban troops in Angola.[5]

The report asserts that presidential security adviser Zbigniew Brzezinski argued that this would allow the United States "to pin down the Cubans" and limit their role in Africa. Aid was to be funneled through an unnamed "third party."

These reports and the rebellion in Shaba have inspired a controversy over the Cuban presence in Angola. Less attention has been paid to the ominous undercurrents suggested by the Carter Administration's public trial balloon.

The CIA's previous covert interventions in Africa have all been marked by ever-growing cooperation, direct or indirect, with the white-minority regimes in southern Africa, especially South Africa. Analysis of these earlier interventions provides a useful picture of the CIA which can aid in understanding its probable present and future role there.

This chapter first outlines the overall structure and decision-making procedures of the CIA and briefly describes the way the CIA initiated its covert activities in Africa, and the links it established with the intelligence networks of former colonial powers and the white-minority regimes of southern Africa. Then it reviews the character of the CIA's on-going "low-level" activities. Finally, it summarizes the evidence relating to three instances of "high-level" CIA intervention—in the Congo (now Zaire), Ghana and Angola—to illustrate the possible patterns of current and future covert United States activities in the context of the crisis in southern Africa.

Overall Structure and Decisionmaking Procedures

CIA covert operations[6] are sub-divided into two closely related functions, "intelligence collection, primarily espionage"; and "covert action, attempting to influence the internal affairs of other nations."[7] Espionage is especially important for the creation of the groundwork for covert action. Since the early '50s, the CIA's classic espionage techniques have been more effective in the Third World than in the Soviet Union or China. Every CIA station in a Third World country has developed an agent network which sometimes includes the highest state officials.

CIA activities in Ecuador in 1961 exmplify its "classic espionage" activities in a Third World state.[8] With a total staff of 12, the CIA station there penetrated virtually every major political party in Ecuador. The personal physician of the president of Ecuador and the chief of national police intelligence were CIA agents. All diplomatic communications from Eastern Europe and China were monitored by the CIA. Travel into and out of the country was closely watched. Anti-communist youth movements were deeply penetrated. "Assets" were in place for clandestine propaganda. The CIA Ecuador station also provided safe "letter drops" for agent networks in Cuba handled by the CIA base in Miami.[9]

The development of a large and varied number of "assets" allows the CIA to carry out several functions.[10] First, they supply "timely intelligence of the internal power balance," which gives the CIA "a chance of careful prediction" as to the local political situation. Second, these assets present an expanding basis for instant mobilization of covert action, as the need arises. "Assets" for minor interventions "can be recruited simply with money"; for "larger and more sensitive interventions," covert assistance may be rendered directly to allies who "must have their own motivation."

Richard Bissell, head of the CIA's Clandestine Services in 1958-'62, defined covert action as:

> 1. political advice and counsel; 2. subsidies to an individual; 3. financial support and "technical assistance" to political parties; 4. support of private organizations, including labor unions, business firms, cooperatives, etc.; 5. covert propaganda; 6. "private" training of individuals and exchange of persons; 7. economic operations; 8. paramilitary [or] political action operations designed to overthrow or to support a regime [such as the Bay of Pigs or the programs in Laos.][11]

Typically, the normal operations of a CIA station in the Third World include categories one through seven. "Low-level" covert operations occur simultaneously and overlap. "High-level" covert actions—paramilitary and political action programs—are introduced where low-level covert action operations have failed or do not exist.

The key difference between low and high level covert action is that the latter seeks to alter the internal power balance radically in the short-term, rather than merely influence it. The coups in Chile in 1973, Guatemala in 1954, and Iran in 1953 illustrate high-level covert action. Covert operations are easier to introduce in Third World countries because,

> governments are much less highly oriented; there is less security consciousness; and there is apt to be more actual or potential diffusion of power among parties, localities, organizations and individuals outside of the central governments.[12]

The impact of covert actions is increased if

a comprehensive effort is undertaken with a number of separate operations designed to support and complement one another and to have a cumulatively significant effect.[13]

This operational integration can involve cooperation with other intelligence agencies. Given the CIA's development of a large apparatus for covert intervention, it is not surprising that the executive branch has turned to it first in most crisis situations.

The command and control procedures for covert operations encourage the use of the CIA's "violent option." First, the decision-making process for covert operations is highly secretive and elitist, and hence vulnerable to excess and abuse. More important, institutional momentum tends to push the CIA into questionable actions. CIA officials frequently urge covert escalations which push our foreign-policy apparatus along the path to high-level covert intervention.

Theoretically, the system of command and control over covert operations is tightly controlled. The NSC monitors all CIA covert operations through a group once known as the 40 Committee, and renamed the Special Coordination Committee by the Carter Administration. This committee usually includes the Director of Central Intelligence, the national security advisor, the chairman of the Joint Chiefs of Staff, the Deputy Secretary of Defense, and the Under Secretary of State for Political Affairs, as well as other high officials. Despite some additions and increased Congressional concern, however, decision-making is still limited to a small body of people.

From 1965 to 1975, covert action projects approved by the 40 Committee were divided into four major categories.[14] The largest (32 per cent) involved projects "providing some form of financial election support" in foreign countries. The second largest category (29 percent) represented "media and propaganda projects." The third (23 percent) covered paramilitary and arms transfers projects, including "secret armies, financial support to groups engaged in hostilities; paramilitary training and advisers; and shipment of arms, ammunition and other military equipment." These projects were the most expensive. The fourth category (16 percent) financed organizational support for "a plethora of foreign, civic, religious, professional and labor organizations."

Covert action may initially be sparked at either the station or division level. It passes up the chain of command to the area division chief, the Director of Operations, the Director of Central Intelligence, and finally the NSC decision-making body.[15] This process strictly limits input from the CIA's own Directorate of Intelligence, as well as from policy-making officials in other agencies, including the State and Defense Departments. The use of special ultra-secret security clearances further limits the number of participants in the decision-making process. Approval for covert action proposals is practically routine. One former CIA official reported the 40 Committee was,

> like a bunch of schoolboys. They would listen and their eyes would bug out. I always used to say I could get $5 million out of the 40 Committee for a covert operation faster than I could get money for a typewriter out of the ordinary bureaucracy.[16]

The gathering of intelligence through the Clandestine Services—that is, through CIA "assets" and their case officers in the field—further strengthens the CIA's inclination for risk-taking activities.[17] The biases and self-interests of intelligence gained by classic espionage cannot be reviewed. The failure of the Bay of Pigs operation was initiated because CIA assets (anti-Castro forces inside and outside Cuba and their case officers) insisted Castro's grip on power was fragile.

All covert operations are designed to give the president the option of "plausible deniability." The president is informed of all covert operations, but does not sign any documents approving them. Suitable "covers" are constructed to hide United States involvement. During the war in Angola, for example, the CIA supplied the FNLA and UNITA with osbolete, Second World War, United States weapons. Since these are available everywhere in the world, the CIA felt their use in Angola would not automatically indicate United States involvement.

The CIA implements covert operations through area divisions or by creating special task forces. During the Indochina War, the Far East area division expanded gradually until it became the largest of the area divisions by the late '60s.

If a crisis arises, the CIA may deal with it through a task forces. Stockwell provides a good description:

> In 1960, a small, quiet office handling several central African countries suddenly became the Congo Task Force and then, as the Congo crisis dragged on for years, the Congo Branch. The Cuban Task Force eventually became the Cuban Operations Group. The Libyan Task Force in 1973 faded almost as quickly as it was assembled. A task force supporting a serious paramilitary program would normally have a good GS 16 at its head, with senior GS 15 as its deputy chief, and twenty-five to one hundred people on its staff, including half a dozen senior case offices to write the cables and memos, sit in on the endless planning sessions, and undertake the numerous individual missions that inevitably arose.[18]

The CIA can use the $50-million to $100-million contingency fund at the disposal of the Director to implement the early stages of this type of operation in relative freedom.[19]

Morton Halperin, perhaps the most influential public critic of the CIA, argues[20] that the CIA's decision-making apparatus inevitably increases the chances that "risky" operations will be chosen over more desirable alternatives; reduces the effectivness with which the operations are designed and carried out; distorts decision-making within the executive branch in general; and lowers the quality of intelligence evaluation, supposedly the CIA's primary responsibility.

CIA Links in Africa

The Africa Division of the CIA's Clandestine Services is the smallest of all the area divisions. Only 300 to 400 people are in the divisions, based at CIA headquarters in Langley or stationed in Africa. This small size reinforces a strong sense of "clubbishness."[21]

Until the late 1950s, clandestine operations which concerned Africa were handled in the European or Middle Eastern division. The de-colonization of Africa in the 1960s, however, spurred the CIA to consolidate and expand the newly created Africa division. From 1969 to '63, "the number of CIA stations in Africa increased by 55.5 percent."[22] The main focus was halting "Communist advances through propaganda and political action." Intelligence operations were also directed at recruiting the socialist countries' personnel in Africa.[23] In 1960, the CIA's first major covert operation in Africa began, in the Congo.

The CIA effort in Africa initially depended on liaison relationships with other, more established, intelligence services. The French intelligence service, *Service de Documentation Exterieure et de Contre-Espionage* (SDECE) still played an important role in the internal politics of the former French colonies.[24] Relationships between the SDECE and the CIA were "difficult and sensitive" while De Gaulle was in power,[25] but with his departure the situation changed. Giscard d'Estaing's government initiated a new era in United States-French cooperation in covert operations in Africa, in particular during the Angolan war. France supplied funds and paramilitary advisers for the Front for the Liberation of the Enclave of Cabinda (FLEC).[26] But although the CIA informed the French of its activities, SDECE did not reciprocate.[27] The liaison could also have been more open at higher levels in the CIA or the National Security Council.

A close liaison between the British intelligence agency, MI-6, and United States intelligence services when dealing with South Africa and Rhodesia has existed for several decades. The oldest and "most important liaison operation of the CIA,"[28] this link dates back to before World War II.[29] The CIA has benefited from Commonwealth intelligence agreements fostered by MI-6 over the years. As a result, the CIA had extremely close contacts with South African intelligence services through a special agreement, known as UKUSA, as well as with the Rhodesian regime's intelligence.[30]

In 1970, when the National Security Council deliberated closing the United States consulate in Salisbury, Richard Helms, then the CIA director, was "one of the strongest proponents of a pro-white policy in Africa." When President Nixon asked his opinion on the Salisbury question, Helms replied,

> ...we do have useful and workable relationships in Salisbury with our counterparts there. I think it would be a shame to sacrifice those if we didn't have to..if we got rid of the consulate in Salisbury, we would have to run our operations out of some other context..I would like to see us keep a hand in there.[31]

The deeper relationship between the CIA and the intelligence services of the white-minority regimes remains hidden, but some aspects are known.

The South African Bureau of State Security (BOSS) was formed in 1968-'69. It grew rapidly; between 1969 and 1975, its budget increased over 300 percent.[32] From the start, BOSS sought to strengthen relations with other intelligence services. In July 1969, the Rhodesian and Portuguese secret police and BOSS held a week-long conference in Lisbon[33] to discuss their growing collaboration in the war against the southern African liberation movements. BOSS also cooperates with the CIA. Stockwell points out,

> The CIA has traditionally sympathized with South Africa and enjoyed its close liaison with BOSS. The two organizations share a violent antipathy toward communism and in the early sixties the South Africans had facilitated the Agency's development of a mercenary army to suppress the Congo rebellion. BOSS, however, tolerates little clandestine nonsense inside the country and the CIA had always restricted its Pretoria station's activity to maintaining the liaison with BOSS. That is, until 1974, when it yielded to intense pressures in Washington and expanded the Pretoria station's responsibilities to include covert operations to gather intelligence about the South African nuclear project. In the summer of 1975 BOSS rolled up this effort and quietly expelled those CIA personnel directly involved. The agency did not complain, as the effort was acknowledged to have been clumsy and obvious. The agency continued its cordial relationship with BOSS.*[34]

The white-minority regime in South Africa and the CIA cooperated closely in both the Congo and Angola in dealing with a common "enemy."

The CIA's self-imposed restrictions on covert operations inside the white-ruled countries of southern Africa led to its failure to predict the April 1974 coup in Portugal. In part, this failure was also due to the CIA's close links with the Portuguese secret police, the Direccao Geral de Seguranca (DGS).** When

* See Chapter Nine for a further discussion of U.S. intelligence agencies' relationship to South Africa's nuclear power program.
** The DGS originated in the 20s, as Salazar's political police. In the 30s it received advice and training from Hitler's Gestapo and Mussolini's OVRA.[35]

nationalist resistance in Africa grew in the late '50s, the Portuguese secret police expanded their operations there. Relations between the CIA and the DGS were developed during Allen Dulles' directorship in the CIA (1953-'61). Many Portuguese travelled to the United States for four-month CIA training courses.[36]

Under Kennedy, the CIA began to finance Holden Roberto and the FNLA in Angola in 1962, as a "moderate" alternative to the Portuguese colonialists.[37] The Johnson Aministration, however, ended this policy. The CIA mounted a clandestine effort to smuggle B-26 bombers to Portugal in 1965, and had delivered seven before United States customs officials discovered the scheme.[38]

Under NSSM 39,[39] the Nixon Administration shifted further towards support of the Portuguese and other white-minority regimes in southern Africa. The CIA suspended major subsidies to Holden Roberto in 1969, and closed down its stations in Mozambique and Angola as an economy measure and a gesture of faith in Portuguese rule. It also reduced its personnel in Portugal itself, becoming almost entirely "dependent upon the official Portuguese security service for information."[40]

The CIA built up another highly controversial, extremely secret liaison relationship which affected Africa, with the Israeli intelligence service, the Mossad. Israeli foreign policy began to develop a sophisticated foreign aid program for independent African states, starting with Ghana in the late '50s. This foreign aid program was crucial to Israel's effort to end its diplomatic isolation in the Third World. The program presented the United States with an unprecedented opportunity to utilize the "favorable" image in the Third World for its own ends.[41] The CIA handled its Israeli links through the Counter-Intelligence Staff of Clandestine Services, under James Angleton.[42]

Starting in 1960, the CIA paid the Israelis "tens of millions" of dollars. These funds were "regularly funneled to Israel's intelligence services for control and disbursement by the Prime Minister's office." CIA backing aimed "to give the anti-communist West, through the highly effective good offices of Israel, competitive equality in political penetration of newly independent states in black Africa."[43] At least half Israel's aid funds came from non-Israeli sources.[44] The increase in funding by the CIA coincided with an expansion of Israeli military and paramilitary assistance to Africa. Most of this assistance went to Ethiopia, Zaire, Tanzania and Uganda.[45] Israeli military assistance played an important role in Idi Amin's rise to power in Uganda.[46] CIA financing of Mossad activities in Africa gave an enormous boost to CIA activities throughout the continent.

Although liaison operations with "allied" intelligence agencies are important, in the final analysis the CIA's unilateral operations are its most significant. All the low-level covert operations are aimed at maintaining a favorable *status quo* in the African nations where CIA stations have been located.*

Low-Level Covert Operations

The CIA conducts on-going low-level covert operations affecting all aspects of the political life of the African states where it has stations. In 1965, the CIA set up the African-American Labor Center to encourage anti-communist labor leaders and unions.[48] In the early '60s, the CIA helped the governments of Rwanda and Burundi to defeat pro-Chinese dissident movements. The CIA was especially interested in eliminating Burundi as the base for Congolese rebels in 1964-'65.[49] Stockwell, who was the chief of station in Burundi in 1970, argues that CIA activities there contributed to the ethnic hatred between the Watusi and Hutu, which led to wholesale killing of the Hutu in 1972.[50]

The CIA helped Muhammed Egal to become premier in Somalia in 1967. Egal's allies in the Somali Youth League Party received extensive covert CIA backing before the 1967 presidential elections. Egal concluded a border agreement with Ethiopia, then a close United States ally. Two years later, the army overthrew him, charging that he collaborated with the CIA.[51]

These scattered examples illustrate the broad character of low-level CIA operations in Africa. These activities aim to maintain

---

* The CIA also sought to use its African bases to recruit Soviet, Chinese and Eastern European diplomats and intelligence agents, but this effort has proved a dismal failure.[47]

the existing web of dependent and manipulted relationships. When these relationships have been threatened locally and/or regionally, the CIA has initiated higher forms of intervention. These major interventions reflect the decision makers' world view, which remains similar to that which led to Vietnam.[52]

CIA Intervention in the Congo

The CIA initiated its first high-level action in Africa in the Congo in the 1960s. The first major task of the Africa division when it was established in 1960 was to create a Congo Task Force to install a pro-Western government there. From 1960 to '64, the CIA carried on intensive covert action. From 1964 to '68, it conducted a "secret war" involving extensive use of mercenaries in paramilitary operations.

From the start, the CIA viewed Patrice Lumumba as a willing dupe of the communists.[53] In June 1960, Lawrence Devlin arrived in the Congo as the new CIA chief of station. He cabled CIA headquarters in August,

> Embassy and station believe the Congo experiencing classic communist effort takeover government. Many forces at work here: Soviets, Communist Party, etc....decisive period not far off. Whether or not Lumumba actually Commie or just playing Commie game to assist his solidifying power, anti-West forces rapidly increasing power Congo and there may be little time left in which take action to avoid another Cuba.[54]

The CIA dispatched agents to the Congo to "learn Congolese politics from the bush on up, to recruit likely leaders and to finance their bids for power."[55] In late August, the NSC gave Devlin wide latitude to "carry out any crash programs on which you do not have the opportunity to consult HQS." The major goal was Lumumba's "removal."[56]

Within days, the CIA helped stir up labor unrest and to bribe members of the Congolese senate to isolate Lumumba. The CIA played a major role in the September coups which helped propel Colonel Joseph Mobutu, the Congolese army's chief of staff, to power. Throughout the fall, large sums of CIA money were used to buy the loyalty of Mobutu and his colleagues in the "Binza Group."

On August 18, 1960, Eisenhower gave the green light for "an order for the assassination of Lumumba."[57] Various schemes were then implemented. Several days after Mobutu seized power, on September 15, a Congolese in contact with the CIA "implied he was trying to have Lumumba killed but added this most difficult as job would have to be done by African with no apparent involvement with white man." Lumumba was in U.N. protective custody at the time. The CIA dispatched a scientist to the Congo with toxic materials to try to kill Lumumba. Two CIA agents, code-named QJ/WIN and WI/ROGUE, tried to have Lumumba abducted or murdered. When Lumumba tried to escape to Stanleyville in late November, the CIA helped Mobutu's troops to capture him.[58] He was then removed to Katanga (now Shaba). The CIA station and the embassy, however, continued to view him as a serious threat. A CIA cable to headquarters on January 13 aptly expressed these sentiments:

> The combination of Lumumba's powers as demagogue, his able use of goon squads and propaganda and spirit of defeat within Government coalition which would increase rapidly under such conditions would almost certainly insure Lumumba victory in Parliament.. Refusal take drastic steps at this time will lead to defeat of U.S. policy in Congo.[59]

Four days later, Lumumba was dead, shot by Mobutu's troops. The CIA misled the Senate Intelligence Committee as to their involvement in Lumumba's death, arguing that the Congolese had killed him. This view, however, ignores the massive covert action program directed against Lumumba, in the course of which he died. Further indication of the CIA's involvement was revealed by a CIA officer, who told Stockwell how he had "an adventure in Lubumbashi, driving about town after curfew with Lumumba's body in the trunk of his car, trying to decide what to do with it."[60]

The struggle between the Western-backed Binza group and the Lumumbists continued after Lumumba's assassination. The CIA furthered the establishment of a regime under Cyrille Adoula and contributed to his power base through "connected trade union and youth groups, public relations and security apparatus."[61] This aid allowed Adoula to establish a political party named RADECO. Consistent bribery of the Congolese parliament helped maintain his fragile grip on power, and to force Lumumbist ministers out of government.[62] Yet even with this support, the Adoula regime faced growing internal problems.

By late 1963 and early '64, Adoula faced an armed rebellion in western and eastern Congo. Mulelist and Lumumbist rebels took control of roughly half the Congo in several months. In the absence of U.N. forces, the United States wanted an African troop presence to meet this new threat. But Mobutu, who feared domestic implications, opposed this option. In 1964, Cuban exiles working as pilots with the CIA Cuba Task Force in Miami were sent to the Congo to fly fighter-bombers against the rebels. They were brought into the Congo by WIGMO, a CIA proprietary cover based in Lichtenstein. These mercenaries helped beat back rebel attacks in February 1964.[63] By the spring, nearly 100 United States military advisers were assisting the Congolese Army to combat the rebels. Fighter-bombers, transport aircraft and helicopters were also sent to the Congo.

Belgians, South Africans and Rhodesians cooperated with the United States in this "secret war." The Belgians sent an airforce group to main the transports and helicopters. South African and Rhodesian intelligence forces began to help the CIA to recruit a mercenary force.[64] The Number Five mercenary commando, led by Mike Hoare, was formed partly by veterans of the Katanga gendarmerie. The United States urged the Organization of African Unity (OAU) to form a force to help the Congolese regime fight the rebels.

There is uncertainty, however, about the United States role in replacing Adoula. The installation of Moise Tshombe as the new leader of the Congo disturbed many African leaders, since Tshombe had led Katanga's secession from the Congo. The CIA-sponsored Binza group had brought him back because he still had the allegiance of the Katangese gendarmes in the Congo and Portuguese-ruled Angola. The French SDECE encouraged this move when the chief of the Congolese Surete, Nendaka, was in Europe. The United States did approve plans for the Belgians to cooperate with Tshombe in directing the mercenary force to crush the rebels.

By mid-August, the United States had airlifted to the Congo many light armored vehicles and a Special Forces detachment to help consolidate efforts against the rebels. By October, a mercenary force of nearly 500 men was organized and in action. They were equipped with United States weapons and supported by Cuban-piloted fighter-bombers.

Belgium and the United States cooperated closely in the airborne operation against the rebel capital of Stanleyville in late November 1964. Accompanying the mercenary column was a small force of emigre Cubans, who moved ahead of the force to "rescue" United States diplomatic officials.[65]

The United States was sensitive to the international complications of depending on white South Africans and Rhodesians to do the fighting, and sought to phase them out.[66] Israeli advisers were sent to the Congo to train paratroopers; a year earlier, a cadre of 243 Congolese had been sent to Israel for training. These activities were partially financed by the United States.[67] The CIA also used its ample finances to attempt to create "elite" Congolese units that could replace the mercenaries. In the '70s, they became Mobutu's personal bodyguard.[68]

While the CIA was pursuing an active paramilitary war against the Lumumbist rebels, it also conducted a political action program against President Kasavubu. Kasavubu's desire to dismiss the mercenary force and improve relations with the socialist countries and radical nationalist states was apparently considered threatening to United States interests. With the Binza group's cooperation, Devlin organized a coup against Kasavubu in November 1965. This coup placed Mobutu in power.

The CIA continued to maintain a strong presence in the Congo against the rebels between 1965 and '67. In 1965, Che Guevara was reportedly in the Congo with a group of 100 Cuban advisers. He operated on the ground with the rebels that spring, but reportedly was disappointed with their effectiveness.[69] He also traveled to Congo-Brazaville and helped train the Angolan MPLA forces for their first operatins against the Portuguese in Cabinda. The CIA began a paramilitary operation to kill him.[70] A successful CIA "hit" would have indirectly aided the Portuguese in their fight against the MPLA.

In 1967, continuing cooperation between the CIA and the white regimes in southern Africa was revealed. A Vietnam Green Beret veteran, Ted Braden, seeking to fight in the Congo, was directed to southern Africa in January, seven months before a mercenary revolt threatened Mobutu. Braden discovered that cadre from the Rhodesian Light Infantry provided training for mercenary replacements. Two commando groups were then in operation against the Congolese rebels, Number Five and Number Six. Number Five was composed of South Africans, Rhodesians, English, Canadians and a few Americans. Six consisted of Belgian mercenaries. CIA financing was "routed through the Congo government machinery to make it appear that the Congolese are running their own country."[71]

The leaders of the mercenary units were divided when Katangese gendarmes and Belgian mercenaries, supporters of the ousted Tshombe, launched their own revolt in July 1967. The South African and Rhodesian regimes took a dim view of the revolt, and Five Commando remained loyal to Mobutu. The United States rushed air transports and advisers to help Mobutu put down the mutiny, although, according to then-Special Group member Cyrus Vance, the CIA paramilitary campaign had wound down by the middle of 1967. The revolt was crushed, and the Katangese involved were executed. Throughout this period, Mobutu was receiving financial payments and political support from the CIA.

The Coup Against Nkrumah

The CIA carried out another high-level intervention in the 1960s, contributing to the overthrow of Kwame Nkrumah of Ghana. Nkrumah was one of the foremost pan-Africanist leaders in Africa. He played an important role in the non-aligned movement, the formation of the OAU, and spoke out boldly against neo-colonial activities in the Congo as well as elsewhere on the continent. His government provided the Algerian and southern African liberation movements with vital political and military aid.

Nkrumah faced severe internal problems. His style of "social-ism" suffered from contradictions stemming from Ghana's continued integration into the world capitalist political-economy.[72] These internal difficulties contributed to conditions favoring the plotters of the military coup. Nevertheless, the CIA role was significant.

The CIA's intervention illustrates the dangers of uncontrolled covert action. Stockwell reports that,

> The 40 Committee had met and rejected an agency proposal to oust Nkrumah. The Accra Station was nevertheless encouraged by headquarters to maintain contact with the dissidents of the Ghanaian army for the purpose of gathering information on their activities. It was given a generous budget, and maintained contact with the plotters as the coup was hatched.[73]

The CIA station in Accra expanded to ten officers, controlling a network of perhaps 100 agents.[74] This included extensive contacts throughout the security forces. The chief of station, Howard T. Banes, adopted the aggressive style of leadership esteemed in the Clandestine Services. At one point, he proposed that a "hit team" of paramilitary experts assault the Chinese Embassy in Accra during the coup, kill all the Chinese personnel, destroy the building and steal the embassy's code books.[75] When headquarters turned this proposal down, Banes's comment was: "They didn't have the guts to do it."[76]

The CIA did purchase Soviet intelligence information and material from the post-coup military regime, reportedly for $100,000. United States policy makers, however, perceived the most important result as the removal of one of Africa's foremost nationalist leaders. Within the CIA, "the Accra Station was given full, if unofficial, credit for the coup."[77]

Howard Banes was not satisfied with the mere removal of Nkrumah. After the coup, he urged the chief of station in Guinea to set in motion a similar covert action to topple Sekou Toure of Guinea, and "liberate" West Africa from "communism."[78] Banes was later rewarded by the CIA with promotion to Chief of Operations for the Africa Division.[79] His behavior exemplified standard operating procedure for an upwardly mobile bureaucrat in Clandestine Services.

The CIA in Angola

After the downfall of the Portuguese regime in April 1974, events moved rapidly in Angola, as rival political factions vied for power. Behind the scenes, representatives of South Africa and various Western powers used their ties with former agents of the Portuguese secret police to play an increasingly important role in an effort to influence the outcome. About 12,000 of the Portugese DGS agents were active in Angola shortly before the 1974 coup.[80] Many had infiltrated African political groups, where they had allegedly already contributed to divisive trends.[81]

The CIA used its contacts with the DGS to strengthen the anti-MPLA forces. In the period of Spinola's rule (April to September, 1974), the overseas components of the DGS were not dismantled but re-integrated into the Portuguese Army. In Angola, they sought to weaken the MPLA. On September 14, Spinola, Mobutu, and all the Angolan nationalist movements discussed a settlement isolating the MPLA. Spinola had underestimated the shift to the left in the army, however, and was toppled several weeks later. The CIA's role in this early period in Angola is vague. Stockwell reports that,

> In July 1974, the CIA began funding Roberto without 40 Committee approval, small amounts at first, but enough for word to get around that the CIA was dealing itself into the race..During the fall of 1974 the CIA continued to fund Roberto, still without 40 Committee approval, and its intelligence reporting on Angola was predominantly from Zairian and FNLA sources.[82]

During the summer and fall of 1974, the CIA formed the Portuguese Task Force to deal with the "alarming" events which moved Portugal politically to the left.[83] Given the close relationship between events in Portugal and Africa, it is likely that the CIA coordinated its operations against "communism" in both areas.

In the fall of 1974, the French SDECE became "more adventurous than any other Western power" in Angola.[84] Former DGS officials based in Gabon helped FLEC plan the seizure of Cabinda, the oil-rich Angolan province,[85] and facilitated the "walkover" of nearly 1000 DGS-controlled "Flechas" to join FLEC.[86] These commandos were similar to the CIA's Nung, Cambodian and Meo mercenaries in Indochina. French mercenaries, such as Robert Denard and Jean Kay, were involved in the creation of a FLEC military force.[87] These efforts led to an abortive FLEC coup in November 1974.

As the left became stronger in the Portuguese Armed Forces Movement, the South African BOSS and the Rhodesian Special Branch sought to preserve as much as possible of the intelligence networks and paramilitary capability of the DGS.[88] Top DGS officials fled from Mozambique and Angola to Rhodesia and South Africa in the summer and fall of 1974. The bulk of the Flechas in Mozambique were encouraged to leave for Rhodesia and South Africa. Many joined the Rhodesian Selous Scouts, while others help form bogus anti-Frelimo groups in Mozambique under joint Boss/Rhodesian control.

On July 7, 1974, the CIA began to increase its covert funding of Roberto, without 40 Committee approval.[89] On January 26, 1975, the 40 Committee officially approved $300,000 of further funding, marking the beginning of what was to develop into a $31-million covert war.[90] In March, the CIA reopened its Luanda station. From that station and those in Kinshasa (Zaire), Lusaka (Zambia) and elsewhere, it supplied the Angola Task Force at CIA headquarters in Washington, D.C.—and through it, Henry Kissinger and other policymakers—with intelligence reports.

It has been argued that the CIA's renascent interest had results of "infinitely greater significance than the U.S. government has claimed."[91] In monetary terms, the amount spent represented a thirty-fold increase in CIA support for Roberto.[92] At the time, CIA reports—apparently based primarily or solely on information from Mobutu and Roberto—suggested the FNLA was militarily stronger than the MPLA or UNITA. The expansion of United States aid "gave rise to speculation that the U.S. was intent on trying to assure FNLA dominance."[93] Stockwell points out that,

> the original 40 Committee options paper acknowledged the United States' vulnerability to charges of escalating the Angola conflict when it stated that a leak by an American official source would be serious, that we would be charged with responsibility for the spread of civil war in Angola.[94]

Furthermore, it was clear that accelerated United States aid *preceded* the expansion of Soviet arms shipments to the MPLA, which began only in March 1975, after a lull of nearly two years.[95]

The situation in Angola was clearly linked to events taking place in Portugal. On August 19, the Portuguese Foreign Minister, Mario Soares, maintained in an interview with *Der Spiegel*,[96] that he had engaged in negotiations with the PAIGC of Guine-Bissau and Frelimo in Mozambique, but not with the liberation movements in Angola because of the "cleavages" between political groups and the mobilization by conservative whites of "armies of mercenaries against the liberation movements." He dismissed the possibility of a Rhodesian-style coup by white settlers in Angola, however, explaining it could occur only if there was a "rightist coup in the motherland." If these activities were not resisted, they "would put in question the entire process of our decolonization, our credibility and our good will." Moreover, he argued, "such a solution could facilitate the return of fascism to Portugal."

United States officials, on the other hand, viewed internal developments in Portugal and Africa with growing alarm. Kissinger voiced his opinion that Portugal was on the verge of a Communist takeover. In the early days of September, the 40 Committee met to consider possible actions by the CIA to counter the "Communist danger."[97] In late August, Lt. General Vernon Walters, deputy director of the CIA, visited Portugal.[98] Critics insisted the CIA was collaborating with right-wing elements. In mid-October, another CIA mission, including experts on currency problems and the Portuguese colonies, went to Portugal.[99] Kissinger was known to be advocating a policy of isolating Portugal in order to "bring the leadership back to its senses."[100]

The extent to which heightened CIA activity accounted for growing divisions in Angola over the next months is hard to determine.[101] Throughout the CIA, the Kinshasa station was known for its "flagrant, semiovert activities," which "ensured that American support of the FNLA would be widely known."[102] These activities were clearly carried out in direct opposition to official Portuguese efforts to achieve a coalition in Angola to take up the reins of government. They also ignored the expressed view of United States diplomats in Luanda that the MPLA was the best organized group, the movement most qualified to run the country.[103]

After the political divisions in Angola broke out into open warfare, CIA stations and bases in the region were made responsible for coordinating and distributing the influx of war materiel. On July 17, 1975, the 40 Committee met and authorized $14 million for further paramilitary operations.[104] On July 19, the first C-141 flight of arms went out. Cargoes for additional flights were assembled in South Carolina from CIA warehouses in Texas.[105] A shipload of arms for FNLA docked in Matadi, Zaire on September 12.

During a two-week reconnaissance trip to Angola as CIA task force commander for that country, Stockwell met with both Holden Roberto and the president of UNITA, Jonas Savimbi, to evaluate the state of affairs in order to guide future policy. He concluded that the United States should either opt for a swift military victory via tactical air support and provision of advisors for the FNLA and UNITA, or should sharply de-escalate its involvement to a diplomatic level.[106] Kissinger, however, rejected a similar State Department recommendation,[107] and on December 9 acknowledged at a press conference that "U.S. aid to curb the success of the MPLA is being channeled through neighboring countries (Zaire, Zambia, England and France)."[108]

At the end of 1975, the CIA's Angola Task Force consisted of the following units: (a) an intelligence gathering section; (b) a reports section; (c) a paramilitary section; (d) a propaganda section; and (e) a supporting staff of assistants and secretaries.[109] As Stockwell explains,

> From the outset we were deeply involved in managing the war from Washington, from Kinshasa, and from advance bases inside Angola...[the] intelligence effort was always subordinate to their [CIA officers'] advisory activities. CIA communications officers trained FNLA and UNITA technicians at the Angolan advance bases. Kinshasa cables reported that CIA paramilitary officers were training UNITA forces in Silva Porto and the FNLA in Ambriz...A retired army colonel was hired on contract and assigned full time to the FNLA command at Ambriz.[110]

The CIA propaganda section also had an important role. It disseminated favorable articles to as many news sources as possible. CIA officers in Lusaka and Kinshasa submitted articles to local newspapers. If they were not picked up by international news agencies, the articles were transmitted via agency cable to other stations around the world, who saw to it they were reprinted in the world press. Reuters news agency, for instance, picked up a faked story from Lusaka, which reported the capture of 20 Soviet and 35 Cuban advisors by UNITA forces.[111] The story was carried by the *Washington Post* on November 22, 1975.

Throughout the operation, the white-minority regime in South Africa was continuously informed of all developments by the Chief of Station in Pretoria. On two occasions, the director of BOSS visited Washington and held secret meetings with the CIA's Chief of Africa Division. Stockwell asserts,

> ...without any memos being written at CIA headquarters saying "Let's coordinate with the South Africans," coordination was effected at all CIA levels and the South Africans escalated their involvement in step with our own.[112]

In September 1975, before Cuban troops landed in Angola, South Africa's regular troops and an armored column invaded deep into Angolan territory, in collaboration with UNITA. For some weeks, it did not seem certain that MPLA would stem the column's advance. FNLA troops, aided by regular Zairean soldiers and mercenaries recruited with CIA assistance, attacked from Zaire. Then the MPLA, assisted by the Cubans, began to push the invaders back.

African nations protested bitterly against the South African invasion. Congress rejected Kissinger's request for open armed support for UNITA and the FNLA. Defeated, the South African forces withdrew in January 1976. The South African regime later claimed the United States government had covertly supported the invasion, but had reneged on U.S. promises for overt assistance in the event of difficulties.

Conclusion

Mounting evidence, summarized in this chapter, shows that past United States goverment-sponsored covert activities in Africa have ranged from divisive efforts to disorient the liberation movements and the circulation of false "news" to the press, to the recruitment of mercenaries, encouragement of military coups, and even assassination attempts. In these activities, the United States administration apparently has rarely, if ever, considered whether it was in fact aiding the group with the most popular support. On the contrary, the primary aim of these covert activities has been to install or maintain in power regimes considered favorable to perceived United States interests.

References

1. *The New York Times,* December 22, 1974
2. Gravel, M., ed., *The Senator Mike Gravel Edition—The Pentagon Papers* (Boston: Beacon Press, 1971)
3. Branfman, Fred., "The President's Secret Army: The CIA in Laos, 1962-1972," in Borosage, R., and Marks, J., *The CIA File* (Grossman Publishers, 1976); McCoy, Alfred, *The Politics of Heroin in SouthEast Asia* (New York: Harper and Row, 1972)
4. Sihanouk, Norodom, *My War With the CIA* (Pantheon, 1972); Malcolm Caldwell and Lek Tan, *Cambodia in the Southeast Asian War* (New York: Monthly Review, 1973)
5. *The Washington Post*, May 19, 1978
6. The best published description of covert operations appears in the minutes of the 1968 "Bissell Meeting" of the Council of Foreign Relations. This document was "liberated" by protesting Harvard students in 1971, and was reprinted by the Africa Research Group. At this meeting, in January, 1968, Richard Bissel, chief of Clandestine Services in the CIA from 1958 to 1962, summarized what covert operations are all about. Bissell was head of the Clandestine Services when the Bay of Pigs operation was launched in 1961. The minutes are reprinted in, Marchetti, Victor, and Marks, John, *The CIA and the Cult of Intelligence* (New York: Alfred Knopf, 1974), pp. 380-398.
7. *Ibid.,* p. 382
8. Agee, Philip, *Inside the Company: A CIA Diary* (Stonehill, 1975)

9. See Branch, Taylor, and Crile, George, "The Kennedy Vendetta: Our Secret War on Cuba," in *Harpers* (New York) August 1975; Ayers, Bradley Earl, *The War That Never Was* (Bobbs-Merrill, 1976)

10. For a description, see Marchetti and Marks, *op. cit.*, pp. 386-389

11. *Ibid.*, p. 387

12. *Ibid.*, p. 386

13. *Ibid.*, p. 391

14. "The Pike Papers," in *The Village Voice* (New York), February 16, 1976, pp. 83-84

15. CIA organization chart as of 1975, in Marchetti and Marks, *op. cit.*, pp. 69-70

16. *The Washington Post*, May 26, 1973

17. Marchetti and Marks, *op. cit.*, p. 392

18. Stockwell, John, *In Search of Enemies—A CIA Story* (New York: Norton, 1978), p. 169; see also p. 201 fn.

19. Marchetti and Marks, *op. cit.*, p. 63

20. Halperin, M., "Covert Operations—Effects of Secrecy on Decision Making," in Borosage and Marks, *op. cit.*; Marchetti and Marks, *op. cit.*, pp. 32-55, 325-334. The analysis of these authors is highly recommended.

21. Marchetti and Marks, *op. cit.*, p. 70; Stockwell, *op. cit.*, p. 105

22. "History of the Central Intelligence Agency," in, U.S. Senate, *Supplementary Detailed Staff Reports on Foreign and Military Intelligence: Book IV*, 94th Congress, 2nd Session, April 13, 1976, p. 68

23. *Ibid.*

24. See Chairoff, Patrice B. *Comme Barbouzes*(Paris:1976), pp. 69-91

25. Agee, *op. cit.*, p. 54

26. See a series of articles by Robert Moss in *The Sunday Telegraph* (London), January 30 through February 20, 1977

27. Stockwell, *op. cit.*, p. 181; see also, pp. 164, 192, and 220-221

28. Agee, *op. cit.*, p. 54

29. See Stevenson, W., *A Man Called Intrepid: The Secret War* (New York: Harcourt Brace Jovanovich, 1976); Hyde, H. Montgomery, *Room 3603* (Farrar, Strauss and Co., 1963); Smith, R. Harris, *OSS: The Secret History of America's First Central Intelligence Agency* (Berkeley: University of California Press, 1972), pp. 1-35; Brown, Anthony Cave, *The War Report of the OSS* (Berkley Medallion Books, 1976), chapters 1 and 2.

30. Szulc, Tad, *The Illusion of Peace: Foreign Policy in the Nixon Years* (Viking, 1978), pp. 224-225

31. *Ibid.*

32. For an excellent brief description of BOSS, see International Defence and Aid for Southern Africa, *BOSS: The First Five Years* (London: 1975). All work on BOSS is sorely in need of updating.

33. *Daily Telegraph* (London), July 26, 1969

34. Stockwell, *op. cit.*, pp. 187-188

35. del Boca, Angelo, and Giovana, Mario, *Fascism Today* (New York:

Random House, 1969), p. 258; de Oliviera Marques, A.H., *History of Portugal* (New York: Columbia, 1976), 2nd edition, pp. 187-188

36. Maxwell, K., "Portugal Under Pressure," in *The New York Review of Books,* May 29, 1978

37. *The New York Times,* September 25, 1975

38. Welsh, David, "Flyboys of the CIA," in *Ramparts,* December 1966

39. Lake, Anthony, *The "Tar Baby" Option: American Policy Toward Southern Rhodesia* (New York: Columbia, 1976); El-Khawas, Mohammed, and Cohen, Barry, eds., *The Kissinger Study of Southern Africa* (Westport: Lawrence Hill, 1976)

40. "Pike Papers," *op. cit.,* p. 79

41. For a devestating critique of Israeli foreign policy in Africa, see, Africa Research Group, "David and Goliath" (Boston: 1969); for a defense of Israel's policies, see Curtis, M., and Gitselson, S., eds., *Israel in the Third World* (Transaction Books, 1976)

42. This relationship was secret even within Clandestine Services; see Colby, W., *Honorable Men: My Life in the CIA* (New York: Simon and Schuster, 1978), p. 387; see also Hersh, Seymour, "The Angleton Story," in *The New York Times Magazine,* June 25, 1978

43. See column by Evans and Novak in *The Washington Post,* February 25, 1977

44. Laufer, Leopold, *Israel and the Developing Countries: New Approaches to Cooperation,* Twentieth Century Fund, 1968

45. Silverburg, Sanford, *Israeli Military and Paramilitary Assistance to Sub-Saharan Africa: Harbinger for the Role of the Military in Developing States,* M.A. Thesis, American University, 1968, pp. 50-75; data reprinted in Africa Research Group, "David and Goliath," *op. cit.*

46. Martin, David, *General Amin* (Faber and Faber, 1974), Chaper 9.

47. Stockwell, *op. cit.,* pp. 237-238; Penkovsky, Oleg, *The Penkovsky Papers* (New York: Doubleday, 1965)

48. Peck, Winslow, "The AFL-CIA," in *Uncloaking the CIA*, pp. 231-236, 260, 264

49. Lemarchand, R., "The CIA: How Central? How Intelligent?" in Lemarchand, R., ed., *American Policy in Southern Africa: The Stakes and the Stance* (University Press of America, 1978), pp. 350-351; Larkin, Bruce, *China and Africa: 1949-1970* (Berkeley: University of California Press, 1971), pp. 72-74, 127-128

50. Stockwell, *op. cit.,* pp. 63, 110-111, 80-81

51. Morris, Roger, and Mauzy, Richard, "Following the Scenario," in Borosage and Marks, *op. cit.,* pp. 37-39

52. Barnett, R., *Roots of War* (Atheneum Press, 1972); Kolko, Gabriel, *The Roots of American Foreign Policy* (Boston: Beacon, 1969)

53. For a sympathetic view of Lumumba and his political writings, see Van Lierde, Jean, *Lumumba Speaks: The Speeches and Writings of Patrice Lumumba, 1958-1961* (Little Brown, 1972)

54. U.S. Senate, Select Committee to Study Government Operations with Respect to Intelligence Activities, *Alleged Assassination Plots Involving*

Foreign Leaders: Interim Report, 94th Congress, 1st Session, November 20, 1975, p. 14
55. *The New York Times,* April 29, 1966
56. *Alleged Assassination Plots, op. cit.,* pp. 15-16
57. *Ibid.,* p. 55
58. *Ibid.,* pp. 48-49
59. *Ibid.*
60. Stockwell, *op. cit.,* pp. 105, 160 fn., 201 fn.
61. Weissman, Stephen, "The CIA and U.S. Policy in Zaire and Angola," in Lemarchand, *American Policy in Southern Africa, op. cit.,* p. 390
62. Weissman, Stephen, *American Foreign Policy in the Congo, 1960-1964* (Cornell, 1974), pp. 185, 201, 210; *The New York Times,* April 26, 1966
63. *The New York Times,* April 26, 1966
64. Stockwell, *op. cit.,* pp. 187-188; Mockler, A., *The Mercenaries* (New York: Macmillan, 1969), pp. 155-253; Hoare, M., *Congo Mercenary* (R. Hale, 1967); Vandewalle, Col. Frederic, *L'Ommegang: Odysee et reconquete de Stanleyville, 1964* (Le Livre Africain, 1970)
65. Vandewalle, *op. cit.,* p. 313
66. *Ibid.,* pp. 207-208
67. *Ibid,* p. 203
68. Weissman, "The CIA and U.S. Policy," *op. cit.,* p. 394
69. Marchetti and Marks, *op. cit.,* p. 126
70. Borosage and Marks, *op. cit.,* p. 51
71. Braden, Ted, "Mercenary Job Wanted," in *Ramparts,* October 1967, pp. 21-26
72. See Fitch, R., and Oppenheimer, M., *Ghana: End of an Illussion* (New York: Monthly Review, 1975)
73. Stockwell, *op. cit.,* p. 201 fn.
74. *The New York Times,* May 9, 1978; op-ed page, May 17, 1978
75. *The New York Times,* May 9, 1978
76. *Ibid.*
77. *Stockwell, op. cit.,* 201 fn.
78. Interview with John Stockwell, June 1978
79. *The New York Times,* May 9, 1978
80. United Nations, *Mozambique,* A/8423/Add 3 of October 5, 1970 (New York: 1970); and Humbaraci, A., and Muchnik, M., *Portugal's African Wars, 1974*
81. *See Afrique-Asie* (Paris), July 8, 1974
82. Stockwell, *op. cit.,* p. 67
83. Szulc, Tad, "Lisbon and Washington: Behind the Portuguese Revolution," in *Foreign Policy,* No. 21, Winter 1975-'76; Hammond, J., and Szulc, Nicole, "The CIA in Portugal," in Frazier, H., ed., *Uncloaking the CIA* (Free Press, 1978)
84. Robert Moss, *op. cit.*
85. *Foreign Broadcast Information Service, Sub-Saharan Africa,* November 25, 1974; hereafter referred to as FBIS.
86. *The Washington Post,* July 17, 1975; Adelman, K., "Report from Angola," in *Foreign Affairs,* April 1975

87. Collings, R., *Africa Contemporary Record, 1974-1975,* p. B536

88. The New York Times, June 11, 1974; personal interview with former DGS agent, November 1977; FBIS—Sub-Saharan Africa, June 12, 14, 27, 1974

89. Stockwell, *op. cit.,* p. 258

90. This money came from the CIA Contingency Reserve Fund, and does not include additional unknown amounts in operational expenses incurred by CIA staff and facilities.

91. Lemarchand, *op. cit.,* p. 76

92. This increase must be evaluated in conjunction with supplies already being forwarded to Roberto from his ally and brother-in-law, President Mobutu of Zaire.

93. Stockwell, *op. cit.,* p. 67 fn.

94. Stockwell, *op. cit.,* p. 68

95. *Ibid.*

96. Der Spiegel (Bonn), August 19, 1975

97. Szulc, Tad, "Lisbon and Washington," *op. cit.*

98. *Ibid.,* p. 33

99. *FBIS-Western Europe,* October 7 and 11, 1974

100. Szulc, "Lisbon and Washington," *op. cit.,* pp. 29-30, fn. 8

101. See *FBIS—Sub-Saharan Africa,* August 23, 1974; *Star* (Johannesburg), August 24, 1974

102. Stockwell, *op. cit.,* pp. 67-68

103. *Ibid.,* pp. 63-64

104. U.S.-House of Representatives, Special Subcommittee of the Committee of International Relations, hearings on Mercenaries in Africa, 92nd Session, 1976, p. 42

105. Stockwell, *op. cit.,* pp. 58-59

106. *Ibid.,* p. 158

107. Lemarchand, *op. cit.,* p. 83

108. House Committee on International Relations, *op. cit.,* p. 49

109. Stockwell, *op. cit.,* p. 168

110. *Ibid.,* p. 177

111. House Committee on International Relations, *op. cit.,* p. 47; Stockwell, *op. cit.,* p. 194

112. Stockwell, *op. cit.,* pp. 187-188

Chapter 6

Mercenarization

Cynthia H. Enloe

The United States public would clearly reject sending troops to support the white-minority regimes of southern Africa. There is, however, extensive evidence that United States citizens, many of them Vietnam veterans, are fighting in Zimbabwe as "khaki" mercenaries, while "white collar" mercenaries help the white-minority regimes in Rhodesia and South Africa overcome the shortage of white skilled manpower.

EX-MARINE SEEKS EMPLOYMENT as mercenary, full time or job contract. Prefer South or Central America but all offers considered. Contact Palo, 2101 Willoughby, Las Vegas, NV.
EXPERIENCED, MATURE, BONDABLE, seeks assignment anywhere for covert operation, foiling industrial theft, etc. Experienced with land and water transport, ex-police officer. Available on contract or fee basis. Bob Strohm, 5690 Williams, FMB, Fl.
WANTED: Skilled, ex-military personnel seeking overseas assignments. Also invited, information concerning available para-military equipment. Resumes information to: Action International, c.o. 8135 Engineer Rd., San Diego, Cal 92111.[1]

Mercenaries are as old as organized warfare. Most of the literature on mercenaries concentrates on the hired soldiers themselves, presuming they are "colorful," freewheeling adventurers. In fact, this portrayal is erroneous. Most mercenaries come from groups—Gurkhas, Irish, Hessians, Meos—that are economically and politically disadvantaged. Being a mercenary is not so much an indication of an adventurous spirit as it is a testimony to minimal opportunities available to an individual.

The common concentration on the hired combatants diverts our attention away from the states that hire mercenaries or allow their citizens to be hired. In southern Africa today, it is especially important that we focus on those who recruit and hire foreign soldiers. The mercenaries themselves are certainly not the crucial elements in determining the scope and intensity of violence in the region.

By defining the problem as one of "mercenarization," rather than as one of mercenaries, we can insure that we focus on politically significant aspects of the issue. Mercenarization is a slow, gradual process, in which, first, a government under siege relies more and more heavily on hired combatants (usually from outside its own territory) for state defense, and second, foreign governments supporting the besieged regime depend increasingly on military assistance that is not supplied directly by the supporting governments. Mercenarization is, therefore, an historical phenomenon; it reflects growing contradictions within both the state system where violence is escalating and the foreign states that are convinced the threatened regime's survival is crucial for their own self-interest.

In southern Africa in the late 1970s, we can discern an intensification of contradictions on both of these levels. Mercenarization is proceeding in Rhodesia and South Africa, and it is being made possible by implicit and explicit support from governments such as the United States.

"Will the Real Mercenary Please Stand Up?"

In earlier centuries, regimes hired or sold soldiers in a relatively open fashion, to supplement inadequate manpower or to fill depleted state coffers. But today's state policymakers operate in a different ideological setting, in which the general legitimacy of a state's military depends on the extent to which it is perceived as acting in the people's interest. An admission that the state is defended by hired, alien soldiers not only undercuts the military's legitimacy, but also weakens the (probably already very tenuous) legitimacy of the state authority itself.

If mercenarization is a process in which the embattled state misrepresents its domestic defense policy, it also allows the supporting governments to follow increasingly covert foreign policies. Supporting governments must also hide their sanction of mercenary exports, since much of foreign alliance maintenance depends on some sense that the allied regimes are legitimate nation-states. The Prince of Hessia openly bargained over the price per head of the soldiers he supplied the British to help subdue the American rebels; but the United States government today would rather portray mercenary recruitment as a shady entrepreneurial enterprise carried on by private citizens in Colorado or San Diego.

Because both the hiring and the supplying states have some stake in denying their reliance on mercenaries, it is difficult to trace the mercenarization process. Several tactics are used to disguise mercenaries and thus to cloud the contradictions in the states' survival formulas. One common tactic is the use of "third party" soldiers, recruited from a group which is not directly involved in the conflict. This method was employed on numerous occasions during the Indochina war by the United States, especially to prop up the anti-communist regime in Laos. Meo tribesmen were recruited and equipped by the United States Central Intelligence Agency, but were kept in units separate from the regular Laotian Royal Army and deployed chiefly in remote hill areas. For the Meos themselves, this experience as tools of mercenarization resulted in even greater hardship than in the past.

The United States also utilized an additional tactic in Laos, involving the recruitment of allegedly demobilized, "laundered" Thai soldiers to fight in Laos. The Bangkok regime cooperated with Washington in this scheme. Thai officers, non-commissioned officers and enlisted men were ordered first to "resign" from the regular army and then to go to Laos—as part of their duties as Thai servicemen. One Thai soldier explained the process of becoming a mercenary.

> We would all sign papers resigning but the papers would be shoved in some desk and never processed. That way if anything happened to us they could say, "Look, this guy resigned two years ago."[2]

Perhaps the most common form of mercenarization is described by Wilfred Burchett and Derek Roebuck in their detailed account of how British and American combatants were recruited to fight for the FNLA in Angola.[3] This was essentially the "private entrepreneur" tactic. Recruiting agents in Britain and the United States operated as private citizens. They placed ads in newspapers and worked through private networks to contact other private citizens, typically demobilized soldiers on the fringes of the tight labor market. Although nominally private, these recruiting efforts could not have succeeded without considerable governmental funding for equipment and transport, as well as official tolerance, especially by security and customs agencies. As in Laos, the supplying states also had a third-party state ally, in this case the Mobutu regime in Zaire, which permitted the use of Zaire as a staging ground from which the newly mobilized mercenaries could invade neighboring Angola.

There are other mercenarization tactics as well, which are becoming more significant as counter-insurgency becomes more sophisticated in terms of broadening the definition of "security" and employment of ever more complex technology.

In particular, these developments in counter-insurgency have fostered "white collar" mercenarization. This is the process by which a state hires technical experts from abroad to maintain newly purchased complex equipment, train local personnel in the uses of that equipment, and occasionally to man the equipment themselves in security operations. The supplying state throws up a protective screen by channelling white collar mercenaries through non-governmental agencies, typically private companies that manufacture electronics equipment or weapons. Since such sales have to be cleared through the supplying state's own foreign or defense ministries, both the supplying as well as the recruiting states must approve the inclusion of technicians in the sales package. In the Persian Gulf today, for example, the British and United States government have promoted white-collar mercenarization by facilitating the recruitment of electronics, chemical and other sorts of experts for the counter-insurgency efforts of Oman, Iran, Saudi Arabia and Kuwait.[4]

Mercenaries From Within and Mercenaries From Without

In the strictest sense, a mercenary is anyone recruited into a military role, whether to carry an M-16 or sit at an electronics control, by the lure of material reward. Mercenarization, therefore, is the process through which, over time, the threatened state and its foreign allies come to depend increasingly on giving material rewards—attractive salaries or bounties—to build up and maintain a security apparatus that will keep the threatened regime in power.

Historically, states have created and maintained their security forces at manpower levels deemed adequate in four principal ways: (1) *coercion*—conscription through use of force; (2) *ideology*—recruitment by appeals to publicly sanctioned values (patriotism, nationalism, anti-communism, etc.); (3) *status*—promising upward social mobility for members of the security forces; and (4) *material reward*—reliance on monetary or other remuneration that is more attractive than is available in the civilian labor market.

Clearly, mercenarization in this strict sense is not exclusively an external process. One of the debates that went on when states gave up the draft to rely instead on paid volunteers, like Britain and the United States in the 1970s, was whether such a change would produce in effect a mercenary force. in countries whose state systems are rapidly losing public legitimacy because of rising anti-colonial sentiment or racial or ethnic disaffection, mercenarization from within may occur at the same time as mercenarization from without. As the central state progressively loses support, it will have to appeal more and more to the immediate monetary needs of potential recruits. Furthermore, as the anti-state insurgency itself escalates and military service entails greater and greater risks for soldiers, the level of salaries and benefits offered must escalate.

At just what point state recruiters will draw on domestic mercenaries in the overall mercenarization process is not certain. But state security planners may initially prefer to recruit mercenaries from abroad, and to rely on domestic mercenarization only as a last resort. Domestic mercenarization presents a paradox: while the targets of domestic mercenarization are likely to be those most compelled to take any job no matter how risky or socially despised, these domestically marginal people are not apt to be perceived by security planners as a desirable manpower pool in the face of spreading insurgency.

Mercenarization from within and mercenarization from without may occur simultaneously. But it is likely that regimes will prefer to use external recruits as long as feasible, and to deploy them in the most strategically sensitive points (as, for example, pilots, officers, communications specialists). Domestically recruited mercenaries are usually seen by central elites as cannon fodder.

Mercenarization in Rhodesia

In April 1978, it was estimated that 80 percent of the army of the Smith regime in Rhodesia was black.[5] One of the most blatant contradictions in Rhodesian politics was becoming, if possible, even more acute on the eve of the so-called "internal settlement:" the reliance of a white-dominated state apparatus on security forces—both police and military—composed largely of Africans. The Smith regime was expanding the African Rifles, the chief unit into which blacks traditionally were recruited. For the first time, it instituted conscription for blacks (national service heretofore had been a white-only recruitment). At the same time, it stepped up recruitment of mercenaries abroad, especially from the United States, Britain and South Africa.*

Manpower politics is never simply a matter of a state's ability to fill its military ranks. As the Rhodesian situation in 1978 clearly revealed, manpower politics is related to the labor needs of the entire political-economic structure on which the current state system depends for its maintenance.

* For the importance of foreign corporations in providing advanced technology and personnel, as well as capital, see Chapter Ten below.

Table 2: Population of Zimbabwe/Rhodesia, 1970-'77 (in thousands)

Year	1970-'71	1972-'73	1974-'75	1976-'77
Total population	5,250	5,600	6,070	6,530
White population	250	259	280	270

Source: International Institute of Strategic Studies, *The Military Balance* (London, 1977), p. 37

Table 3: The Armed Forces of South Africa and Rhodesia, 1973-'77 (in thousands)

A. Size of South African armed forces

1973	1974	1975	1976	1977	Reserves 1977	Paramilitary*
46	47.5	50.5	51.5	55	165.5	125.5

* Paramilitary forces consist of the commandos and South African Police (SAP). They are charged with protection of local industry and urban areas. Active military service is 12 months.

B. Size of Rhodesian Armed Forces

1973	1974	1975	1976	1977	Reserves 1977	Paramilitary*
4.7	4.7	5.7	9.2	9.6	55.0	44.0

* Paramilitary consist of British South African Police (BSAF) and Territorial Police.

Source: International Institute of Strategic Studies, *The Military Balance 1977-'78* (London, 1977)

Rhodesia's white-dominated state system had always required a steady infusion of white immigrants. But immigration policy and military manpower policy are intimately related, today more than ever. Whites comprise less than 5 percent of the Rhodesian population. Whites-only conscription could insure state survival as well as economic dominance only so long as the security of the state was not in immediate jeopardy. Mobilization of Zimbabwean dissidents and escalation of Patriotic Front guerrilla activities in the 1970s shed a harsh light on that fundamental condition for maintenance of the present system. In 1977, Rhodesia experienced a net loss of 10,908 whites. A total of 16,638 whites left the country, while only 5730 came as new immigrants.[6] Emigration grew at the very time when the state needed whites to satisfy the twin manpower needs of military recruitment and economic management. In fact, many white Rhodesians left to avoid military service, which had become both more dangerous and more lengthy.

Foreign mercenaries have become a principal means used by the Smith regime to reconcile the increasingly acute contradictions evident in the Rhodesian political economy. Mercenaries are intended to fill out the depleted military ranks. They are also meant to relieve local whites, whose services are needed in the ever more strained commercial and production sectors, from military service. Mercenaries from abroad are also recruited because of the skills they bring to a regime that must increasingly employ advanced technologies to offset manpower shortages. Finally, they are needed because the insurgents are widening the definition of "war." It is no longer a matter of filling the ordinary ranks, but of having security personnel who can guard against the guerrillas' growing emphasis on economic disruption. Mercenarization has increased in Rhodesia in the late 1970s because, as the basic contradictions in the system have deepened, the state's security needs have expanded.

Mercenaries have become an integral part of the Smith regime's general security formula for several years, but especially since the launching of the guerrilla war and the mounting pressure from Smith's traditional allies, Britain and the United States, to reach some sort of settlement with the African majority. In October 1976, secret security plans were distributed to Rhodesian politicians and military officers. The plans were designed to exploit the period of transition from white to majority rule. This period was built into the U.S.-British proposals and looked upon with great skepticism by the militant Zimbabwean leadership. Rhodesia's secret plans, published in the British press in mid-1977, explained to government officials that any interim period would be used to restock government armories, boost the economy and recruit more foreign mercenaries.[7] In other words, any interim period between white rule and majority rule would, if it were not explicitly and intimately supervised by Africans themselves, be used to hasten mercenarization.

In mid-1978, two articles appeared in the U.S. magazine for mercenaries, *Soldier of Fortune*, describing how the Patriotic Front's insurgency, which includes economic disruption, had increased the regime's reliance on foreign mercenaries. Both articles were written by United States mercenaries who were then employed in Rhodesia. In the first article, the author described his job as a security officer protecting white-owned ranches whose cattle had become a target for African guerrillas.[8] The author and his partner on the range patrol were both U.S. Special Forces veterans with experience in Vietnam. The white ranchers, with obvious approval from the white regime, hired mercenaries for ranching security because the Rhodesian police and army were already over-extended. Many white ranchers were themselves being called away from their operations to fulfill military obligations. The mercenaries did not, however, simply guard valuable cattle. As described by the author, their job also included tracking down African guerrillas. Thus the utilization of foreign ex-military personnel in what are apparently simply "guard" capacities must, in reality, be conceived of as mercenarization of state security forces.

The second article reinforced this interpretation. It too was written by an American mercenary serving as a security officer in Rhodesia.[9] He claimed he and his fellow officers were not part of the regular military. Instead, they were deployed in teams of a dozen men, all white, mostly foreign mercenaries, from South

Africa, Britain and Canada, as well as the United States. They were equipped with Belgian F.N. rifles and described their unit as a "private anti-terrorist security force." They guarded ranches, coffee plantations and mines, all white-owned.

The superficial distinction between private and public (state) security, then, cannot hide creeping mercenarization. The funnelling of funds to pay foreign mercenaries through private white businesses cannot disguise the actual state security function that such soldiers fulfill for the Smith regime. Nor can British, United States or South African governmental reliance on such superficial distinctions between hiring for private security guards and for government military forces provide sufficient excuse for permitting such mercenary recruitment.

The proposed "internal settlement" in 1977 between the Smith regime and three African spokesmen did not reconcile the contradictions that made mercenarization a necessity for the white government. Just prior to the agreement, the white government was forced to extend the military draft to Africans, a step it had resisted for several years. It had been proposed previously when manpower shortages had become most serious and the drain of white manpower was most harmful to the economy. Before the extension of the draft to blacks, the Rhodesian military depended on what amounted to a combination of military recruitment by coercion and mercenarization. Africans were pressed into service as "volunteers" through threats against their families (especially if they did not agree to renew their military service contracts at the end of their tour) and through offers of improved wages. Even so, black soldiers received only a fraction of white soldiers' wages. A black sergeant, for example, received only $135 per month in 1978, barely more than half the $320 paid a white enlisted man.[10] Yet given the economic insecurity suffered by most Africans, even low and unequal pay might appear attractive enough to some to permit the white regime to continue mercenarization from within. The institution of the draft for blacks, on the other hand, suggests that reliance on economic appeals, even when coupled with coercion, is not sufficient to maintain the military as more Zimbabweans are mobilized politically and as the Patriotic Front makes clear its position that any blacks serving in the government forces are considered traitors.

Following the "internal settlement," another sort of mercenarization move appeared, again aimed at Africans. This time it was directed at the Patriotic Front guerrilla forces. Mercenarization was proposed under the guise of "military integration." There were reports that white security planners in Salisbury were pressuring Bishop Muzorewa, the leading black involved in the "internal settlement," to approach guerrillas based in Mozambique. Muzorewa was to urge them to accept positions in the Rhodesian regime's regular security forces. The choice to be presented to the guerrillas was "between a rough and disorganized life in the bush, and a well-paid job in the army."[11] This was to be presented as consistent with British-United States guidelines for an integrated military. In essence, as the *Manchester Guardian* suggested, "military integration" in Rhodesia, outside the context of genuine majority rule, could be little more than a new form of mercenarization. The basic contradictions that made mercenarization necessary would still remain.

Mercenarization in South Africa

Mercenarization does not seem to be as blatant or as developed in South Africa as under the illegal Rhodesian regime. This is true for several reasons. First, the South African state system is based on a larger white majority, comprising 20 percent of the total population. Consequently, more whites are available to fill military quotas. Second, the South African regime has had a stronger and far more elaborate economic base on which to build its security apparatus. This has meant, on the one hand, that national service for white South Africans has not drained the economy so seriously; and, on the other, that the government can turn more readily to expensive technology to make up for manpower limitations.

Nonetheless, mercenarization is proceeding in South Africa. As in Rhodesia, immigration and state security are intimately related. Thus it was disturbing to security planners in Pretoria to receive the 1977 immigration figures, which revealed that 26,000 people—mostly whites—had left South Africa, while only 24,822 whites entered as immigrants. (The tens of thousands of black migrant laborers brought in from neighboring countries are not counted.) Even more significant for the formulation of security policy, particularly given the current stress on substituting technology for personnel in the counter-insurgency efforts, was a large exodus of white professionals. In the first ten months of 1977, 3182 professional personnel left South Africa.[12]

In 1977, South Africa's regular armed forces included 55,000 people, an increase of 4000 over 1976. But 38,400 of these—that is, the overwhelming majority—were conscripts.[13] Furthermore, within the army there was a drain on the officer corps. More and more career officers were leaving to enter the private sector, where Afrikaners now have an increasing opportunity for advancement, in part because of deliberate efforts by the Afrikaner-dominated Nationalist regime to help them become more economically competitive with English-speaking whites.[14] Thus, if foreign mercenaries are more necessary to fill particular officer posts in the future, it will be, ironically, a consequence of the regime's own success in promoting the economic interests of its immediate ethnic constituency.

Manpower politics have been prominent in South African military development, perhaps even more than in Rhodesia, because of the ethnic split between Afrikaner and English whites and because the white-ruled state is not sure how best to use the Coloureds and Asians. Beginning in the late 1930s, the Afrikaners have looked upon the military—especially the army—as a state institution that was particularly their own. Ethnic compositions of the various services reflect this. While in 1974, only 50 percent of the navy's permanent staff was Afrikaans-speaking, 75 percent of the airforce's permanent staff and 85 percent of the army's permanent staff spoke Afrikaans.[15] In one effort to forestall mercenarization, the government has appealed to English-speaking white South Africans to pursue military careers. In other words, mercenarization might be retarded if white ethnic unity replaced the older ethnic communalism that often divided whites.

In addition, the South African government has sought to overcome military manpower shortages by bringing more blacks into the traditionally all-white military. But these moves have been taken gingerly and with ambivalence.[16] They do not represent a clear-cut tactic of mercenarization from within, in that the regime is not simply appealing to the economic needs of prospective Asian and Coloured recruits. The regime has tried to convince the established accomodationist leaders of these groups that they and their rank and file have an ideological stake in defending the current state system. They should see the new chance to serve in the South African military—mostly in unarmed logistical units— as an opportunity to support the existing system and perhaps even win gratitude from white South Africans. If this ideological appeal does not succeed, the regime will have to make the mercenarization dimension of its non-white recruitment even clearer.

As in Rhodesia, the sharpening contradictions produced by white intransigency and growing black militance have resulted in the extension of military duty for whites, at the same time that greater numbers of whites are leaving the country and new white immigrants are proving harder to attract. In June 1977, the South African government decided to double the period of compulsory military service for white citizens. Beginning in January 1978, white males had to serve two years instead of one.[17] In February 1978, the government passed a bill that made white immigrants subject to immediate conscription, although traditionally new entrants were granted a "grace period" before having to serve. The bill was introduced at a time when white South Africans were becoming increasingly resentful of newly arrived young white immigrants who were immune from conscription. More than two-thirds of the new immigrants to South Africa in the 1973-'78 period were British, a fact which added fuel to the resentment among Afrikaner whites.[18]

In addition to inter-white cleavages and the reluctance to give non-whites *entree* into the military (although they are heavily used in the police) another constraint pressing more mercenarization in South Africa is the traditional white—especially Afrikaner—resistance to serving outside South African borders. When the government deployed South African troops in Angola in 1975, it aroused the anger of some of the Nationalist regime's most ardent supporters. When the intervention also proved a military fiasco, the opposition to such deployment grew even stronger. It was not a matter of opposition to intervention *per se*, and certainly not to white support for the anti-MPLA forces in Angola, but rather resistance to the deployment of white conscripts outside their homeland. In 1976, the government decided to confront the white opposition directly, taking this opportunity to confront the question of what constitutes "security" in the 1970s. In the end, it managed to pass a new defense act that abolished the stipulation that only volunteers could be deployed outside the country. The act also redefined the area of "national defense" to encompass "Africa south of the equator."[19] Nonetheless, the political realities are such that the Nationalist regime, burned by the failure of its Angolan expedition and the white criticism it provoked, will be reluctant to deploy regular troops outside South Africa. It is therefore likely that it will have to utilize mercenaries from within—South African soldiers attracted by high salaries—and mercenaries from without in extraterritorial operations. (Already there are South African mercenaries in Rhodesia.)

"White collar" mercenarization is perhaps more important to monitor than conventional "khaki" mercenarization in South Africa, because it reveals the basic counter-insurgency strategy of the white regime and the limits of South Africa's racially exclusive industrialism*on which such a strategy depends. South African defense orientation has recently been twofold: to develop both a long-range attack capability and an urban counter-insurgency capability. The latter is clearly contradictory, for it relies on a police force that is approximately 40 percent black to put down rebellions in entirely black townships such as Soweto. The long-range strike orientation in the military's current planning also involves serious contradictions, contradictions that have been addressed, if not resolved, by mercenarization. Such a long-range strike capacity demands sophisticated electronic communications equipment and censoring devices; it also requires well equipped and trained transportation units and commando-like special forces. These are precisely the areas in which mercenaries can be found in the current South African

---

* For the importance of foreign corporations in providing advanced technology and personnel, as well as capital, see Chapter 10 below.

security apparatus.

British, United States and, increasingly, West German firms producing electronics, aircraft and armored vehicles have supplied white collar mercenaries—that is, highly paid technicians sent to South Africa to set up and train South Africans in the use of these technological systems adapted for security purposes.[20] Companies such as IBM, ITT and Siemens are not usually thought of as hiring or deploying mercenaries; but in this era of electronic, chemical and nuclear warfare, the roles played by these companies in state security must be addressed explicitly.

The South African government's security formula is constrained by: (1) a defense strategy that calls for countering guerrilla forces over a vast territory; (2) severe limitations on the military manpower available to deploy over large areas; and (3) a military-industrial base that is sophisticated and well financed but still heavily dependent on foreign capital and technical expertise. It is the simultaneous existence of these three conditions that has made it analytically imperative to consider white-collar employees of overseas security-related firms as mercenaries. As the white-minority regime tries to solve its racially derived manpower shortages by increasing its strategic reliance on high-level technology, the state may be expected to shift further from "khaki" to "white-collar" mercenarization.

Mercenarization and Covert Foreign Policy

All transfers between states have political repercussions in terms of technology, intelligence, weapons, capital and personnel. In southern Africa, mercenarization has involved, increasingly, the transfer of security-related personnel from Western states to Rhodesia and South Africa. Some of these personnel wear uniforms; others perform their security missions in white shirts; but all should be considered mercenaries. The specific roles these mercenaries play is determined, first, by the acuteness of contradictions within the threatened state systems. In Rhodesia and South Africa, the decline in white immigration and the mobilization of resistance have made the foundations of state security ever more shaky. Second, mercenaries' role will be determined by the other transfers from allies upon which the state can draw. If, as in South Africa, there has been considerable influx of technology, capital and intelligence, mercenaries are likely to be deployed in highly specialized ways, particularly in technical installation and training.

Mercenarization has become a more pronounced aspect of United States foreign policy implementation because the deepening contradictions in southern Africa have made more open and direct forms of inter-state transfers less tenable or justifiable. Mercenarization is essentially an attempt to "privatize" foreign policy, at least nominally. But in reality, mercenarization reflects the public power's underlying strategy. Men are recruited, funded and transported with the aid—or at least the complicity—of public agencies; it is important to look beyond the job-seeking ex-marine in Las Vegas or his agent in San Diego. Mercenarization is a process by which the uses of public power and authority are camouflaged. The United States policies toward Rhodesia and South Africa are, at bottom, policies intended to reconcile the contradictions, not only within white-dominated southern Africa, but between those state systems and Western capitalism.

References

1.   These notices appeared as classified advertisements in *Soldier of Fortune: The Journal of Professional Adventurers* (Calif.), Summer, 1976, p. 79
2.   Burgess, John, "Thai Mercenaries in Laos," in *Ronin*, No. 16 (Winter 1974-Summer 1975), p. 66
3.   Burchett, Wilfred, and Roebuck, Derek, *The Whores of War: Mercenaries Today* (New York: Penguin Books, 1976)
4.   Halliday, F., "British Mercenaries and Counter-Insurgency," in *Race and Class*, XIX.2 (Autumn 1977); Halliday, F., *Mercenaries: Counter-Insurgency in the Gulf* (Nottingham, U.K.: Spokesman Books, 1977); NACLA, *Latin America and Empire Report: The Pentagon's Proteges*, "From MAAGs to Mercenaries," X.1 (January 1976), pp. 19-20
5.   *The New York Times*, April 26, 1978
6.   *The New York Times*, January 24, 1978
7.   Martin, David, "Smith's Secret Plans Revealed," in *The Observer* (London), June 19, 1977

8. Earp, Wyatt Jr., "Pros at Work: Bounty Hunting in Africa," in *Soldier of Fortune*, March 1978, pp. 36-40

9. Allen, Richard, "Rhodesia's Secret Army," in *Soldier of Fortune*, July 1978, pp. 36-38

10. *The New York Times,* February 12, 1978

11. *Manchester Guardian Weekly,* "Rhodesia—A Way Out of the Maze," April 2, 1978

12. Burns, J.F., "Apostles of Apartheid Aren't Yet Marching From Pretoria," in *The New York Times,* April 30, 1978

13. International Institute of Strategic Studies, *The Military Balance 1977-'78* (London), p. 47

14. Baker, Pauline H., "South Africa's Strategic Vulnerabilities: The 'Citadel Assumption' Reconsidered," in *African Studies Review*, XX.2 (September 1977), p. 93

15. Enloe, C.H., "Ethnic Factors in the Evolution of the South African Military," in *Issue*, V.4 (Winter 1975). This article is reprinted in, Enloe, C.H., *Police, Military and Ethnicity* (New Brunswick, N.J.: Transaction Books, forthcoming, January 1979)

16. *Ibid.,* p. 24

17. *Guardian* (U.K.), June 4, 1977

18. *Guardian* (U.K.), February 27, 1978. For an analysis of the historical linkages between military and immigration politics and English-Afrikaner politics in South Africa, see Stone, John, "The 'Migrant Factor' in a Plural Society: A South African Case Study," in *International Migration Review*, IX.1 (Spring 1975), pp. 15-28

19. Grundy, K.W., *Defense Legislation and Communal Politics* (Athens, Ohio: Ohio University Center for International Studies, 1978)

20. On the West German operations, see, African National Congress of South Africa, *Conspiracy to Arm Apartheid Continues: FRG-SA Collaboration* (Bonn: Progress Dritte Welt, 1977)

Appendix*

Sections 958, 959 and 960 of Title 18 of the U.S. Federal Code expressly forbid United States citizens to recruit for or enlist in foreign armed forces. The Code imposes various fines and prison terms for violation of these laws. As the following cases indicate, there are numerous publicized instances of involvement by U.S. citizens in the white-minority Rhodesian regime's military and police. Yet there is no evidence that any citizen has been prosecuted for serving as a mercenary in post-colonial Africa.

* This appendix was compiled from information supplied by Professor Richard Lobban.

The precise number of mercenaries serving in Rhodesia, and their nationalities, is kept secret by the illegal regime. In July 1976, however, a BBC program indicated that 80 percent of the regime's newest recruits are foreign. The greatest number come from Britain; the second largest group is from the United States. Most others come from West Germany and South Africa. The report described an international recruitment network, although this was denied by the Rhodesian regime.[1]

Later in 1976, Robin Wright, a freelance journalist in southern Africa, revealed that 400 United States citizens had already enlisted, and that the number of applications was increasing daily.[2] The British *Sunday Times* estimated the total mercenary force had already reached 800, and that five new applications were received every day.[3] The African press counted 1400 mercenaries, representing a significant share of the regime's entire troop strength, including soldiers from "New York and Tucson, Arizona."[4]

Mercenaries are usually recruited for the Rhodesian Light Industry (RLI), but sometimes for the police, the Special Air Service, or an elite commando group, apparently something like the notorious Selous Scouts.[5]

Recruitment of mercenaries for Rhodesia has been openly carried out in several United States magazines, including *Shotgun News, Gun Week, Sports Afield, Shooting Times* and *Gun Magazine*, as well as through individually addressed letters or word-of-mouth.[6] Reportedly, the "Phoenix Associates" of U.S. Marines in Quantico, Virginia,[7] and the chairman of the Department of Military Science of the University of California at Berkeley[8] were also involved in recruiting mercenaries. Both parties have fiercely denied these reports.

Shotgun News suggests applicants write Frank Abbot Sweeney in Tenafly, New Jersey, to serve in the Rhodesian Light Infantry, as he did for three years.[9] An organization known as "Anubis Ltd." of Highlands, Texas, has also advertised in *Shotgun News*.[10] Frank Renzi of Long Beach, California, has placed recruiting ads in *Shooting Times* and *Sports Afield*.[11] Former U.S. Special Forces Major Robert K. Brown of Arvada, Colorado, organized his own recruitment organization, which included a glossy, gory magazine, *Soldier of Fortune*, in which he published a recruitment contact in Salisbury, Rhodesia.[12] None of these individuals or organizations have been prosecuted. An April 1977 advertisement in the *Fresno Bee* (California) describes "high risk" military work in Africa. This might be recruitment for southern Zaire or Rhodesia.[13]

Mercenaries typically arrive on a tourist visa in Salisbury, Rhodesia,[14] and seek out Major Nick Lamprecht[15] at the King George VI Barracks, the central recruiting office. The rate of pay is determined on the basis of experience and former rank in the United States military. Wages have been reported as low was $800 a month,[16] although they may reach $3000 a month[17] for high-ranking officers.

The Rhodesian regime frequently fails to report casualties, either for regular soldiers or mercenaries. A few cases have, however, been reported. The first known U.S. mercenary killed in action in Rhodesia was John Coey of Hideway Hills, Ohio, a member of the Rhodesian Light Infantry, who had originally joined the Special Air Services in March 1972. For official services, Coey said he had emigrated to Rhodesia and then been drafted.

The State Department responded to the publicity surrounding Coey's death by saying, "we can discourage them, but we can't prohibit them"[18]—although U.S. citizens were long prohibited from visiting Cuba, Vietnam, North Korea and other countries.

In November 1977, Keith Nelson, aged 26, returned home. A Vietnam veteran from Sycamore, Ill., who had served in the U.S. Special Forces, Nelson had lost both legs on a military patrol in Rhodesia in June 1977. Nelson said he went to Rhodesia because he loved military adventure, and that he participated on raids into Mozambique. Nonetheless, there have been no reports that he is being prosecuted.[19]

Two other Americans, Joe Belisario and Craig Acheson, were arrested in Botswana, allegedly on a mission for the Rhodesian secret police. Both men were leaders of the anti-communist formation known as "Veterans and Volunteers for Vietnam." No United States prosecutions followed their arrest, however.[20]

The success of the liberation movement has demoralized some of these "soldiers of fortune." Three United States mercenaries stole a Piper Cherokee plane from Salisbury airport in February 1977. Two of the three had deserted from the Rhodesian Light

Infantry; the third, from an air cavalry unit.[21] Another deserter, Lawrence Meyers, fled to Gaberone, Botswana. He said the nationalists will win, the Rhodesians are losing.[22] Meyers was deported to the United States.[23] The FBI has reportedly begun an investigation, but Meyers has been granted immunity from prosecution. No reasons were given.

In September 1977, S. Dravitts, aged 25, a deserter, claimed many others had left already, "because they do not want to die for a futile cause."[24]

David Bufkin, a mercenary recruiter for the CIA,[25] was reportedly assigned to spy on the Cuban Embassay in Montreal. The CIA believed the Cubans were seeking to organize fake mercenaries to infiltrate the Rhodesian military. Bufkin was to bug the Embassy and break this alleged network. Mercenaries recruited by the Cubans were reported to have deserted to Botswana.[26]

Finally, the case of Major Mike Williams, aged 52, of San Antonio, Texas, may be cited. Williams served in the U.S. Army for 12 years, including a period in Vietnam as a Special Forces Captain. In 1977, he commanded the Rhodesian Grey Scouts, an elite horse-mounted unit which specialized in counter-insurgency activities. Apparently, Williams has also not been prosecuted by the United States government.[27]

References

1. *Zambia Daily Mail* (Lusaka), July 20, 1976; *International Herald Tribune*, July 23, 1976
2. *International Herald Tribune*, December 10, 1976
3. *Sunday Times* (London), November 28, 1976
4. *Daily News* (Dar-es-Salaam), December 21, 1976
5. Thobhani, A.H., "The Mercenary Menace," in *Africa Today*, XXIII.3 (1976), p. 65
6. Anable, D., "The Return of the Mercenaries," in *Africa Report*, XX.6 (1975)
7. *The New York Times,* June 22, 1975
8. *The Guardian* (U.K.) March 11, 1977
9. Anable, *op.cit.*
10. *Ibid.*

11. *Ibid.*
12. *Ibid.*
13. *The Christian Science Monitor* (Boston), May 1977
14. *The Daily News* (Dar-es-Salaam), December 21, 1976
15. *The International Herald Tribune*, July 23, 1976
16. *The Guardian* (U.K.), March 11, 1977
17. *The Sun*, July 18, 1976
18. Anable, *op.cit.*
19. Providence Sunday Journal (Rhode Island), November 20, 1977
20. Anable, *op.cit.*
21. *The Times of Zambia* (Lusaka), February 20, 1977
22. *International Herald Tribune*, January 10, 1976
23. *The Star* (Johannesburg), weekly edition, February 12, 1977; *The Guardian*, (U.K.), March 11, 1977
24. *The Times of Zambia* (Lusaka), September 8, 1977
25. *International Herald Tribune,* January 12, 1977
26. *The New York Times*, January 11, 1977
27. *Chicago Daily News*, December 8, 1977

Part III
The United States Contribution to South Africa's Military Build-Up

Chapter 7

Breakdown of the United States Arms Embargo

Sean Gervasi

The United States and other Western powers pledged to impose a volunteer arms embargo in 1963. Nonetheless, extensive evidence exposes the continued funneling of military supplies and equipment to South Africa and even to the illegal Smith regime.

Introduction

The material presented in this chapter shows the extent of the failure of the United States government to adequately enforce the U.N. voluntary arms embargo on South Africa of 1963. It is an edited version of testimony originally presented to the Subcommittee on Africa, Committee on International Relations, U.S. House of Representatives, on July 14, 1977. The testimony demonstrates that, despite the U.N. embargo, U.S.-produced and U.S.-licensed weapons have contributed importantly to the continued clandestine flow of foreign weapons to South Africa.

The facts set out in the testimony were at the time heatedly contested by the Department of State. On July 20, 1977, six days after the testimony was presented, William H. Lewis, director of the Bureau of Inter-African Affairs of the State Department, spoke before the Subcommittee on Africa. In his testimony, Lewis said, concerning the data presented in this chapter, that, "Allegations...that the U.S. has assisted South Africa in building a stockpile of sophisticated weapons, including aircraft, tanks and artillery, are utterly false." Lewis avoided challenging specific allegations, however. He did not contest any of the statistics regarding the number and kind of U.S.-produced weapons which have been added to the South African arsenal since 1963.

Many of the statistics cited in the testimony have since been confirmed independently by authoritative sources in both Britain and the United States. The July testimony brought to the House subcommittee's attention the fact that standard sources did not even list many important weapons systems which had been acquired from abroad by South Africa. Many of these were produced in the United States, or in third countries under U.S. license. The following sources have now confirmed the acquisition of these previously unlisted U.S. weapons systems by South Africa, as first revealed in the July testimony:

Jane's Weapons Systems, 1977 edition (M-7 105 mm self-propelled gun, 155 mm howitzer)

The Military Balance, 1977-'78 (M-41 tank, M-3A1 scout car, 105 mm self-propelled gun, 155 mm gun/howitzer)

Arsenal of Democracy, by T. Gervasi, 1978 (M-47 tank, M-41 tank, V-150 armored personnel carrier, M-113A1 armored personnel carrier, M-3A1 scout car, M-7 105 mm self-propelled gun, M-109 155 mm self-propelled gun, F-104G Starfighter, F-51D Cavalier COIN aircraft, Agusta Bell 205A helicopter)

Armed Forces of the World, 4th edition, ed. R. Sellers (V-150 Commando armored personnel carrier)

Defense and Foreign Affairs Handbook 1976-'77 (V-150 Commando armored personnel carrier, 155 mm howitzer)

United States government spokesmen have openly begun to acknowledge the fact that the United States provided arms to South Africa after the 1963 embargo. In the February 21, 1978 edition of *The Inter Dependent*, a publication of the United Nations Association, U.S. Deputy Ambassador to the United Nations Donald McHenry stated that at the time of the Soweto demonstrations in June 1976, the previous U.S. administration was in fact *relaxing* the arms embargo. In describing the problems of diplomatic cooperation with South Africa at the time, McHenry said:

> We were put in the very difficult position of being relatively quiet on the situation in Soweto where 600 kids were being killed while we were speaking with South Africa on Rhodesia and Namibia. And it's very difficult to follow that kind of approach. *We were making changes in our arms embargo, being more lenient with South Africa, while 600 children were being killed in Soweto.* [emphasis added]

The failure of the 1963 voluntary arms embargo suggests the need to examine two sorts of issues. The first, considered to some extent in Robert Sylvester's essay, is its implication for the mandatory embargo voted by the United Nations Security Council on November 4, 1977.* Specifically, have the enforcement mechanisms adopted by the United Nations been changed to ensure an effective embargo? More importantly, is the United States government sufficiently committed to the embargo to prevent its violation and the abuses of power which led to the CIA involvement in Angola, illegally and contrary to Congressional policy decisions?**

Second, one must examine the nature of the contribution of the United States violations of the voluntary embargo for the South African government's military build-up, how arms reaching South Africa secretly are likely to be used. The political-military geography and concentration of population in southern Africa dictate that the apartheid regime will have to be "prepared" over the next five to ten years for three kinds of conflict.

First, the eastern areas of South Africa, bordering Swaziland and Mozambique, are mostly savanna and grasslands, with some forest cover. They are suited to traditional, small-unit counter-insurgency warfare. As in Vietnam, this implies the need for a certain kind of "capital-intensive" warfare: location devices, sophisticated communications equipment, small aircraft and helicopters.

The western Cape and Namibia are mainly desert and karoo.

---

* See Chapter 11. Appendix B gives the resolution's text.
**See Chapter Five.

Distances between cities are considerable. Here, a second, more or less conventional type of armored warfare would be more appropriate. The distances also suggests that South Africa must have a long-range rapid airlift capability. In the central areas of the country, which have a mixed terrain, a combination of these types of operations seems likely to be used in future war.

Third, in urban areas, the South African military will need to support the police with two kinds of operations: those against mass demonstrations and large-scale strikes, and those against small groups of urban guerrillas seeking to attack strategic targets. As demonstrated in Soweto and elsewhere over the last two years, this implies the need for relatively large numbers of small, high-speed armored cars and armored personnel carriers.

As the following testimony indicates, the military hardware required for these three types of operations is exactly the kind of hardware that the United States and other Western powers have covertly supplied to South Africa over the past decade.

Finally, it should be noted that none of the items secretly provided to South Africa could be covered by the "exceptions" to the voluntary arms embargo that the United States made at the time of its adoption in 1963. That is, the weapons cited in this text as having "slipped through" the arms embargo neither promote international peace and stability, nor provide for the external defense of South Africa. Rather, these weapons were intended to be, and have been, used to suppress the legitimate liberation struggles of the black majority, and to destabilize neighboring governments which support this struggle. The wave of repression following the murder of Steven Biko and the May 1978 attack on Angola are only the most recent examples of the uses to which South Africa puts foreign weapons which it acquires through the channels of the "secret arms trade."

The Testimony

The 1977 testimony was as follows:

Evidence has recently come to light that makes it clear that the arms embargo is practically nonexistent. By all accounts, South Africa has had a thriving international trade in arms for nearly a decade. Reliable sources indicate that in recent years the government of South Africa has spent hundreds of millions of dollars abroad each year in order to purchase arms and defense equipment. Almost all its purchases have been made in Western countries.

In some cases, South Africa has been able to purchase arms quite openly. The French government, for instance, has allowed the sale of aircraft, helicopters and missiles through normal intergovernmental channels. A great deal of weaponry has, however, been sold secretly to South Africa. Arms have moved through other channels, known only to a small circle of government officials and arms dealers. The South African Defense Forces have been able to acquire hundreds of aircraft, tanks and armored vehicles that they could not easily purchase directly from Western governments or corporations.

South Africa has thus been able to add to its known stock of arms a large "secret arsenal." A good proportion of this additional weaponry is reconditioned but very serviceable equipment of United States origin. The breakdown of the arms embargo is no insignificant matter. The major Western powers have flouted the will of the United Nations Security Council and have, in effect, declared their contempt for the United Nations itself. Instead of isolating South Africa, they have secretly assisted it. And South Africa has now built a formidable military force with a long-range strike capability. It could not have done so without Western arms and technology. If South Africa now threatens peace and international security in Africa, the responsibility lies in large measure with those states which have been assisting it militarily.

How has major U.S. equipment, whether produced in this country or under license abroad, been able to reach South Africa? Was it the policy of previous administrations to allow the shipment of major weapons systems to South Africa? Did they deliberately ignore the United Nations arms embargo? Or are the regulations governing the arms trade so loosely drafted that they permit sales to South Africa? Were the regulations adequate but simply not enforced for a long period of time? Are they being enforced now?

Africa is nearing the final confrontation over apartheid. The

South African government is preparing for war. It is serious enough that South Africa has used Western arms to build a modern military force in the last 15 years. Continued sales of Western arms to South Africa at this time will be seen throughout the world as evidence of a commitment to support apartheid. In the present circumstances, the actions of the United States government constitute military collaboration with South Africa.

In the strict sense of the term, the United Nations 1963 resolution on arms sales to South Africa *was not an embargo*. It began when the United Nations requested all states to stop the sale of arms and of equipment for making arms to South Africa. In August 1963, the Security Council passed Resolution 181, which called upon all states "to cease forthwith the sale and shipment of arms, ammunition of all types and military vehicles to South Africa."[1] A few months later, in December, the council widened its call for an embargo by requesting that states also stop the shipment of equipment and materials for the manufacture and maintenance of arms and ammunition. Thus the embargo has been, from the beginning, strictly voluntary.*

The original call was framed in the most general terms. The United Nations has never really elaborated on it. It has never suggested standards and procedures for implementing an embargo. Indeed, it has never even established machinery for monitoring movements of arms and military equipment to South Africa. Everything was left to individual governments. They decided how to translate the general terms of the original Security Council resolutions into specific prohibitions on the sale of arms; they decided how to formulate, apply and enforce, the particular provisions of a national embargo. Governments have been free to do as they saw fit—in particular, to allow whatever exceptions and loopholes seemed to them to be necessary and appropriate.

The United States declared its intention to adhere strictly to the embargo from the very beginning. In announcing the U.S. intention to institute a national embargo in 1963, Ambassador Adlai Stevenson said at the United Nations that the United States

*See Chapter 11. Appendix B gives the text of the resolution.

expected "to bring to an end the sale of all military equipment to the Government of South Africa by the end of this calendar year..."[2] At the same time, Stevenson noted two exceptions to this policy. He pointed out that the United Nations would have to fulfill existing contracts for "limited quantities of strategic equipment for defense against external threats." He also stated that the United States, "as a nation with many responsibilities in many parts of the world," would naturally have to reserve "the right in the future to interpret this policy in the light of requirements for assuring the maintenance of international peace and security."[3] Consequently it was not at all clear that adoption of this new policy would ensure the cessation of all shipments of arms and equipment to South Africa.

In fact, there has been a great deal of confusion about how the United States implements the arms embargo. Quite large quantities of U.S. military equipment were sent to South Africa and the then-Portuguese territories in Africa in the late 1960s and early '70s. At the end of hearings before the House Subcommittee on Africa in 1973, the chairman stated,

> We find that there has been what we consider to be a massive erosion of the principles established during the 1960s, with significant sales of equipment, aircraft, herbicides, even crop-spraying aircraft, to the South African and/or Portuguese military, and to civilian users who are likely to be connected with the military, especially in an emergency.[4]

The subcommittee's efforts to find out exactly what was happening met with resistance. The chairman of the subcommittee requested a copy of the guidelines for implementation of the embargo from the Department of State. A representative of the department agreed that such guidelines existed. The department would not, however, say anything about them publicly. When asked formally whether there were guidelines for the implementation of the embargo, the department replied that it had to treat the answer to that question as classified.[5]

Nonetheless, government witnesses strongly rejected any allegation that the United States had failed to implement the embargo properly. They argued that the United States had pursued and was pursuing a policy of strict compliance with the terms of the United Nations resolutions. Former Assistant Secretary of State for African Affairs David Newsom denied there were any "hidden areas of policy toward southern Africa."[6] In his view, the United States had not in any way ignored the U.N. arms embargo. He argued that,

> ...over a period of a decade, we have maintained strict arms embargoes toward both South Africa and the Portuguese territories. We have done so as a tangible demonstration of our support for self-determination and *our desire to avoid any support for the imposition of apartheid.* Our desire is *to avoid giving any encouragement to any side to rely on military solutions* to the complex of southern African problems. The arms embargo policy has been reaffirmed and enforced by succeeding administrations since the early 1960s. [Emphasis added][7]

It is generally recognized that South Africa has become an important military power in the last decade. It has a large standing army, and a very large pool of trained manpower which can be quickly mobilized. It has a large, modern airforce with an impressive strike capability. Its army possesses hundreds of tanks and other armored vehicles which can be moved rapidly to any part of the southern African region.

The prevailing view among military experts is that South Africa has achieved this capability through long, hard effort. South Africa has an industrial base with which to manufacture modern arms and ammunition. It has close ties to countries willing to sell it the technology needed to expand and modernize its armed forces. And finally, it has made great sacrifices in order to carry out an extensive program of military expansion over the last ten years.

This view is, however, quite misleading. It is true that South Africa has devoted much energy to the defense effort. The government has given military expansion first priority for some time. In 1963, defense expenditures were less than $200 million.[8] By 1976, the country was spending 20 percent of the national budget and more than 5 percent of the national domestic product on the military. The 1977 budget projects defense expenditures of nearly $2 billion.

The scale of this effort has clearly been important in helping South Africa to build a modern armed force. But South Africa has not been producing the weapons it now uses. It has purchased them overseas. In fact, South Africa has spent large amounts of foreign exchange every year in order to purchase arms. In recent years, the equivalent of two thirds of the military budget has been spent on defense imports each year.[9] In 1973, the defense import bill was already more than $450 million. By 1975, over $800 million in foreign exchange was being spent for defense. The projected defense import bill for 1977 is in excess of $1.2 billion.[10]

Almost all this money has been and is being spent in Western countries, or in countries used for the transshipment of Western arms. Industry and government sources indicate that South Africa has been able to buy almost anything it wants, if it was willing to pay the price. And the South African government has been willing. It has purchased every kind of weapon and type of equipment, from tanks and radar, to helicopters and self-propelled guns.

The principal sellers of arms to South Africa have been Great Britain, the United States, France and Italy. It was generally believed until now that France had supplied South Africa with almost all its imported arms in recent years. This now seems doubtful, however. While figures on the value of the arms trade are not yet available, it appears that Great Britain, the United States and France have accounted for the bulk of sales to South Africa since 1963. As the South African defense import figures indicate, the volume of the arms trade with South Africa has been far larger than it was thought to be. French sales have accounted for only a small part of the actual arms trade with that country.

Little has been known until now about British, United States and Italian arms sales, for the simple reason that they have been kept secret. It is not possible, at this time, to say precisely why the public and the Congress have been told almost nothing about these arms sales. There is not sufficient information available about the organization of the South African trade. It has been suggested, however, that some governments have found it difficult to create the machinery needed to monitor the arms trade properly. They themselves, it is said, have little information on the development of the South African arms trade.

This argument is quite unconvincing, particularly with respect to the United States and United Kingdom governments. These governments follow the movement of arms on the international market very closely. They have vast resources for information-gathering. And there is abundant evidence that extensive information on the sale of arms to South Africa has been available in government circles since the United Nations embargo began. Moreover, it appears that in more than a few cases governments themselves have been directly or indirectly involved in selling arms to South Africa.

The tables which follow give a rough indication of the extent of the "invisible" arms trade with South Africa. Tables 4 and 5 provide data on major weapons systems used by the South African air and land forces. They give a rough description of the South African arms inventory.[11] This must be the starting point for any thorough analysis of the "invisible" arms trade, for one can estimate the volume and importance of that trade only when one knows precisely what is in the arms inventory.

The difficulty until now has been that published figures on the South African inventory were inaccurate. The International Institute for Strategic Studies (IISS) in London publishes figures annually which indicate the quantities of different kinds of equipment in the inventories of most countries. The IISS figures are generally regarded as authoritative. Their data on South Africa, however, provide a misleading view of South African strength in equipment. The institute's figures on South Africa are inaccurate in two respects. First, the institute has failed to list many major weapon systems currently in use in South Africa. Second, the figures on weapons that it does list often understate the quantites actually in use.

Table 4 attempts to provide a more accurate summary of the South African arms inventory. It indicates which weapon systems the IISS lists as part of that inventory. It indicates the cases in which the institute has given figures which understate the quantity of a particular kind of equipment in use. Finally, Table 4 lists important weapon systems now in the South African inventory that are not listed by the institute. The data for this table have been drawn, as is indicated, from a wide variety of

*Table 4: Major Weapons Systems in Use By South African Army and Air Force **

Used in the South African Army

Listed by IISS	Quantity Understated by IISS
Centurion tanks[1]	yes
Comet tanks	no
Eland armored cars	no
Ferret sct/armored cars	yes
Saracen APC	yes
Ratel APC[2]	?

Not listed by IISS

Centurion Mk 10 tank
Patton tank
Walker Bulldog tank
AMX-13 tank
Staghound armored car[3]
Shorland Mk3 armored car
M-113A1 APC
V-150 Commando APC
Piranha APC
Short SB 301 APC
M3A1 APC
Sexton 88 mm SP gun
M-7 Priest 105 mm SP gun
M-109 155 mm SP gun

Used in South African Air Force[4]

Listed by IISS	Quantity Understated by IISS
Buccaneer bomber	no
Canberra bomber	no
Mirage F-1 strike/interceptor	yes
Mirage III strike/interceptor	yes
Impala I strike/trnr[5]	yes
Shackleton patrol	no
Albatross patrol	no
Alouette III helicopter	yes
Puma helicopter	yes
Super Frelon helicopter	no
Wasp helicopter	yes

Not listed by IISS

Impala II jet strike[6]
F-104G Starfighter
F-51D Cavalier COIN
Iroquois helicopter
Gazelle helicopter

* References on bottom of p. 144.

Table 5: *Deliveries of Weapons Systems Known to be in Service with the South African Defense Forces*
(end 1976)

Item	Manufactured/ Licensed by	Numbers Deliveries	IISS*
Mirage III fighter/bomber trainer/recce	France	95 plus	57
Mirage F-1 all-weather multipurpose fighter	France	48 plus	16
Aermacchi MB-326M Impala I strike/trainer	SA/Italy	300	145
Aermacchi MB-326K Impala II	SA/Italy	100	22
Aerospatiale Alouette III armed attack helicopter	France	115 plus	40
Aerospatiale/Westland 330 Puma assault helicopter	France/UK	40 plus	25
Centurion Mk 7 heavy tank	UK	150	141
Daimler Ferret Mk 2 scout car/anti-tank armored car	UK	450	230
M-3A1 White armored personnel carrier	US	400	n.s.
Saracen FV603 and FV610 armored personnel carrier	UK	700	n.s.
T-17 E1 Staghound armored car	US	450	n.s.

n.s.—not specified
*The Military Balance, 1976-'77   Source: As for Table A.

[1] Most military publications list the MK 7 as the most recent model of the Centurion in the South African inventory.
[2] This is supposed to be a domestically produced model. It may be a South African name for an imported model.
[3] These armored cars, which are still in service with the Citizen Force, were listed by the IISS in previous editions of *The Military Balance*.   [4] Combat aircraft and helicopters only.
[5] South Africa has 300 Impala I trainer-strike jet aircraft. These can be used as combat aircraft when armed.
[6] IISS listed the Impala II as a "trainer" in 1976. It is a jet strike aircraft.

Source: The Military Balance 1976-'77 (London: International Institute for Strategic Studies); *Almanac of World Military Power* (New York: T.M. Depuy and Associates, 1974); *Southern Africa, The Escalation of a Conflict* (Stokholm: Stockholm International Peace Research Institute, 1976), Appendix I; *International Military Aircraft and Aviation Director*, 1970 and 1976 (Essex: Aviation Advisory Services); *AAS Milavnews*, monthly, 1975 and 1977; *Foreign Military Markets*, South African Force Structure, 1974 and 1976 (Greenwich, Conn.: Defense Marketing Services); diverse industry and government sources.

industry and government sources in several countries.

Thus it is clear that two kinds of transactions have been taking place in the South African arms trade. First, suppliers have been selling far larger quantities of certain weapons to South Africa than is generally reported.[12] Second, suppliers have been selling South Africa many items of equipment which are not generally believed to be part of the South African inventory. Both kinds of transactions are politically secret, although the latter tends to be shrouded in particular secrecy.

Table 5 provides some details on the sale of "extra quantities" of equipment to South Africa. The weapons systems listed are all generally known to be in use at the present time. It was not known until recently that, in many cases, large numbers of these weapons have been delivered to South Africa. Table 5 gives figures for estimated cumulative deliveries of certain weapons. It also gives the currently available IISS figure for the number of each of these weapons actually in use. The figures are not, strictly speaking, comparable. Everything which has been delivered is not necessarily in use. As most deliveries have been relatively recent, however, the rate of attrition through accident and retirement cannot possibly account for the low figure given by the IISS in most cases. The new data on deliveries therefore make it clear that South Africa has far larger quantities of the weapons in question than it is believed to have.

Table 6 indicates that many important arms deals have been kept entirely secret until now. It lists weapons systems now in the South African inventory which are not credited to South Africa by standard sources such as *The Military Balance*.[13] These weapons are all major items of considerable military significance. The arms listed in Table 6—aircrafts, helicopters, tanks, armored cars and armored personnel carriers—have all, with one exception, been delivered to South Africa since the arms embargo began. Many have been delivered within the last eight to nine years. Orders for some are still on the books in Great Britain, Portugal and Italy.[14]

The data set out in these tables show that France, the United States, the United Kingdom and Italy have failed altogether to heed the Security Council call for an arms embargo against South

Table 6: Deliveries of Weapon Systems Not Generally Known
to be in Service with the South African Defense Forces (end 1976)

Item	Manufactured/ Licensed by	Deliveries
Lockheed F-104G Starfighter fighter/bomber	US/ex-Luftwaffe	40
North American F-51D Cavalier counter-insurgency strike	US	50
Aerospatiale/Westland 341 Gazelle general purpose helicopter	France/UK	2(?)
Agusta/Bell 205A Iroquois utility/s.r. helicopter	US	25
Lockheed P-2 Neptune anti-submarine patrol	US	12
Centurion Mk 10 heavy tank	UK	240
M-47 Patton main battle tank	US/Italy	100
M-41 Walker Bulldog light tank	US	100
AMX-13 light tank	France	80
M-113A1 armored personnel carrier	US/Italy	(400)
Commando V-150 armored personnel carrier	US/Portugal	(300)
Piranha armored personnel carrier	Switzerland	(100)
Shorland Mk 3 armored car	UK	(200)
Short SB 301 armored personnel carrier	UK	(300)
Sexton 25 pdr self-propelled gun	Canada	200
M-7 105 mm self-propelled gun	US	200
M-109 155 mm self-propelled gun	US/Italy	(50)

Note: Figures in brackets indicate orders on which delivery continues.
[1]In service with the South African Police.

Source: As for Table 4.

Africa. There may be "arms export control" regulations of some kind in force in various countries. But they are entirely ineffective. Those regulations have not stopped the flow of arms to South Africa. Suppliers in Western countries have shipped vast quantities of arms to South Africa throughout the last decade. In recent years, the arms trade with South Africa has reached levels which even the most skeptical would have thought impossible.

And governments have allowed arms to be shipped in secret.

In the circumstances, the protests of government officials in various countries that they are implementing the U.N. embargo can hardly be taken seriously. An arms embargo which is ignored by not one but several major arms-producing countries is to all intents and purposes a dead letter.

The breakdown of the arms embargo has had very serious consequences, although that fact is not yet generally understood. Perhaps the most serious is that South Africa has been able to build a modern military force on the African continent, a force which in the present circumstances affords it formidable power. When the arms embargo began, South Africa had a relatively small military establishment. There were less than 13,000 men in the Permanent Force, which provides the cadre of the armed forces on active duty.[15] Total military expenditures were approximately R120 million. The airforce had few modern aircraft and only a few helicopters. The army had a collection of old British and U.S. equipment. It had some Centurion and Comet tanks, some U.S. tanks and armored cars, and some British artillery. It had relatively few armored personnel carriers. On the African continent, the South African Defense Forces seemed quite large enough; but they were far from formidable. Moreover, the Defense Forces had essentially a defensive capability. They did not have even a small mobile attack force.

Today, the situation is different. South Africa now has an awesome military capability. Table 7 indicates the general kinds and quantities of modern equipment in service with the Defense Forces today. The airforce possesses more than 600 combat aircraft, including nearly 150 Mirage III and Mirage F-1 aircraft, as well as some 300 Aermacchi MB-326 strike-trainer and strike jets, 40 Lockheed F104G fighter-bombers and 50 North Ameri-

*Table 7: Arms Inventory for South African Defense Forces
(end 1976)*

	IISS*	Currently in service
combat aircraft	133	625
helicopters	92	215
tanks	161	525
armored cars	1,050	1,430
armored personnel carriers	250	960
self-propelled guns	not listed	294
medium and light artillery n.a.		380

*The Military Balance, 1976-'77
n.a.—not available

can F-51D Cavalier counter-insurgency strike aircraft.[16] It also
has more than 200 helicopters.[17] There are well over 1000 aircraft
in service with the South African Air Force.*

The army possesses more than 500 tanks. A large number of
these are Centurion MK 10s with a 105 mm gun and better armor
and engine than the MK 5 and 7 models that South Africa is
usually listed as having. Some are United States Patton tanks,
and some are French AMX-13 light tanks. The Patton tanks are
an improved model fitted with a British 105 mm gun. The army
also has nearly 200 Panhard armored cars fitted with 90 mm
guns. These are made in South Africa under French license. In
addition, the army possesses several hundred other armored cars
and nearly 1000 armored personnel carriers. Some of the larger
are very recent U.S. and British models. The army also has a large
number of self-propelled guns. These are medium and heavy
artillery, of 88 mm, 105 mm and 155 mm, mounted on tank
chassis. These guns are an important element in South Africa's
armored forces.

Table 7 indicates the extent to which standard sources
generally underestimate South African power. It gives the figures
for each type of major weapon actually in service. And it gives the
same figure for each category as listed in the most recent edition
of *The Military Balance*. It will be seen that in each case the IISS
has understated actual South African strength. The discrepancies

* For specifics on aircraft sales, see Chapter Eight.

are quite large. The institute lists less than a quarter of South Africa's combat aircraft as such. Its figure for helicopters is less than half the actual figure. It indicates South Africa has less than one third of the tanks which are currently in service. Its figures for armored personnel carriers are very wide of the mark, and it fails to list self-propelled guns at all.

South Africa has now emerged as a significant power in world terms. One can obtain a clearer idea of its real military capability by comparing its strength in various major weapons with that of other powers. Table 8 provides data for a rough comparison with Iran, Brazil, Egypt and Japan, all of which are significant military powers with a dominant influence in important regions of the world.

It is true, of course, that South Africa has a relatively small standing force, since until recently it recruited men for the Defense Forces from the white population alone. The manpower pool is still quite large, however. It has been estimated that it contains some 450,000 trained personnel.*[18] More importantly, South Africa can mobilize large numbers on relatively short notice by calling up the Citizen Force reserves, units composed of men with military experience who are re-trained every year. At the present time, Citizen Force units are being rotated continuously through the standing forces (those on active duty) in order to maintain a high degree of readiness. There are well over 200,000 men in the Citizen Force reserves, and anywhere from 25 to 35 percent may be on active duty at present. The Defense Forces are in fact in a state of permanent semi-mobilization.[19] Thus, the relatively small size of the standing forces is not as important as it might seem.

The data in Table 8 makes it clear that South Africa must be ranked with such powers as Iran, Egypt and Japan, rather than with middle-capacity powers like Poland, Argentina and Nigeria, with which it is usually compared. It is obviously far stronger than Brazil, which is generally considered to be quite powerful militarily. Its airforce is apparently more powerful than that of Egypt, Iran or Japan. And although South Africa might be considered weak in tank strength, its combined strength in tanks

---

* A breakdown for this figure is supplied on p. 115. The dual use of white skilled personnel is discussed in Chapters Six and Ten.

Table 8: Comparative Strength of Selected Armed Forces (end 1976)

	Iran	Brazil	Egypt	Japan	S. Africa
total armed					
total armed forces (thousands)	281	254	322	236	130[1]
combat aircraft	450	190	600	500 plus	625
helicopters;	125	50 plus	160	n.a.	215
tanks	1,990	350 plus	1,975	750	525
armored cars	n.a.	120	100	n.a.	1,430
armored personnel carriers	1,960	500	2,500	46	980
self-propelled guns	n.s.	n.s.	200	660	294

n.a.—not available

n.s.—not specified

[1]Estimate by the author based on South African source material. South Africa can mobilize 200,000 men with two days in an emergency.

Source: Defense and Foreign Affairs Handbook 1976-'77, Washington, D.C. and London, 1977; and various industry sources.

and armored cars, which have advantages over tanks in African terrain, is equivalent to that of any of the powers in question. South Africa is also weaker than Iran and Egypt in armored personnel. In the near future, however, it expects delivery of approximately 1000 additional armored personnel carriers. On the African continent, this means that South Africa has achieved the strongest military power south of the Sahara.

Some observers have suggested the Western equipment in the South African inventory is largely old. Some go on to say that almost all of it was shipped to South Africa before the arms embargo began. There is very little truth to this claim. Some of the Western equipment still in service, such as the Walker Bulldog tank and the Staghound armored car, is quite old; but much of it is still serviceable. More importantly, a good deal of equipment which may seem old, such as the Patton tank, has recently been reconditioned and improved. And most of the major weapons now in service with the regular airforce and army have been delivered in the last ten years.

Table 9 lists the principal weapons systems now in service with the regular South African Army. These include Centurion MK tanks, Panhard armored cars, Ferret scout cars armed with anti-tank missiles, Commando V-150 armored personnel carriers, M-113A1 armored personnel carriers and the M-109 155 mm self-propelled gun. The table gives the numbers of these and other major weapons now in service with the regular army. It also gives the approximate date when deliveries of each weapon began. It can be seen from the last column that almost every item was delivered after 1968. One armored car is produced under license in South Africa. The Sexton self-propelled gun was purchased 30 years ago; and the Saracen armored personnel carrier was imported in part before the embargo began.

Almost all the first-line armor of the regular army, then, has been imported from Western countries within the last ten years. Many important items such as the M-113A1 armored personnel carrier and the M-109 self-propelled gun have been imported quite recently. This equipment may not be entirely new, but it is far more modern than that usually found in Africa. It is also far heavier, and there is a great deal of it. All the Frontline States

Table 9: *Major Weapon Systems in Service with the South African Regular Army (early 1977)*

Item	approx. number in service	approx. date of delivery
Centurion Mk 10 tank	180	1967-68
Panhard AML 245 H60 armored car	800	produced under license
Panhard AML 245 H90 armored car	170	produced under license
Daimler Ferret Mk 2/Vigilant ATGW	160	1968-'69
Saracen armored personnel carrier	280	1962-'66
Commando V-150 armored personnel carrier	110	post-1971
Piranha armored personnel carrier	?	delivery beginning
M-113A1 armored personnel carrier	150	1973/4; delivery continuing
Sexton 25 pdr self-propelled gun	150	1946
M-109 155 mm self-propelled gun	24	1972/3; delivery continuing
Shortland Mk 3 armored car	60	1973; delivery continuing
M-47 Patton tank[1]	70	1971

[1]assigned to Citizen Force, but major equipment.

combined could not hope to match South Africa's firepower on the ground. That fact is largely the result of the shipment of arms from Western countries over the last decade.

What is the responsibility of the United States in the breakdown of the arms embargo? It is clear from the tables that a great deal of United States military equipment is now in service with the South African Defense Forces. The major items about which we know at this time are the following:

M-3A1 armored personnel carriers
T-17 El Staghound armored cars
M-47 Patton main battle tanks
M-41 Walker Bulldog light tanks
M-113A1 armored personnel carriers
Commando V-150 armored personnel carriers
M-7 105 mm self-propelled guns
M-109 155 mm self-propelled guns
Lockheed F-104G Starfighter jets
North American F-51D counter-insurgency aircraft
Agusta-Bell 205A Iroquois helicopters
Lockheed Hercules C-130B transport aircraft

It was not known outside official circles until last year that these weapons were in the South African inventory. Mention has been made from time to time of the use of the Staghound armored car and of the M-3A1 armored personnel carrier by South Africa. But it has certainly never been mentioned that large numbers of them remain in service with the Citizen Force. Virtually nothing has been said anywhere about the other arms listed above. That the United States has made an important contribution to the expansion and modernization of the South African Defense Forces therefore comes as a surprise to many people. Yet the facts make that conclusion inescapable.

It is not clear when all these arms were sent to South Africa. A large proportion appears, however, to have been shipped after 1963. The M-3A1 personnel carriers and the Walker Bulldog tanks were apparently sold to South Africa in the early 1950s, along with the Staghound armored cars and the M-7 self-propelled guns. The Hercules transports were sold the year before the embargo began. All the remaining U.S. items are believed to have been sold thereafter. The M-47 Patton tanks, the Commando personnel carriers, the M-113A1 personnel carriers and the M-109 155 mm self-propelled guns were all sold in the 1970s. The date of sale of the Starfighter jets and the F-51D Cavaliers has not yet been ascertained.

Weapons made in the United States or in other countries under U.S. license are today an important element in South Africa's arsenal. South Africa has large numbers of some of these weapons. All are operational. All are in service with the regular forces or the Citizen Forces. Still more important, deliveries of some items of United States equipment are continuing now.

Typically, United States corporations do not, so far as is known, sell directly to South Africa. Arms move to that country by an indirect route. At present, the preferred channel for getting U.S. arms to South Africa appears to be licensed production. By these arrangements, United States corporations agree to let foreign manufacturers produce U.S. weapons under license. The foreign manufacturer then ships the item in question to South Africa. In theory, this traffic should be controlled by the Office of Munitions Control (OMC) in the Department of State.* The OMC, however, apparently does not control foreign sales when production takes place under U.S. license. The FMC Corporation, for instance, has licensed Oto Melara, a major Italian arms manufacturer, to produce a version of the M-113A1 armored personnel carrier. It is the Oto Melara models which have been sold to South Africa recently. They were shipped from Italy. Oto Melara also produces or refurbishes the M-109 self-propelled gun under license, and then sells it to South Africa. Bravia, a firm in Portugal, produces the V-150 Commando personnel carrier under license from Cadillac Gage of Detroit. The Commandos are then sent to South Africa. These weapons are all now in the process of being delivered. So far as is known, no attempt has been made to stop this traffic.

It is clear that the United States and other Western powers

---

* For a discussion of the prosecution of Colt, the first after 15 years of embargo violations by a number of United States corporations, see Chapter 11.

have simply ignored the Security Council's call for an arms embargo against South Africa. There is no other construction to be put on their actions. For, while stating that they have implemented an embargo, they allowed vast quantities of arms to be sent to South Africa. These countries, then, did precisely what they said they were not doing. They helped South Africa to impose apartheid. They encouraged a state whose policies they profess to abhor "to rely on military solutions to the complex of southern African problems." These states, including the United States, have taken the side of the white-minority state in the military confrontation which is now developing. And they have done so in secret.

References

1. Resolution 181 (1963) of August 7, 1963 (S/5386)
2. Statement by Ambassador Adlai E. Stevenson, United States Representative in the Security Council on the South African Question (U.S. Mission to the U.N.: Press Release No. 4233, August 2, 1963)
3. *Ibid.*
4. Subcommittee on Africa of the House Committee on Foreign Affairs, Hearings on "Implementation of the U.S. Arms Embargo" (Washington, D.C.: Government Printing Office, 1973), p. 137

5. *Ibid.,* p. 53, footnote.

6. Testimony of David Newsom, Assistant Secretary of State for African Affairs, in *ibid.,* p. 148

7. *Ibid.*, p. 143

8. Barakat Ahmad, "South Africa's Military Establishment" (New York: Unit on Apartheid, United Nations, December 1972), p. 3

9. The South African Minister of Defense recently indicated that 45 percent of the defense budget is spent internally. See *White Paper on Defence, 1977* (Pretoria: Department of Defense), p. 12. Reliable sources indicate that in addition to the 55 percent of the budget used on foreign purchases, South Africa also spends large sums outside the defense budget on defense imports—as much as R200 million. A U.S. journalist has concluded that the equivalent of two thirds of the defense budget is spent on defense imports. See Hoagland, Jim, "U.S. Firms Imprint on South Africa Deep," in *The Washington Post,* January 16, 1977

10. This figure is given by U.S. Senate sources.

11. There are, of course, other weapons in the inventory which have been left out of account here, notably artillery, anti-aircraft guns, missiles, non-combat military aircraft, etc.

12. In many cases it is possible to arrive at much larger totals for individual items simply by collating all the available industry sources.

13. The reference is to the 1976-77 edition.

14. It is not clear whether the Carter Administration has allowed further deliveries of U.S.-licensed items produced in Italy and Portugal. Deliveries were apparently continuing at the end of 1976, however.

15. Ahmad, *op.cit.*, p. 5

16. The SAAF has 300 MB-326M strike/trainer and 100 MB 326M strike jets. It has been assumed that only 200 of the MB-325M dual-role jets can be used for combat. In theory, they could all be used for that purpose.

17. Confidential industry sources indicate that 35 more Alouette III and Puma helicopters have been transferred to South Africa in 1977.

18. This is an estimate based upon data from South African sources.

19. See Kaplan, I.,*et.al., Area Handbook for the Republic of South Africa* (Washington, D.C.: U.S. Government Printing Office, 1971), p. 731. The figure is bound to be considerably larger today, but 200,000 is used in the text as a reasonable estimate.

Chapter 8

Evading the Embargo: How the U.S. Arms South Africa and Rhodesia

Michael T. Klare and Eric Prokosch

United States interests have taken advantage of loopholes in the 1963 and 1977 embargoes to continue the profitable business of shipping arms to the white-minority regimes in southern Africa. In-depth analysis of one case—the provision of aircraft—illustrates the channels used.

Although the United States agreed to honor both the 1963 U.N. embargo on arms deliveries to South Africa and the 1966 U.N. arms embargo on Rhodesia, vast quantities of United States arms have been shipped to the two countries through a variety of clandestine and semi-legal channels.

Strict enforcement of the U.N. embargoes is critical for two reasons: first, to demonstrate the unity of the world community in opposing white-minority rule in southern Africa; and second, to prevent the delivery of those weapons and systems needed by the minority governments to preserve their dominance in the face of growing domestic opposition. Indeed, while these regimes may require a wide variety of externally supplied resources to persevere—including technology, capital investment and loans—their racial policies ultimately rest on the possession of overpowering military and police capabilities. The sincerity of Washington's commitment to the anti-apartheid effort can thus be measured by its performance in enforcing the arms embargo.

Given the fact that the Carter Administration has now subscribed to a new, more rigorous embargo on South Africa,[1] it is particularly important to examine the loopholes that have been used to evade the 1963 and 1966 measures. Unless Washington acts forcefully to close existing breaches in the original U.N. decrees, it will not be able to halt the flow of arms to the minority regimes and our country will become ever more implicated in the preservation by violent means of the racist *status quo*.

Our research on the arms traffic indicates that a variety of channels—legal and illegal, direct and indirect, overt and covert—are used by United States and foreign corporations to evade the 1963 and 1966 U.N. sanctions. In this paper we attempt to describe the various channels and the arms that have been shipped through them. For convenience, and because of the greater availability of information, we will concentrate on transfers to the South African Air Force (SAAF), but most of the channels we describe are also used to supply the South African Army and Navy. Some of these routes are further used to arm Rhodesian military units. To illustrate the use of these channels, we will identify some of the U.S. arms that have been transferred to South Africa and Rhodesia over the past few years. Research by other analysts suggests that additional U.S. arms have been furnished through the same routes.[2] We will confine ourselves to cases which have been confirmed by internationally recognized sources.

Each year, the International Institute for Strategic Studies (IISS) in London publishes a survey of world military forces, *The Military Balance*. Of the 362 combat aircraft (excluding trainers) listed as being in the SAAF's active inventory in the 1977-'78 edition, at least 161—more than 40 percent—are partly or fully of United States origin. Some of these, such as the C-130 Hercules transports, were delivered prior to the 1963 embargo; most, however, have been delivered over the past 15 years.

Aircraft of United States origin delivered to the SAAF *after* the embargo was imposed include 16 L-100 transport, seven

Swearingen Merlin-IV medium transports, and at least 22 Cessna Model-185 Skywagons. U.S.-designed and U.S.-powered aircraft delivered during this period include 19 Piaggio P-166S patrol planes, 40 AM-3C Bosbook utility craft, and 20 C-4M Kudu liaison planes. These planes may not be the most advanced aircraft in the SAAF's inventory, but they play a key role in the kind of scattered, sporadic fighting in which South African forces have been engaged. United States planes were used, for instance, to airlift supplies to South African forces fighting in Angola in 1975, and to ferry troops from one embattled city after another following the 1976 black uprising in Soweto.

Still other United States aircraft which are not listed in *The Military Balance* are flown by an all-white, voluntary militia known as the "Air Commandos." These forces, trained by SAAF instructors at government expense, are called up periodically to help patrol border regions and to augment regular counter-insurgency forces in Namibia (South-West Africa).

The existence of these United States aircraft in South African hands cannot be denied. The real question is: how did they get there in the face of an embargo which Washington is pledged to support? Following is a description of the principal loopholes used by United States firms and government agencies to evade the 1963 sanctions.

Loophole No. 1: "Civilian" Aircraft Sales to the South African Air Force

In some cases, U.S. planes have been delivered from the United States directly to the SAAF with the blessing of our government. Such, at least, was the case with the Lockheed L-100s and Swearingen Merlin-IVs, delivered under the Nixon Administration, and the Cessna 185s, delivered in the mid-1960s. These aircraft were declared "civilian" products by the State Department, and thus exempt from the 1963 embargo—even though United States officials knew they would be used by the SAAF to support military operations.

The January 7, 1964 White House memorandum governing United States participation in the 1963 U.N. embargo outlawed the transfer of conventional *weapons*, but gave the State

Department wide latitude in determining whether auxiliary items, such as transport and communications equipment, were to be included in the ban.*[3] By stretching this discretionary power to its limits, the Secretary of State permitted sales of major combat-support equipment to South African military forces.

Under the Nixon Administration, this practice became official policy. In a secret 1969 National Security Council memorandum, known in government circles as the "Tar Baby"** document, President Nixon agreed to provide substantial quantities of support equipment to the South African military. According to the published version of this document, the administration decided to "enforce the arms embargo against South Africa," but to accord "liberal treatment of equipment which could serve either military or civilian purposes."[4] The L-100s and Merlins fit into this category.

The Lockheed L-100 "Commercial Hercules" is an almost exact replica of the Lockheed C-130 Hercules cargo plane flown by the U.S. Air Force and many other military agencies around the world. Both the L-100 and the C-130 can carry some 43,000 pounds of cargo or 92 combat troops over distances up to 2500 miles. The military version has slightly superior range and payload characteristics, additional electronics and a paratroop door, but otherwise there is little to distinguish it from the civilian version.[5] Aircraft of this type were reportedly used to carry supplies to the South African units fighting in Angola during the 1975 war, and they may well have been used during the 1978 attack on Angola.

The Swearingen Merlin-IV is an all-weather, pressurized, executive-type transport plane. It is powered by two AiResearch turboprop engines and can carry 15 to 20 paratroopers or 5000 pounds of cargo over distances of several hundred miles. Although the Merlin is not configured specifically for military use, it is included in the airforce inventories of several countries, including Oman, Argentina and Chile. According to the July

* See Chapter 11, pp. 222-3, 226, and 231.
** For the story of how this sale was managed to avoid Congressional action, see Chapter 3, p. 41.

1976 issue of *Milavnews*, a private intelligence newsletter published in England, the SAAF received seven Merlins in 1975-'76, and assigned them to the 21st Transport Squadron based at Zwartkop. Reportedly these planes have also been used to support military operations in Namibia and southern Angola.

Like the Lockheed L-100/C-130, the Cessna Model-185 Skywagon is produced in both civilian and military versions. The military version, designated U-17 by the U.S. Air Force, is used for a variety of support functions, including liaison, reconnaissance and light transport duties. Both versions are powered by a single 300-h.p. piston engine, and can carry up to six passengers for distances of over 1000 miles. Although the SAAF's Skywagons cannot be considered major combat systems, they do play an important role in guarding the South African border against liberation fighters. According to the South African military magazine *Paratus*, Cessna 185s "keep the 1000-mile border under constant surveillance." The planes were being used for road surveillance, medical evacuation, light transport and radio relay posts, and were used for low-level visual reconnaissance with a pilot and observer because of their "maneuverability and low fuel consumption." The magazine also noted that "Cessnas can be used to control ground fire on to specific targets and to report subsequent enemy movement."[6]

Other significant support equipment, including computers, communications systems, navigational devices and military vehicles, have also been supplied to South African military forces via Loophole No. 1. Like the transport planes described above, these items were deemed "civilian" systems and thus exempted from the embargo even though they were intended for military use.

Loophole No. 2: U.S.-Powered Aircraft

The 1963 embargo applies both to complete aircraft and to major components and subsystems such as engines. Many of the aircraft in the South African Air Force inventory, however, are powered by U.S. produced or designed piston engines, including the Piaggio P-166, the AerMacchi AM-3C and the Atlas C-4M. These aircraft were assembled outside the United States. The engines used to power them were deemed non-embargoed products under a 1968 State Department memorandum allowing sales of United States components to "third countries" for use in combat support equipment of the type covered in Loophole No. 1.[7]

The role of U.S. engines is particularly critical because, despite reports that South Africa has its own aircraft industry, the fact is that the country still cannot produce aeronautical engines. Following are descriptions of the aircraft and engines involved under Loophole No. 2.

The P-166 is a light transport plane produced by Piaggio of Italy and powered by two Avco-Lycoming IGSO-540-AIC piston engines produced in Williamsport, Pennsylvania.[8] The basic P-166 carries up to 12 passengers or 2500 pounds of cargo, and can be armed with a variety of bombs, rockets and other munitions. The SAAF has also acquired a specially equipped version, the P-166S Albatross, which is used for coastal surveillance missions.

Piaggio also produces the U.S.-designed Lycoming engines used to power the AM-3C and the C-4M under license. The AM-3C, known in South Africa as the Bosbok, is a three-seat utility plane manufactured in Italy by Aeronautica Macchi SpA (Aer-Macchi), an affiliate of Lockheed Aircraft. According to *Jane's All the World's Aircraft*, the AM-3C is used for observation, liaison and training missions. It is powered by a single Lycoming GSO-480 piston engine, and can be fitted to carry small bombs, rockets, and napalm.

The C-4M Kudu is a light short takeoff and landing (STOL) transport used to support ground operations. Like the AM-3C, it is powered by a Lycoming GSO-480 piston engine produced under license in Italy by Piaggio. The Kudu is produced in South Africa by Atlas Aircraft, a company set up by the Pretoria regime to promote self-sufficiency in arms production, and thus to lessen the impact of the arms embargo.

Although Prime Minister J.B. Vorster has boasted frequently of South Africa's domestic arms-making capabilities, Pretoria is still dependent on foreign suppliers for key components, raw materials, and design technologies. The Kudu is a case in point:

not only is it powered by a U.S.-designed engine imported from Italy, but it is itself modeled after a United States aircraft, the Lockheed L-60, which is discussed further below.

Loophole No. 3: Overseas Production of U.S.-Designed Aircraft

We have already seen, in the cases of the AM-3C and C-4M, that US.-designed engines, produced in Europe, are used to power aircraft destined for South Africa. In still other cases, European producers have sold the SAAF aircraft of wholly U.S. design. To be permissible under United States law, such sales would have to be of unarmed support planes of the sort described under Loophole No. 1. An aircraft in this category whose delivery to the SAAF can be documented is the AerMacchi-Lockheed AL-60 Conestoga transport, the Italian version of the Lockheed L-60.

The AL-60 is a single-engine STOL transport produced in Italy by Aermacchi under license from Lockheed, which also owns a considerable block of AerMacchi stock. Powered by a single Lycoming 10-720-A1A piston engine, it is designed for operation out of unimproved airstrips in rugged areas. Approximately 20 AL-60s were sold to the SAAF in the 1960s and later transferred to the Rhodesian Air Force, where they are known as the Trojan.[9] Reportedly, these aircraft are used by the Rhodesian Air Force to support outlying anti-guerrilla forces.

Loophole No. 4: Aircraft Sales to Civilians[10]

The 1964 Executive Order governing United States compliance with the 1963 U.N. embargo did not cover sales of "civilian" planes to civil buyers in South Africa. Over the years, United States producers have enjoyed a booming trade in light business-type" planes and helicopters with South African civilians and airplane dealers. South Africa is reported to be the world's tenth largest market for such aircraft, and United States firms normally sell some 150 light planes per year to South African buyers.[11]

These aircraft, many of which also exist in military versions, are nominally owned by private citizens and firms, but can be seized for military use under the emergency decree adopted by the Pretoria regime on November 10, 1977, in response to the new U.N. embargo of November 4, 1977. Such aircraft can also be used for military purposes by the Air Commandos, an all-white citizens' militia which can be called on to fly its own planes in support of regular army units.

The Air Commandos participate in annual two-week training sessions subsidized by the government and supervised by SAAF instructors. These units—currently numbering 13 squadrons, according to *The Military Balance*—can also be called up in emergencies to augment regular government forces.

Jennifer Davis, research director of the Africa Fund, testified before the Subcommittee on Africa of the Senate Foreign Relations Committee in 1975 that the Air Commandos' training,

> entails radio cooperation with army and mobile police striking forces, reconnaissance, practice bombing, and general cooperation in maintaining the internal security of both South Africa and South-West Africa...
>
> Many of these Commando members fly U.S. light planes, such as Pipers and Cessnas. Thus, even if the licensing procedures were adhered to technically in the sense that no planes were sold to the military, such planes would become available to the military, and, most important of all, form part of the "security planning" of the government.[12]

Although it is impossible to determine from publicly available sources which U.S. aircraft have been assigned to the Air Commando squadrons, data recently released by the United States Export-Import (Ex-Im) Bank on loans provided for civilian aircraft sales to South Africa indicate many deliveries of planes with dual military/civilian capabilities. In 1973, for instance, the Ex-Im Bank guaranteed loans for sales of several Beechcraft Model-55 and 58 Baron twin-engined business planes to South African buyers. A militarized version of the Baron, the T-42A Cochise, is used by the U.S. Army as a basic instrument trainer. The Baron is also used as a military trainer by the airforces of Spain and Turkey.[13]

In May 1976, the Ex-Im Bank approved a $163,000 discount loan for the sale of two Helio Aircraft Model-295 Super Couriers to a South African firm. The Super Courier is a short takeoff and landing transport which is particularly suited for operation in rugged country. Several military versions exist, one of which is equipped with paratroop doors and "has been operated in Southeast Asia, South America, and in other parts of the world, on a wide variety of military missions," according to *Jane's All the World's Aircraft*. Under its military designation, the U-10, several were assigned to the U.S. Tactical Air Command for "counter-insurgency duties," presumably in Southeast Asia.

Other United States aircraft sold to South African buyers since 1972 with Ex-Im Bank funding include: the Beechcraft A36 Bonanza, a single-engine utility plane used by the airforces of Iran, Mexico and Spain; the Rockwell Turbo-Commando, a twin-engined turboprop which is in the Iranian airforce inventory; Cessna Executive, Golden Eagles, Conquests and Citations; Piper Super-Cubs; and the Mitsubishi MU-2 twin-turboprop STOL transport, produced in San Angelo, Texas, by Mitsubishi Aircraft International.[14]

Although these are nominally commercial transactions, involving U.S. firms and private buyers in South Africa, the United States government is directly involved, both through the Commerce Department which must grant permission for all such "civilian" exports to South Africa, and through the Ex-Im Bank, which assumes the risk, at United States taxpayers' expense, for loans provided by local banks for these sales. The State Department is also involved by default, since it is responsible for monitoring the 1963 U.N. embargo and for ensuring that military equipment is not misrouted to South Africa.

On December 14, 1977—only five weeks after adoption of the new U.N. embargo—the State Department announced that it was recommending approval of an aircraft sale to South Africa that reportedly involved six Cessna planes valued at about $500,000. As in the case of earlier sales, the decision was defended on the ground that the aircraft involved were nonmilitary products destined for civilian users. Announcing the recommendations, State Department spokesperson John Trattner said, "it would be incorrect to infer that a decision has been made to discourage the export of civilian aircraft to South Africa."

Press reports of the December 14 announcement indicated that Cessna was planning to sell another 44 planes, valued at $3 million, to South Africa.[15] Reportedly, many of the planes involved are Cessna Model-172s, used for military training by the airforces of Ecuador, Honduras and Peru.

Illegal/Clandestine Arms Deliveries

In addition to the aircraft and support equipment sold to South Africa through the loopholes described above, large quantities of arms have been shipped to both South African and Rhodesian military authorities through illegal and clandestine routes. In most cases, such transactions have involved the delivery of United States weapons to "third countries" which are not covered by any embargo, and then their transshipment to individuals, firms or agencies inside South Africa. Such was the situation in the case of the Olin Corporation, which was convicted in March 1978 of selling 3200 firearms produced by its Winchester division to South Africa via transshipment points in Mozambique, Austria, Greece and the Canary Islands.[16] This was the first time a United States corporation was indicted for violating the embargo on South Africa, although in 1976 an employee of Colt industries, Walter S. Plowman, was sentenced to a year in prison for selling handguns to South Africa via several third countries.*[17]

Arms of U.S. design are also sold to South Africa and Rhodesia by subsidiaries and partners of United States corporations in Europe. We have already discussed the production and sale of U.S.-designed aircraft engines and cargo planes by European firms, but here we are dealing with the sale of aircraft or other systems that have been designed for specific combat functions. Since United States firms provided the technology and in some cases key components for these arms, their delivery to South Africa and Rhodesia represents a serious erosion of United States adherence to the 1963 and 1966 embargoes.

Several researchers have reported the sale of U.S.-designed combat planes and armored vehicles to South Africa by Euro-

---

* For a fuller discussion of this case, see pp. 238-9.

pean firms. Such arms reportedly include: the Lockheed F-104G Starfighter, produced by a consortium of firms in West Germany; Bell Model 205A troop-carrying helicopters, produced by Agusta of Italy; and FMC Corp. M113 armored personnel carriers, produced by Oto Melara of Italy.[18]

In one significant case, there are strong indications that U.S.-designed combat planes have been sold to the Rhodesian Air Force by a United States affiliate in France. The British newsletter *Milavnews* reported in June 1977 that Rhodesia had received 20 militarized versions of the Cessna 337 aircraft from Reims Aviation, a Cessna affiliate in France. According to *Milavnews*, the 337s "arrived in Rhodesia by circuitous routes in mid-1976 when they were ostensibly ordered by a 'Spanish fishing company' in the Canary Islands."[19] These presumably are the 18 337s listed as being in Rhodesian Air Force hands in the 1977-'78 edition of *The Military Balance*. (No such aircraft were listed in the 1976-'77 or earlier editions.)

The Cessna 337 is a light, twin-engined aircraft with a dual fusilage. It was at one time produced in a military version, the 0-2, and saw wide service in Vietnam as a forward air-control, target-spotter plane. A civilian version is produced by Reims Aviation, which is 49 percent owned by Cessna.[20] The 337s shipped to Rhodesia were reportedly fitted with underwing armament racks and special avionic gear, thus converting them, in effect, to 0-2 configuration.

Several of the Rhodesian 337s have been used as spotter planes in raids on neighboring Mozambique, according to Tony Avirgan, an American journalist based in Dar-es-Salaam, Tanzania. One 337 has reportedly been shot down in Mozambique. The use of this aircraft by the Rhodesians is one of the clearest cases of the importation of United States counter-insurgency tactics and equipment, originally developed for Vietnam, into southern Africa.

The Cessna 337 sale to Rhodesia has been denied by Cessna officials, although Pierre Klostermann, president of Reims Aviation, told the London *Sunday Times*,[21]: "If I could have done this deal legally, I would have done it."

In its March 1978 issue, *Milavnews* reported that four more

Reims 337s, nominally destined for Panama, "were believed to have arrived in Rhodesia towards the end of last year." The Department of Commerce and the United Nations Committee on Sanctions are now investigating the alleged sales of 337s to Rhodesia.

There are indications that the Olin and Cessna-Reims cases are only the tip of the iceberg. Although some United States firms involved in clandestine arms sales to South Africa and Rhodesia may be tempted to violate the embargo out of sympathy for the white-minority regimes, it is likely that most do so simply out of a desire for profit. As long as private firms judge it to be in their interest to take advantage of any loopholes or laxity in the enforcement of arms restrictions, the burden of responsibility for assuring compliance with the embargo must fall on the United States government. The relative ease with which Olin was able to circumvent the embargo (its one mistake, apparently, was to ship arms repeatedly through the Canary Islands, which presumably has a relatively limited market for firearms, thus triggering the suspicions of U.S. officials) suggests that government enforcement has, up to now, been rather lax.

If the United States government were truly committed to strict adherence to the United Nations embargo, it would be extremely vigilant in monitoring corporate arms transactions in order to preclude any violations. Conversely, the lack of such vigilance suggests the government is, through inaction, prepared to allow such violations. During court proceedings connected with his prosecution for violating the embargo, Walter S. Plowman alleged that the government had undermined the embargo by "closing its eyes" to corporate misbehavior. According to press accounts of the case, Plowman charged State Department officials "acquiesced" in his South African sales by failing to investigate questionable transactions.[22]

Plugging the Loopholes

In response to widespread protests from members of Congress and opponents to the Pretoria regime in the United States, the Carter Administration agreed to reevaluate government regulations concerning civil aircraft sales to South Africa in light of the

U.N. embargo of November 4, 1977. The new regulations were issued on February 17, 1978, and while they go a long way to curb the abuses noted under Loopholes One through Three above (it will no longer be permissible, for instance, to sell "civilian-type" aircraft like the L-100 to South African military and police units), they do *not* prohibit sales of civilian aircraft to non-governmental buyers in South Africa. Indeed, the General Aircraft Manufacturers' Association announced on March 22, 1978, that the Carter Administration had approved the sale of another 70 to 80 light aircraft, worth over $3.5 million, to buyers in South Africa.[23]

In letters to members of Congress, the State Department has promised to impose new language in all licenses issued for the export of civilian aircraft to South Africa prohibiting their use by military or police units. Critics of the administration's policy charge, however, that such language would not be heeded by the Vorster regime in the event of a crisis, at which time, the emergency decree described above—which allows the government to seize the assets of any private individual or firm—could be put into effect. Accordingly, several Congresspeople, led by Cardiss Collins of Illinois, have introduced a bill (H.R. 10722) prohibiting the sale of aircraft, aircraft engines and helicopters to South Africa.

In the absence of such legislation, it is safe to assume that U.S. aircraft sold to South Africa will be used for military purposes in the event of intensified struggle against the Vorster regime. The same is true, of course, of United States vehicles, computers and other military-related products sold to corporations in South Africa.

Unless the links between United States firms and their overseas subsidiaries and partners are closely monitored by United States officials to prevent violations of the U.N. arms embargo of the types described above, it is obvious that such supply routes will remain in operation. It is up to us, therefore, to generate public support for the Collins bill and to pressure the Carter Administration to take effective action to enforce the November 4, 1977 U.N. arms embargo against South Africa, and the 1966 embargo against Rhodesia. If it fails to enforce the embargoes, the United

States government will be providing *de facto* support to South African and Rhodesian efforts to strengthen their military capabilities.

References

1. U.N. Security Council Resolution No. 418 of November 4, 1977, which requires all member states to halt all transfers to South Africa of "weapons and ammunition, military vehicles and equipment, paramilitary police equipment, and spare parts for the aforementioned..."
2. See Gervasi, Sean, "Breakdown of the Arms Embargo Against South Africa—Testimony before the Subcommittee on Africa, House of Representatives, Washington, D.C., July 14, 1977," reprinted in *Issue*, Winter 1977.
3. The authors are indebted to Sylvester, R.T., "U.S. Arms Embargo Against South Africa: Is It to be Effective," manuscript, April 12, 1978
4. Study in Response to National Security Study Memorandum 39, Southern Africa, August 15, 1969, cited in El-Khawas, M.A. and Cohen, Barry, *The Kissinger Study of Southern Africa* (Westport, Conn.: Lawrence Hill, 1976), p. 107
5. All data on aircraft performance and characteristics are taken from *Jane's All the World's Aircraft, 1976-'77* (London) and earlier editions.
6. *Paratus* (Pretoria), "Aircraft on the Border," May 1974, pp. 31-32
7. Sylvester, *op.cit.*
8. All data on aircraft engines is from *Jane's All the World's Aircraft.*
9. *Jane's All the World's Aircraft*, 1973-'74 ed., p. 122; *SIPRI Arms Trade Registers* (Stockholm: 1975), p. 84
10. Our thanks to the Washington Office on Africa and the American Committee on Africa for assistance with this section of our paper.
11. *The Washington Post,* March 23, 1978
12. Testimony of Jennifer Davis, as reprinted in, "The U.S. Role in South Africa's Military Build-Up," (New York: The Africa Fund, n.d.)
13. All data on military configurations is from *Jane's All the World's Aircraft.*
14. Information on Export-Import Bank loans to May 1976 as reprinted in U.S. House of Representatives, Committee on International Relations, Subcommittee on International Resources, Food and Energy, hearings on "Resource Development in South Africa and U.S. Policy," 1976, pp. 270-288. Information on subsequent loans as released by the Export-Import Bank to the Washington Office on Africa and to the authors.
15. UPI, "Sale of Planes to South Africa Backed," in *The Washington Post*, December 15, 1977
16. *The New York Times,* March 31, 1978
17. *New Haven Advocate*, October 2, 1976
18. Gervasi, *op.cit.*

19. Earlier, Michael T. Kaufman had reported in *The New York Times* (October 3, 1976) that some "ten new Cessna light reconnaissance and transport planes" produced in Reims, France, under license, had arrived in Rhodesia "through the sanctions net."

20. According to *Jane's All the World's Aircraft,* the "primary structures" of the Reims 337 planes are produced in the United States and then shipped to France for assembly; only some smaller components and equipment are French produced.

21. December 11, 1977

22. *New Haven Advocate*, October 20, 1976; *Wall Street Journal*, October 21, 1975, and January 11, 1977

23. *The Washington Post,* March 23, 1978

Chapter 9

U.S. Policy and Nuclear Proliferation in South Africa

Ronald W. Walters

United States private and governmental interests have played a critical role in transferring nuclear technology to South Africa. The white-minority regime has used this technology to strengthen its ties to other regional sub-centers and to bargain with Western powers for support. Still more dangerous is the possibility that it will employ nuclear weapons in a last desperate effort against the liberation movements and independent African states.

On August 8, 1977, the Soviet news agency Tass began a major story:

> According to information reaching here, work is presently nearing completion in the South African Republic for the creation of nuclear weapons, and preparations are being held for carrying out its tests.[1]

This was the beginning of a major news statement contained in a communique which was delivered to the White House on August 6. Both the news story and the communique from Brezhnev to Carter contained the Soviet view of the urgency of the incident and an offer of cooperation to assist in blocking a probable nuclear test by the South Africans. The Soviets had also notified Britain, France and West Germany simultaneously, requesting their assistance in the matter.[2] The American SR-71 reconnaissance satellite photographs confirmed the Soviet spy satellite's photographic evidence of existence of a small cluster of huts and an instrumentation tower in the Kalahari Desert near Namibia on August 11. At the same time, the South African press suggested that such news was "believed to be the prelude to a world-wide communist-led campaign to stop France selling two nuclear power plants to Pretoria."[3] Nevertheless, the American information was communicated to the British, French and West German governments, and by August 10, all four allied powers had made an official inquiry to South Africa seeking its intentions.

In the midst of this diplomatic crisis, statements from American experts revealed an unusual consensus on the probable possession of a nuclear device by the South Africans. For example, one officials said, "I'd say we were 99 percent certain" that the photographs indicated preparations for an atomic test, and another said, "people were pretty confident that this was what it might be."[4] Murray Marder and Don Oberdorfer concluded their detailed analysis at the time:

> The hoax theory is heavily discounted inside the Carter Administration, which believes that the Kalahari preparations were real. In view of the nuclear sophistication of South Africa, the Carter Administration concluded that what was being built could be used. All U.S. planning proceeded on that premise.[5]

In response to the inquiries, South African Foreign Minister R.F. Botha claimed the "rumors were wholly and totally unfounded," intimating that the Soviets were setting the stage for an attack on South African apartheid at the United Nations conference on apartheid which was to open in Lagos, Nigeria, on August 22. It might also be suggested that the Soviets possessed a powerful issue with which to challenge the entire Western leadership.

The Tass story concerning South African nuclear weapons was carried in an editorial on August 9, and again on August 14. In each instance, reference was made to the French assistance to South Africa that would enable them to manufacture 100 weapons per year in the near future. These attacks caught French Foreign Minister Louis de Guiringaud in Zambia. From there he instructed the French Embassy to issue a formal protest to the Soviets, saying that "the Tass dispatch was nothing but a lie...the Soviet authorities know very well it is a lie."[6] Apparently his embarassment led him into error, for he also declared, "No nuclear weapons can be made out of this plant." Certainly the $1-billion contract with the French firm Framatome,* providing the availability of the two 925-megawatt reactors scheduled to be operational by 1982- 84, is a critical factor in the plans of the South Africans to produce enriched uranium for export. It is well known that nuclear explosives can be made from either highly enriched uranium or plutonium, a by-product of uranium enrichment.[7] In any case, this emotional public response detracted considerably from the French pledge not to sell arms to South Africa, as did the demonstrations against de Guiringaud's presence in Tanzania because of the French role as a major arms supplier to South Africa.

The West Germans were also vulnerable, since the uranium enrichment process utilized by the South Africans had been developed with the assistance of the West German scientist, Dr. Erwin Becker, and the West German firm STEAG. The African National Congress (ANC) of South Africa had previously released documents, taken from the South African embassy in Bonn, which detailed visits by Becker to South Africa, and also revealed meetings between high defense officials from the West German government and South African government officials responsible for the nuclear program. In the week of August 14, 1977, the ANC released simultaneously in London and Bonn a new 92-page set of documents providing additional evidence of a military link between the two countries.[8]

The British have likewise been implicated in the supply of nuclear technology to South Africa and have long-term contracts for the purchase of uranium from the Rossing mines in Namibia. The fate of the South African nuclear industry therefore depends directly upon the way it decides to utilize (illegally) Namibian

---

* The United States firm, Westinghouse, owns 15 percent of Framatome, and provides it with key technological inputs. See Chapter Ten.

uranium production. The proportion it chooses to process and sell as enriched will undoubtedly affect the negotiated price of the British contract for yellow-cake in the future.

Finally, the United States has been instrumental in the build-up of South African nuclear capacity over the years, a matter which will be discussed in some detail below. Suffice it to say that, although some journalists have described this act of cooperation as an example of "detente," the underlying facts of Western complicity in the South African nuclear program sharply call into view a double-edged motive for the Soviets to utilize their discovery as they did. On the one hand, there is the possibility of detente, and on the other, there is the obvious embarrassment which the mandatory response by the Western countries caused them because of their own relationship with South Africa.

To return to the main scenario, by August 15 Carter had made a full reply to the Soviet Union. Each of the Western states had indicated to the South African government their severe displeasure at the recent discovery of the test site. They threatened reprobation if the South African government continued with preparations for the test, which presumably could be monitored by assessing further construction and other preparations for testing. South Africa still continued to deny any intention to test a nuclear weapon. As Foreign Minister Botha said,

> In my statement issued denying the allegations—which I made to the American Ambassador, the West German Ambassador and the French Ambassador—there was no ambiguity. It was a categorical denial.[9]

In direct response to the French foreign minister's repeated warning, Botha said the French statements were inaccurate as to South African intentions, and that,

> I am not alone in believing it. Even the French Ambassador doesn't believe it. How could it have been interpreted in this way after the categorical denial?[10]

This strong denial, apparently, led President Carter to announce at his regular press conference on August 23 that,

> In response to our own direct inquiry and that of other nations, South Africa has informed us that they do not intend to develop nuclear explosive devices for any purpose, either peaceful or as a weapon, that the Kalahari test site which has been in question

is not designed for use to test nuclear explosives and that no nuclear explosive tests will be taken in South Africa now or in the future.[11]

President Carter indicated that there would be continued "monitoring" of this situation. It is logical to ask why such monitoring had not occured previously. That is to say, was this an "oversight" of U.S. intelligence institutions, or evidence of covert cooperation with the South African government? The latter suggestion arises naturally from the fact that the United States has for some time maintained, in close cooperation with the South African government, satellite tracking facilities, such as Project Syncom, and other facilities, such as the Minitrack Radio tracking station at Esselen Park and the Baker-nun optical tracking station at Olifantsfontein, all in South Africa. Could it be that in exchange for the operation of these facilities there was an agreement that South Africa would not come under the scrutiny of high-flying photographic surveillance?[12]

Further, the statements by the South Africans and the other concerned parties did not indicate either the exact nature of the facility in question, whether it would be dismantled or completed and available for use at a later date, or just what were the intentions of the South African government with respect to it. Of course, the most important point to be considered is that construction of a test facility comes at the *end* of the fabrication sequence (that is, the nuclear explosive device has already been developed at that point), and such a device could therefore be utilized without testing if its intentions were military and the risk substantial enough. The inconclusive outcome of the scenario then, has not ended the threat of South African nuclear weapons development, despite the statements by South African officials such as Dr. A.J. Roux, president of the South African Atomic Energy Board, that their nuclear power program is entirely peaceful and geared to civilian uses.[13]

Some question the development of a South African nuclear program for civilian purposes. The enormous costs to the country, whose international debt is already staggering, will not be recouped by earnings from exports of enriched uranium for a considerable period, even though projections are for annual earnings of $250 million. South Africa has other sources of energy. Although it has no known natural oil, it does have abundant coal, which it now exports. Progress is being made on a new project to convert coal into oil.* Completion of the Koeberg nuclear station, a 2000-megawatt electricity generating plant, will add only 10 percent to the total national energy output. This is still less impressive when one considers the recent addition of Cunene hydroelectric power and that the potential power of the Tugela river alone is about 5000 MW.[14]

Table 10: Schedule of Spending by South Africa on the Koeberg Station, 1976-'84 (millions of dollars)

Year	Amount
1976	74.4
1977	103.2
1978	181.2
1979	254.4
1981	241.2
1982	156.0
1983	93.6
1984	60.0

Source: *Nuclear Engineering International*, Sept. 1977, p. 48

The failure of the South Africans to define the nature of the test site, to cite any peaceful or civilian purpose for which it was intended, and the dubious basis domestically for a civilian program all lend circumstantial credence to the possibility that there is a substantial military rationale for the South African nuclear program.

The Nuclear Laager

Following the world's startling glimpse at the all-but-certain confirmation of the existence of a nuclear explosive device in South Africa in the fall of 1977, other occurrences there further exposed the strategic content of the South African nuclear program. The connection of these events to the frequently described "laager" mentality of the Afrikaner ruling elite is shown in the rallies led by Prime Minister J.B. Vorster, who strongly urged South African institutions to join a "war of survival."[15] Government spokesmen approached the country's scientists, industrialists and commercial and professional leaders

* See Chapters Three and Four.

to convince them that South Africa had "its back to the wall," that "government departments closely linked with strategic industries have been ordered to treat the situation as a real crisis and to prepare for the worst."[16] An article entitled, "South Africa to Tell West, 'Back Us or We Make A-Bomb'," appearing in London, reported that South Africa planned to decide before the end of the year whether or not to make nuclear weapons, according to "highly" placed Western officials.[17]

Although this campaign coincided with the exposure of the test site, it was probably also a response to United Nations reactions to two important events in South Africa. These were the killing of Steve Biko on September 12, and the crackdown on the Black Consciousness Movement on October 18, which included massive jailings of individuals, banning of 18 civil rights groups, and the closing of the major black newspaper. The answer of the United Nations came on November 4, in the form of a mandatory arms embargo. Resolution 418 of the Security Council, operative paragraph four, stated: "Further decided that all states shall refrain from any cooperation with South African in the manufacture and development of nuclear weapons."[18]

Operative paragraph four constituted an attempt to include the manufacture of nuclear weapons in the U.N. arms embargo. This issue had been discussed at the August 22 Lagos conference, which resolved that states should take no action to assist South Africa in the manufacture of nuclear weapons. The Organization of African Unity (OAU) had passed several similar resolutions earlier. Operative paragraph four, however, contained a compromise, because none of the countries which trade in nuclear materials with South Africa admits to outright or direct cooperation with that country in the development of nuclear weapons. South Africa's approach seems to be that described by an expert on the subject of nuclear proliferation:

> It is expected that many countries will in the long run wish to narrow the time and cost of converting at least parts of their civilian programs to weapons production. They will wish to keep their options open so as to be able to initiate steps toward the unconditional acquisition of weapons-grade material without clearly being perceived as having done so. In this manner, we may expect countries gradually to constrict the twilight

period between decision and weapon, a process that we believe will hasten a nuclear weapons decision.[19]

The known facts regarding South Africa indicate that it has passed the twilight zone and has apparently made the decision to acquire nuclear weapons. There is wide consensus as to the level of capability required for a nation to produce nuclear weapons:

> Depending on the details of safeguards arrangements for the international nuclear industry and on whether the nation had independent access to uranium supplies and its own reprocessing or enrichment facilities, the time lag could range from months to years, and the probability of detection from moderate to quite high.[20]

From this description, South Africa would qualify on all counts as a country which would only take months to move to the stage of actual production of weapons. It has an unsafeguarded reactor, its own pilot enrichment facility, a supply of uranium and the capability to engage in the process of chemical reprocessing. Given sufficient accumulation of skilled technology and access to raw materials, South Africa can make its own nuclear weapons. A.J. McIlroy, Johannesburg correspondent for the *Daily Telegraph*, points out that,[21]

> While South Africa has not produced enough nuclear scientists of her own to carry through the enormous program necessary to produce the bomb, it is accepted that there are enough committed immigrant scientists in the country, including Americans and Britons, to make it possible.[21]

Clearly, then, from the standpoint of an effective arms embargo, more emphasis should be placed on limiting South Africa's access to *raw materials and technology* needed to develop nuclear weapons. But there is some indication that South Africa may have advanced to the point where it is impervious to even an accurately targeted sanctions program:

> More important, refusing to sell sensitive technology does not deny access to it. Any government capable of managing a commercial nuclear industry could build its own facilities to produce enough plutonium for a modest weapons program. Most of those for which market dissuasion will not succeed can now or would within a decade be able to build their own pilot scale commercial reprocessing or enrichment plants.[22]

The authors of this statement go on to say that states like Brazil and South Africa "are not particularly susceptible" to leverage exercised by the United States over a nuclear development program due to their control over technology and/or materials. They are fast approaching the end of the twilight zone, where decision and weapons merge, based solely on an independent capability. This stage could be reached in the mid to late 1980s.

This judgment about the South African nuclear program is based on the fact that progress in constructing the reactor system provided by the French appears to be on schedule. The 20-story building which will house the reactor is well advanced. The reactor, known as nuclear island, is located on a rocky bluff near the Atlantic, and is supported by 1800 rubber shock-absorbers to protect it from earth tremors.[23]

But while the reactor system is underway, the South African government has apparently substituted a less expensive model for the 5000-ton commercial enrichment plant. Fanie Botha, Minister of Mines, announced in early 1978 that the small pilot enrichment plant at Valindaba would be converted into a "relatively small" uranium enrichment production facility which would "eventually" have the capacity to meet South Africa's needs.[24] This step almost certainly represented the South African government's failure to attract the necessary international financial cooperation, or even the necessary orders for enriched uranium, when it announced its readiness to enter into contracts in both areas at the meeting of the International Atomic Energy Agency at Salzburg, Austria, in the spring of 1977.

Behind the causes listed above for the failure of the original venture lay political and economic problems. American enriched uranium was to fill the gap between the completion of the reactor system and the completion of the uranium enrichment facility, but the Carter policy of requiring full safeguards on all South African nuclear facilities has held up a recent shipment of highly enriched uranium for nearly three years. Also, the original cost of the plant, estimated at roughly $1.2 billion, has been pushed nearer to $2.3 billion with the doubling of steel and power necessary to produce it.*[25] At the moment, long-term investment

---

*Also, this cost should be seen in the light of the cost of additional facilities for ›

in South Africa is drying up, and it has already borrowed heavily on the international market, which would leave the burden of the cost on local capital sources.[26] The drastic reduction in scale of the enrichment plant will affect its revenue projections and its status in the international nuclear materials market. It will also severely reduce the possible number of nuclear devices produced per year.

Delivery Systems

Another aspect of South African strategic planning which is compatible with the utilization of nuclear weapons is the develoment of missile systems, some of which might be nuclear-capable. Dr. Frank Barnaby of the Stockhold Peace Research Institute (SIPRI) has referred to several systems which could, for example, carry a nuclear payload weighing 1000 kg.[27]

A SIPRI analysis of South African missile development indicates that extremely close relations with West Germany have produced a functional capacity in this area. In 1963, an initial contact was made by Herman Abs, a West German banker, offering cooperation in nuclear research. The outcome was the establishment of a rocket research center and an ionosphere station at Tsumeb in Namibia by the Lindau and Harz group. Then, in the same year, it was announced that "South Africa was engaged in research to develop military rockets of an unspecified nature," and that,

> when the Rocket Research Institute was established one year later, Professor A.J.A Le Roux said that South Africa had been

the nuclear program, such as the uranium hexafloride plant at Pelindaba, which provides the processed fuel for the pilot enrichment plant, and increases in the total spending by the South African Atomic Energy Board of 39 percent between 1975 and 1976 fiscal years.

Profile: South African Atomic Energy Board Expenditures
(Research and Development Only)

Type of Research		Sector	
Basic Research	2.30	Energy	10.58
Applied Research	9.66	Gold and uranium	2.87
Development	6.44	Other	3.68
TOTAL	17.13		

Source: Nuclear Engineering International, September 1977, p. 13

forced by events in Africa to enter the missile field. That same year, the Cactus project began in France.[28]

In 1968, the South African Defense Department, in cooperation with an FRG firm, constructed a missile range at St. Lucia, 100 miles north of Durban and 40 miles from the Mozambique border. On December 17, it began test-firing the first missiles. The system produced in 1969 was the Crotale, adopted from the French Cactus ground-to-air missile and manufactured under French license.[29] In 1973, the propulsion division of the South African National Institute for Defense Research was established to work on the various phases of missile develoment, including warheads.

South Africa has acquired the British bombers Canberra and Buccaneer and the Israeli Jericho missile, all of which are capable of transporting nuclear devices. This decision, it should be noted, might have taken place in 1963 in conjunction with a decision to build nuclear weapons, and the "events" referred to be Roux in that year could have been the formation of the OAU and its Liberation Committee, together with the explicit OAU position opposing apartheid. Similar evidence of farsightedness on the part of the South African government is visible in its early anticipation of oil shortages and emphasis on the development of oil-from-coal technology through SASOL, the state chemicals corporation.[30]

The above information, originally exposed by the ANC of South Africa through its West German sources, also contained references to a companion project, Advocaat, a communications project also developed largely with assistance from FRG scientists in the supply of materials and technology. The $25-million facilities were installed by Siemens AG and AEG-Telefunken. Siemens delivered $3 million worth of equipment in 1970 alone. The project equipment consists of short-wave transmitters, relay stations, telephone and telex stations and computerized data processing capability. Its major locations are the Cape Town central headquarters, with regional headquarters at Port Elizabeth, Durban, and Walvis Bay in Namibia.[31] Its uses are apparently versatile. First, it aids the South African government in its internal security by monitoring the identity and movement of the black population. Second, it has the capability to monitor naval traffic in the South Atlantic and Indian Ocean regions. But it has also been suggested that Advocaat could supply information for down-range clearance in missile guidance, making it an indispensable part of the strategic weapons systems inventory.[32]

The coverage of South African missiles and Advocaat early warning and radar monitoring systems in the southern African area is probably very extensive. The creation of a new West German missile firm, Orbital Transport und Raketen AG (OTRAG), with authority to operate until the year 2000 in a vast area of southeastern Zaire, raises further questions about the role of southern-central Africa in the strategic objectives of South Africa, or West Germany, or NATO, or other combinations of powers. No one has suggested that this $80-million project facility fits in with the African states' planning objectives. It has, however, been noted that the extraordinary privileges and status obtained by OTRAG from the Zairian government give it ominous range:

> The implications for neighboring African states are extensive. The route for rockets could easily encompass the airspace of Zambia and Tanzania. Ultimately, most of Central and Southern Africa could be covered from this location.
>
> For West German or NATO intelligence, OTRAG's privileges could be ideal for carrying out reconnaissance espionage. Finally, being situated in volatile Shaba province, serious international repercussions might arise if there reoccured a large-scale revolt by anti-Mobutu forces.[33]

The above objectives are not incompatible with OTRAG's stated purpose of firing low-cost rockets to put communication and observation satellites into orbit around the Earth.

With respect to South African nuclear technology, the growing ties between South Africa and Israel are quite important. A number of sources indicate Israeli possession of several nuclear weapons. If true, this would put South Africa in a position to benefit from Israeli progress in nuclear weapons fabrication. The International Institute for Strategic Studies lists Israel as a major arms supplier for South Africa, and Israeli scientists assisted South Africa in the development of a sensitive electronic surveillance system along its border. In addition, Israel has supplied South Africa with the Jericho missile system, which is nuclear-capable. In 1978, the two countries established a $25-million line of credit for investments, set contracts for the export of between 500 and 800 tons of South African coal to Israel, sponsored a large delegation of Israeli businessmen to visit South Africa, and worked out an agreement setting landing rights between the two countries.[35]

Finally, there is the question, given this strong and expanding relationship, concerning the Israeli attitude toward compliance with Security Council Resolution 418 requiring adherence to the arms embargo against South Africa. The Israeli delegation to the United Nations announced it would "study" the resolution with a view to compliance, but it is widely suspected that the Israeli government is looking for ways to moderate its compliance. For example, one Israeli official asked the following questions of the resolution:

> ...does such an embargo apply to existing arms commitments? Does it apply to raw materials that go into the making of weapons? Does it involve the sale of electronic equipment and other advanced components which are not "military" but which are used in military equipment? Does it involve "know-how" contracts and consultant services?[36]

These questions, of course, conform to our earlier criticism of Resolution 418, paragraph four, regarding prohibition of nuclear cooperation with South Africa. The lack of clarification on them could continue to provide a substantial basis for cooperation in this field between these two beleaguered, volatile nations.

At this point, it may easily be deduced that the adjunct strategic activities discussed above show continued growth and continue to provide the environment and, therefore, support for our assumption of substantial nuclear-strategic activity as a part of the defensive planning process in South Africa. In response to the possibility of nuclear proliferation in all states party to nuclear materials commerce, the United States has enacted the most demanding piece of legislation among the major powers trading with South Africa. It is, therefore, important to understand how such a policy might or might not affect South African strategic weapons development.

United States Non-Proliferation Policy

The picture which emerges from the available data concerning South African strategic activities strongly suggests that the country is competent in the manufacture of devices requiring nuclear testing. It has initiated extensive activities complementary to a nuclear weapons program, involving the construction of missile systems and the guidance and monitoring technology required to ensure that nuclear weapons function at maximum effectiveness. Given this picture, what effect will the U.S. Nuclear Non-Proliferation Act of 1978 have on United States-South African relations?

The United States has maintained an agreement for nuclear cooperation with South Africa since August 22, 1957, which was amended in 1974. Under the terms of 1978 Non-Proliferation Act, Article IV, Section 404, the president is directed to initiate a program of renegotiation of existing agreements for cooperation in an effort to affect compliance with new trade standards compatible with the requirements of the new legislation—the 1954 Atomic Energy Act, as amended. Chief among the concerns expressed in those sections dealing with nuclear export criteria, the conduct requiring termination of nuclear exports, trade in nuclear components, and peaceful nuclear activities, is a concern with bringing all the nuclear facilities of a trading partners under the safeguards system of the International Atomic Energy Agency. This section of the act has been buttressed with "timely warning" provisions in an effort to strengthen IAEA safeguards procedures. South Africa maintains one reactor, Safari I, under international safeguards through a trilateral agreements between South Africa, the IAEA and the United States. The other reactor, Pelindaba Zero, is not safeguarded under any international system of inspection, nor do safeguards apply to its pilot uranium enrichment plant.

Beyond this, however, it appears that South Africa, by virtue of United States and other nations' verification of the existence of a nuclear test site, may have already violated the act by performing "conduct resulting in Termination of Nuclear Exports." Article II, Section 129, No. 1d, clearly provides:

> No nuclear materials and equipment or sensitive nuclear technology shall be exported to any non-nuclear-weapons state that is found by the President to have, at any time after the effective date of this section (D) engaged in activities involving source or special nuclear material and having direct singificance for the manufacture or acquisition of nuclear explosive devices, and has failed to take steps which, in the President's judgment, represent sufficient progress toward terminating such activities.[37]

Critical questions need to be addressed here. First, does the construction of a test site, usually the last process in the sequence of nuclear weapons testing, constitute enough evidence that a nuclear device exists in the possession of South Africa? If so, would South Africa come under the provision of this section with regard to having "engaged in activities involving source or special nuclear material and having direct significance for the manufacture or acquisition of nuclear explosives devices"? How will the United States know, short of an explosion or some other direct provision of evidence by the South African government, that South Africa does or does not possess nuclear devices? Such facilities cannot be inspected, since not all South African facilities are covered by the international inspection system.

Moreover, the Nuclear Non-Proliferation Act of 1978 says, in Article III, Section 128a, no. 1, that:

> ...no such export shall be made unless IAEA safeguards are maintained with respect to *all* peaceful nuclear activities in, under the jurisdiction of, or carried out under the control of such at the time of the export.[38] [emphasis added]

Since the current United States agreement for cooperation with South Africa only covers safeguards on materials—"equipment and devices transferred to the Government of South Africa"—it is clear that it does not meet all the conditions of the 1978 act.

Finally, Article IV, Section 403a, no. 5 says, "No nation or group of nations will assist, encourage, or induce any non-nuclear-weapons state to manufacture or otherwise acquire any explosive device."[39] This clause is potentially broader than operative paragraph four of U.N. Resolution 418. It suggests a prohibition on assisting a non-nuclear weapons state to manufacture explosives devices. This would appear to cover the neglected area of trade or provision of materials and technical assistance necessary in the construction of nuclear explosive devices. In any case, although the act stipulates that the president will "vigorously seek to obtain the application of such provisions" relative to the materials and equipment in question, no punitive course of action is prescribed by either the President or Congress. All actions initiated appear to be wholly discretionary, with the exception of the right to withhold exports due to violations of the act. In fact, Article IV, Section 405 does provide the government with the authority to continue the old agreement for cooperation in force, even where amendments regarding coverage of all peaceful nuclear facilities by IAEA safeguards may be abbrogated.[40]

The essence of this legislation is that it provides the president with a platform of initiative in the area of non-proliferation, if he wants to exercise it, but contains many loopholes and also blocks congressional action if there is no strong desire to implement high standards of non-proliferation performance by prospective parties to international nuclear commercial arrangements. Such lack of firm leverage in law gives South Africa considerable room for bargaining. This is significant in view of the fact that, as suggested earlier, many incentives for South African adherence to supplier states' tough non-proliferation policies are fading due to its increasing status in the field. Part of that bargaining status is derived from South Africa's current position in the market for non-enriched uranium.

It seems to be the premise of the United States, upon which the above legislation rests, that it must avert the spread of national nuclear facilities and materials capable of easy conversion to nuclear weapons, while *at the same time* guaranteeing reliable sources of materials and fuel to the same countries. These goals appear highly contradictory. Access to fuel and materials has already enabled South Africa to develop its nuclear capability, giving it a nuclear weapons option.

It is more important, however, to note that the two goals are related; for the commercial role of South Africa provides the rationale for its relationship with the United States. Between 1953 and 1971, the United States imported from South Africa

43,250 tons of U^3O^8, or non-enriched uranium, at a value of over $450 million, for its nuclear weapons development program.[41] South Africa has two long-term, fixed contracts with the United States for the supply of low-enriched uranium for the two reactors at South Africa's Koeberg station, at an estimated value of $120 million. Of this, South Africa has paid $4.6 million in advance payments by 1976. It had also paid United States firms a total of $1.6 million for the purchase of other nuclear materials and isotopes between 1971 and 1975. This figure would have been increased by $200 million in sales if public pressure had not forced the disruption of the award of license to export two nuclear reactors by General Electric to the South African government.[42] Although the fixed contract with South Africa is large, some indication of the size relative to U.S. global enrichment services is gained by the knowledge that the South African portion represents only 1.2 percent of United States contracts, which total $10 billion.

While Allis-Chalmers provided a reactor to South Africa in 1961 at a cost of $450 million, other firms have since then provided additional materials which are crucial to South Africa's experimental nuclear activities. For example, special nuclear materials, largely enriched uranium fuel and plutonium, have been provided by U.S. Nuclear, Gulf Oil, United States Steel, Texas Nuclear, and Gulf General Atomic. Source materials such as thorium and depleted uranium have been provided by Kerr-Mcgee, Zirconium of America and Picker International, while by-products are traded by Beckman Instruments and Vernon Craggs. Edlow International was licensed to import materials from the South African reactor for reprocessing under the supervision of the United States Energy Research and Development Administration.[43]

In June 1977, hearings were held by the Subcommittee on Africa of the House International Relations Committee on South Africa's nuclear power development. Despite testimony that South African government agents had been in the United States, apparently illegally, seeking the most advanced enrichment technology (which involves the use of lasers), representatives from the Energy Research and Development Authority expressed no concern about either the intended utilization of the technology or the ramifications of civilian development of nuclear power by South Africa, or the possibility of bringing strong measures to prevent such develoment.

A curious thing has happened, furthermore, since the "nuclear crisis" of August 1977. In none of the activities of United States policy formulation does one sense an added element of urgency. The much heralded policy review in the Carter Administration, of all possible relations with South Africa (and thus, leverage points which could be used to influence the South Africa government) has been scrapped. United States spokesmen have specifically ruled out United States nuclear disengagement from South Africa.

Some low-level moves by the United States do appear aimed at bringing South Africa into compliance with the Nuclear Non-Proliferation Act of 1978, placing all its nuclear facilities under international IAEA safeguards, by pressing it to become a signatory to the Nuclear Non-Proliferation Treaty.

The number of South African personnel visiting the United States for studies and consultations related to nuclear science and technology have reportedly been reduced.[44] It had been alleged in hearings before Congressional committees on Africa by witnesses from the Energy Research and Development Authority that such visits were insubstantial, but they were later discovered to have been very numerous. ESCOM (the South African government-owned electricity utility) and United States consular officials in South Africa have, however, denied any reduction.

Late in 1976, partially as a result of anti-apartheid activities in the United States, which exposed the utilization of computers in South Africa and demanded domestic action against such firms as IBM, the United States revoked the multiple transaction licenses of some U.S. computer manufacturing subsidiaries. ESCOM uses computers in the nuclear industry for personnel radiation systems, drawing record systems, and fuel management systems.[45] Washington only re-issued such licenses when declarations were filed that South African purchasers would not utilize U.S.-exported computers in any phase of uranium enrichment.[46]

Next, although application was made by U.S. Nuclear in 1975 for the export of 26 kg. of highly enriched uranium fuel for the

Koeberg power station and some minor quantities for research, these quantities have been held up. This is seen as added bargaining leverage for the United States in its attempt to renegotiate its agreement for nuclear cooperation with South Africa. An added impediment to the granting of a license for this export is the suit which has been filed (by members of the Congressional Black Caucus, other American activisits, and African nationalist groups*) to intervene in the shipment of this uranium by U.S. Nuclear. In the suit, the Lawyers Committee for Civil Rights Under Law argue for the petitioners that the export would be "inimical to the common defense and security"—a previous standard of determination required of the chairman of the Nuclear Regulatory Commission—on the grounds of an unsafeguarded South African nuclear capability juxtaposed against the background of its apartheid policies and the ensuing political situation. They also argue that there were deficiencies in the procedures by which United States officials arrived at findings leading to the shipments. At the present time, the status of this case is indeterminate, since the Nuclear Non-Proliferation Act of 1978 contains new export criteria, the guidelines for which have not been promulgated by the responsible government officials.[47]

The non-proliferation aspect of the International Nuclear Fuel Authority (INFA), determinedly championed by Senator John Glen, was meant to impact on the incentives of states such as South Africa. It would create a pool of nuclear fuel, thus ensuring "reliable supply" and act as a brake on unilateral production of enrichment facilities. While it may not have much direct impact, due to South Africa's growing capability, it may nevertheless multilateralize the pressures against states contemplating clandestine proliferation in additional ways.

Finally, the United States has been engaged, since the passage of the Nuclear Non-Proliferation Act of 1978 in the process of negotiations with South Africa—"jaw-boning"—to persuade it to sign the Non-Proliferation Treaty, in compliance with the 1978 Act:

---

* The list includes such groups and individuals as the American Committee on Africa, the Episcopal Churchmen for South Africa, Elizabeth S. Landis, Esq., Theo-Ben Guriab, South West People's Organization of Namibia, the Wash-

The U.S. intention apparently is to ask SAG (along with Israel and India—also non-signatories of the non-proliferation treaty) to allow periodic inspections of nuclear plants by the IAEA on condition that there will be no inquiry into the amount of plutonium and weapon-grade uranium the plants have produced in the past.[48]

Assuming this statement reflects the content of the discussions underway with South Africa, the resulting agreement would have little effect on, for example, the amount of enriched uranium which may have already been diverted and/or stockpiled since 1965; or upon the plutonium which may have been accumulated since then; or upon the possible nuclear explosive devices fabricated and almost tested in August 1977. It is not, therefore, difficult to agree with the sentence that follows the statement cited above, which relates to the United States approach to the South African nuclear program: "It is really a very small carrot to extend."[49]

The rationale for the "small carrot" policy may be found in the refusal of the Carter Administration to entertain the possibility of nuclear disengagement. United States policy in this matter was set at the time of the debate over the mandatory arms embargo against South Africa in October 1977. Ambassador Andrew Young specifically asserted that, while he might personally favor a cut-off, it would be impractical in the extreme, since "to cut things off now would only encourage separate development of South Africa's own nuclear potential."[50]

Then the Congressional Black Caucus met with Carter to discuss the situation in southern Africa. One of the items requested of the administration was a nuclear disengagement, or a cut-off of all nuclear trade and technology exchanges with South Africa. The caucus received a reply by Zbigniew Brzezinski, the president's advisor on national security affairs, who essentially reiterated the position earlier taken by Young:

> It is our judgment that a complete break now would put South Africa on a go-it-alone path which would compound the already serious problem of nuclear proliferation.[51]

Again, there was no sense of urgency in the policy he enunciated. The "little carrot" approach is apparently rooted in

ington Office on Africa, and Thami Nhlambiso, U.N. representative of the African National Congress of South Africa.

an administration desire not to contribute to a dramatic break-through on the South Africa issue, but rather to follow a measured, incremental policy where possible. In this, Brzezin-ski's introduction to the letter is instructive. Saying that the problem of South African apartheid will not be easy or quick to solve, he says,

> ...we see this situation as one whose progress will be made only by determined effort over the long haul. This is the intent behind our actions in South Africa.[52]

He suggests that the leverage of the United States is not great, so its policy response must be measured.

There is growing admiration in some circles for the ability of the leaders of the white-minority regimes in southern Africa to play their crises off against the strategy of the West, gaining additional time to follow a main-line policy of survival. These machinations are evident in the case of the nuclear issue. Prime Minister Vorster was the first to take advantage of the August crisis of 1977. His tactic was to repudiate guarantees given President Carter that South Africa would not develop nuclear weapons, when he said,

> I am not aware of any promise that I gave to President Carter. I repeated a statement which I have made very often that, as far as South Africa is concerned, we are only interested in peaceful development of nuclear facilities.[53]

Despite the fact that the president insisted that such a pledge was contained in a letter to him from the prime minister on October 13, the political impact of such a tactic was to create—or recreate—an air of uncertainty about South African intentions. It confirmed the possibility that South Africa would produce such weapons to retaliate against Western or other pressures coming from the international system.

It may be that in heeding South African sensitivities with respect to Western pressures, the focus of activity and hence the actual seat of South African motivations is misplaced. The process of subregionalization has been the major factor respon-sible for the strategic responses of South Africa to its political situation. It has been a traditional feature of South African foreign policy to solidify for itself a role in the concert of Western nations by the threat of regional annihilation, the attraction of its economic status, or by emphasizing its military-strategic and scientific importance. Still, the Western powers are not the forces daily exposing its geographic vulnerability, threatening its control over Namibia and Zimbabwe. It is to the more fundamental security threat embodied in the pressure of internal and external black nationalist movements that South Africa's basic defenses are structured.

The courses of action the Western powers, especially the United States, might take to inhibit the development of nuclear weapons by South Africa are at best questionable. It seemed possible in 1978 that steps might be taken to slow down the process of nuclear development in South Africa *by the concerted action* of the Western powers. But it was very clear that continued trading in nuclear materials and technology would only exacerbate an explosive situation, adding to the South African capability to arm itself with weapons of awesome destructive power, with the possibility that they would actually be utilized in some fashion.[54]

The decision of the European states attending the April 1978 Common Market conference in Copenhagen to tighten safeguards for uranium imported from the United States in response to the 1978 Non-Proliferation Act may provide a useful lever against diversion of nuclear materials to South Africa.[55] Nevertheless, the refusal of the Common Market states to consider the renegotiation of existing contracts for uranium supplies may negate the effect of tighter safeguards by weakening the incentive for South Africa to renegotiate its agreement for cooperation with the United States, continuing instead to utilize nuclear materials received from Europe in unsafeguarded nuclear facilities in military-related projects.

It thus appears that United States policy is to multilateralize the actual pressures on South Africa not to proliferate, while going as far as it can with the Nuclear Non-Proliferation Act of 1978, although not in a manner which would upset commercial options in the trade in nuclear materials. This policy remains contradictory. The prominance of the commercial motive and the ideology of "reliable supply" continues to fuel competition among suppliers for the South African market in enrichment and reprocessing services and materials, and renders an effective anti-proliferation posture ultimately meaningless. The United States loss of leverage in its attempts to singularly affect South Africa's proliferation goals clearly internationalizes the problem, but also absolves the United States from taking those bilateral policy actions which would have the maximum impact upon the ability of South Africa to produce nuclear weapons.

The stakes of such production of nuclear weapons by South Africa are fairly obvious, even to the casual observer, and have been discussed elsewhere.[56] The possession of a nuclear option, however crude, by South Africa, and South Africa's ability to greatly increase that capacity by the mid-1980s, should reduce many calculations of the political and human stakes and the time required for corrective strategies to a near-term proposition. Given the existence of nuclear weapons in the international system for some time and the lack of their utilization, no automatic disaster is suggested. But the politics of subregional-ization, the determination of African nationalists, and the nature of the South African regime combine to make the situation in southern Africa a special case in the problem of nuclear proliferation.

References

1. *News and Views from the USSR,* Press Release, Soviet Embassy Information Department (Washington, D.C.), undated.
2. *The Washington Post*, August 23, 1977
3. *The Cape Times* (Cape Town), August 10, 1977
4. *The Washington Post,* August 23, 1977
5. *Ibid.*
6. *The Star* (Johannesburg), August 17, 1977
7. See Greenwood, T., Reiveson, H.A., and Taylor, Theodore B., *Nuclear Proliferation, Motivations, Capabilities and Strategies for Control* (New York: McGraw Hill, 1977), pp. 81-97
8. *The Star* (Johannesburg), August 17, 1977
9. *The Star* (Johannesburg), August 23, 1977
10. *Ibid.*
11. *The Washington Post*, August 28, 1977
12. See: House of Representatives, Subcommittee on Africa, hearings on "United States-South African Relations," Part I, March 8, 1966, pp. 115-126. Also, Subcommittee on Africa, hearings on "US. Business Involvement in Southern Africa," Part 3, April 6, 1973, pp. 183-208. This testimony revealed that an agency of the South African government (the Council for Scientific and Industrial Research) actually staffs and manages a NASA tracking station at Hartbeeshoek. See p. 192.
13. *The Cape Times* (Cape Town), August 23, 1977
14. *The Star* (Johannesburg), August 22, 1977; see also, *Nuclear Engineering International,* September 1977, p. 48
15. *Daily Telegraph* (London), September 14, 1977
16. *Ibid.*
17. *Daily Telegraph* (London) September 12, 1977
18. See United Nations, S/Res/418, November 4, 1977; reprinted in full in Appendix B.
19. Greenwood, Feiveson and Taylor, *op. cit.*, p. 150
20. Gompert, David C., Mandelbaum, M., Garwin, R.L., and Barton, J.H., *Nuclear Weapons and World Politics* (New York: McGraw Hill, 1977), p. 158. This is a new work in the field which scarcely mentions South Africa at all.
21. *Daily Telegraph* (London) September 12, 1977
22. Greenwood, Feiveson and Taylor, *op. cit.*, p. 93
23. *Nuclear Engineering International,* September 1977, pp. 47-8
24. *The Star* (Johannesburg), February 14, 1978, p. 17
25. *The Economist* (London), February 25, 1978
26. *Ibid.*
27. *Africa* (London), November 1977, p. 68
28. SIPRI, *Southern Africa: The Escalation of a Conflict* (New York: Praeger, 1976), p. 143
29. *Ibid.,* p. 131

30. *Ibid.*, p. 119
31. *Ibid.*, p. 134
32. *New African*, "Does South Africa Have the Bomb?" October 1977, p. 971
33. *Ibid.*
34. *International Herald Tribune* (Paris) February 13, 1978
35. *Facts and Reports*, XIII.5 (March 8, 1978), Items 365-70, p. 1
36. *International Herald Tribune, op. cit.*
37. *Congressional Record* (Washington, D.C.), February 9, 1978, p. H 914
38. *Ibid.*, p. H 914
39. *Ibid.*, p. H 916
40. *Ibid.*, p. H917
41. House of Representatives, Subcommittee on International Resources, hearings on "Resource Development in South Africa and U.S. Policy," May 25 and June 8, 9, 1976, p. 297
42. See Walters, R., "The Nuclear Arming of South Africa," in *Black Scholar* (New York), XIII.1 (September 1975), pp. 25-31; also, "Apartheid and the Atom: The United States and South Africa's Military Potential," in *Africa Today*, July-September 1976, pp. 25-37
43. House Subcommittee on International Resources, hearings on "Resource Development in South Africa," *op. cit.*, p. 31
44. *The Star* (Johannesburg), August 17, 1977
45. *Nuclear Engeineering International*, February 1978, p. 11
46. *Ibid.*, August 1977
47. Brief before the United States Nuclear Regulatory Commission, in the matter of U.S. Nuclear Inc., application for special nuclear material export license (No. XSNM-690), July 2, 1976
48. *Nuclear Engineering International*, August 1977
49. *Ibid.*
50. *The Washington Post*, November 1, 1977
51. *The Star* (Johannesburg), March 10, 1978
52. *Ibid.*
53. *The Washington Post*, October 24, 1977
54. For several scenarios which might conceivably induce South Africa actually to utilize nuclear weapons, see Walters, R., *South African Nuclear Development: Political and Strategic Implications* (Social Science Research Center, June 1977)
56. See Walters, R., Testimony before the Special Committee Against Apartheid, United Nations (New York), January 12, 1978

Chapter 10

U.S. Transnational Corporations' Involvement in South Africa's Military-Industrial Complex

Neva Seidman Makgetla
and Ann Seidman

An important feature of the rapid expansion of United States transnational corporate investment in South Africa has been the increased production of machinery and equipment for use by the military-industrial complex. Production within South Africa enables the white-minority regime to alleviate, to some extent, the effects of the arms embargo. The degree of integration of United States firms into the South African military is shown by the designation of some of the largest companies as "National Key Points," which renders their white personnel subject to participation in the regime's commando forces, and requires the companies to supply the regime's army.

In 1977, the governments of the United States, Britain and France finally acceded to a mandatory United Nations embargo against arms sales to South Africa. But they vetoed efforts by the majority of U.N. members to impose sanctions on trade with and investment in South Africa. They claimed transnational corporate investments and loans contribute to economic "development," which will somehow trickle down to better the lives of the African majority. President Carter still seeks to convince a skeptical public that United States investment provides a lever for change in the apartheid regime.*

These claims are false.

Transnational corporations based in the United States serve to prop up the racist apartheid system in several crucial respects. This article examines just one aspect of that support: direct and indirect transfers to the South African regime's military. This aid, as the examples cited below suggest, cannot be separated from the overall involvement of United States transnational corporations in South Africa. Their very presence in that country contributes to the maintenance and expansion of the South African military-industrial complex.

In the years since World War II, and especially since 1960, transnational corporations have multiplied their investments in South Africa. Direct investment in apartheid by United States corporations has more than doubled since 1969 alone. The largest United States and West German corporations, in particular, have expanded their investments in strategic sectors. Sometimes these firms have cooperated, sometimes competed with the British. But they have always collaborated with South Africa's state-capitalist government. United States transnational corporations have provided the regime with sophisticated technologies with important military applications. In recent years, United States transnational corporate banks have loaned the regime billions of dollars to enable it to surmount the political-economic crisis that has been brought about by the prolonged recession in the capitalist world and the growing militance of the people of South Africa.[1]

United States companies have supplied the white-minority regime with direct military supplies, as well as by providing technologies with both military and civilian uses. Locke and Wulf, in their *Register of Arms Production in Developing Countries*,[2] show that transnational corporations have licensed South African firms to produce military equipment and machinery in several areas, including fighter aircraft, jet trainers,

---

* See page 48 above.

aeroengines, helicopters, missiles, rockets, large fighting ships, tanks, small weapons, ammunition and guns. They also list the companies in South Africa which are known to produce parts and materials for military purposes. Examples of United States companies' role in this kind of direct transfer of military know-how and equipment to South Africa are given in other chapters.*

It is difficult, however, to trace either direct or indirect military transfers by United States corporations with investments in South Africa because the regime and corporations have gone to great lengths to conceal them. Direct transfers often go through other countries. United States affiliates in Israel and Iran, for instance, provide a conduit for military equipment and machinery to South Africa. Both these countries are heavily dependent on imports of military equipment from the United States. Together, they are reported to account for about two thirds of all U.S. arms exports. Military equipment constitutes 42 and 62 percent, respectively, of machinery and transport equipment imported by Israel and Iran.[3] Locke and Wulfe assert,

> The recent intensification of cooperation with Israel, whose arms industry faces severe problems because of overcapacities, seems to be a logical step for two reasons. Both governments are very much isolated within the United Nations. Israel has preferential access to American arms technology and the qualified manpower available to assist South Africa. Subsidiaries in Israel provide for quite a few manufacturers in the USA and elsewhere a good cover for exports and sales vetoed by the government of their origin. South Africa in turn can provide a number of essential raw materials (metals) to the Israeli arms industry.[4]

Even more significant than these transfers of military equipment, however, is the transnational corporate contribution to South Africa's industrialization in general, which has in turn assured the regime of domestic sources of military supplies. As Locke and Wulfe explain,

> It is virtually impossible to distinguish between "civil" and "military" technology...

---

* See Chapter 8 for further discussion of these channels.

It should also be mentioned that in the present situation of white-minority rule, many items, usually considered non-military, are of vital importance to the government. As an example [we might refer to] small aircraft and trucks, all subject to requisitioning in case of emergency in order to support the mobility of South African forces.[5]

Transnational corporations in South Africa have helped build the economic and technological base upon which the South African military-industrial complex is built. They own about one-fourth of all capital invested in South Africa. More important still, they provide 40 percent of all investment in South African manufacturing. As outlined below, the role of United States corporations is particularly significant in those sectors which require the most sophisticated technologies, such as auto, oil, electronics and nuclear power. Transnational banks with which United States banks have close ties control almost two thirds of the assets of the 20 largest South African banks. United States banks have played a leading role in helping finance South Africa's military-industrial expansion.

To understand the full extent of the role of United States trans-national corporations in South Africa, it is necessary to examine the complex interlinkages between the South African government, parastatals (state corporations in which private firms hold shares and participate on boards of directors) and the private sector. These inter-relationships are indicated in Table 1.

The South African military market:

South Africa's military expansion stimulated the growth of transnational corporate investment there in the 1960s and '70s, a fact which reflects the close ties between the companies and the white military. Transnational corporations with investments in South Africa benefited directly, through contracts to provide parts and materials for the military, and indirectly, from the general economic expansion that resulted in a number of sectors. In the 1960s, South Africa's military expenditure multiplied more than six times, growing from $65 million to $405 million a year.[6] By 1977-'78, it had more than tripled again, to $1.9 billion.[7]

Since 1970, the South African army has introduced the most

Table 11:

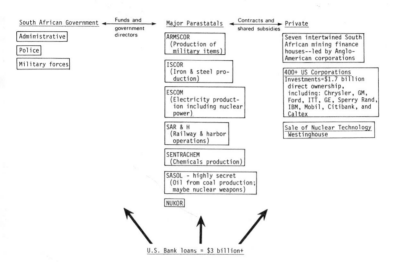

SOUTH AFRICA'S MILITARY-INDUSTRIAL COMPLEX

The Intertwined South African government,
parastatals, and private South African
and transnational corporations

South African Government	Funds and government directors →	Major Parastatals	← Contracts and shared subsidies →	Private
Administrative		ARMSCOR (Production of military items)		Seven intertwined South African mining finance houses--led by Anglo-American corporations
Police		ISCOR (Iron & steel production)		400+ US Corporations Investments=$1.7 billion direct ownership, including: Chrysler, GM, Ford, ITT, GE, Sperry Rand, IBM, Mobil, Citibank, and Caltex
Military forces		ESCOM (Electricity production including nuclear power)		
		SAR & H (Railway & harbor operations)		Sale of Nuclear Technology Westinghouse
		SENTRACHEM (Chemicals production)		
		SASOL - highly secret (Oil from coal production; maybe nuclear weapons)		
		NUKOR		

U.S. Bank loans = $3 billion+

modern equipment available. This was vital for two reasons.
First, the white minority, with its limited numbers, must rely
heavily on advanced military technology to maintain its oppressive rule over the majority. Second, the regime requires a highly
mobile conventional army to police its vast territories, especially
since South Africa now shares long borders with independent
Mozambique and Angola. The share of the defense budget
allocated "for armament procurement and special equipment to
replace obsolete gear" rose steadily, from 12 percent in 1971 to 53
percent in 1973.[8] Between 1970 and 1973, about $280 million was
spent on aircraft, $125 million on ammunition, and $110 million
on radio, radar and other electro-technical equipment. The
regime also took steps to encourage local manufacture of the
parts and equipment needed by its growing military establishment.

The United States publication, *International Defense*, reports that as early as 1971 South Africa could manufacture:

> Explosives and propellants—South Africa is so self-sufficient that she can consider exports.
>
> Ammunition—the position is extremely satisfactory. About 100 different types are being made...
>
> An automatic service rifle...and a submachine gun (unconfirmed reports indicate the Israeli Uzzi) as well as mortars, are already being locally made. A start has been made on a 99 mm cannon.
>
> There are facilities to manufacture almost any armored vehicle.
>
> Aircraft radios, mine detectors and other classified electronic equipment can already be locally designed and made.
>
> More recently it was disclosed that South Africa is building its own 25-pounder guns, manufacturing napalm bombs, and the full range of aerial bombs up to 1000 pounds, and is continuing to develop its own guided missiles (including a Mach 2 air-to-air missile, thought to be IR homing, which was successfully test-fired from a Mirage at a supersonic target in September). The missiles...might be available for export.[9]

South Africa has not, however, achieved complete self-sufficiency in arms production. The *International Defense* report reflects the regime's publicity, and may be exaggerated, as Chapters Seven and Eight suggest. In 1972, the magazine of the Institute for Strategic Studies, *Survival*, reported:

> Although South Africa has made considerable progress towards her goal of becoming more self-sufficient in weapons and equipment, she remains vulnerable to external sanctions, especially in the area of supersonic jet aircraft, heavy armor and warships. So a total, as distinct from partial, embargo of South Africa by the external industrial powers would certainly pose major problems for these programmes, which rely primarily on sophisticated weapons...it can be argued that South Africa's current indigenous production plans provide adequate quantities of small arms and ammunition to overcome a total embargo. All other programmes, even for relatively simple weapon systems such as the locally-produced Italian Impala counter-insurgency aircraft and the French Panhard armoured cars, would probably suffer from a total embargo.[10]

The South African government entered directly into military production in 1969 by creating a parastatal holding company, ARMSCOR. About 70 percent of the government's defense expenditures for armaments went to ARMSCOR's seven wholly-owned subsidiaries and to private industry.[11]

The regime's strict secrecy laws make it impossible to assess the extent to which individual transnational firms have been involved in producing equipment and supplies for the South African military machine, without access to official South African or private company files. Official reports show that private contractors were awarded $52 million worth of contracts for military production in 1971-'72, and double that amount in 1972-'73. Most of these funds were spent on engineering and electronics equipment and machinery, in which transnational corporations have invested heavily.[12]

Domestic military purchases also contributed significantly to the expansion of demand required to stimulate domestic manufacturing industries, benefiting United States and other foreign investors, as well as local firms. In 1973, the Defense Department reported that half its total armaments expenditures were paid to about 200 contractors and subcontractors in South Africa itself. The United States military journal, *Armed Forces Journal International*, observed that South Africa's increasing expenditure on capital goods for the military "has resulted in development and skill locally, and has provided economic growth to the country."[13] United States transnational corporations multiplied their investments in South African manufacturing industries in the late 1960s and early '70s to benefit from this defense-stimulated boom.

In 1977, following imposition of the mandatory arms embargo by the United Nations Security Council, the South African government announced it would not hesitate to take over the plant of any transnational corporation which refused to produce strategic materials upon request.[14] This implied that South African affiliates of any United States company might, at any time, be required to produce military or military-related supplies for the white-minority regime, if so ordered.

Military Implications of United States Investment in South Africa

United States transnational corporations have concentrated their investments in South Africa in the most technologically advanced sectors, producing transport and electronic equipment and other heavy machinery, chemicals and oil (see Table 2). These sectors have important strategic significance. The white-minority regime has tried to use the most modern military equipment to supplement its limited manpower. It has tried to automate skilled civilian jobs as well, aiming to keep blacks out of critical posts while freeing whites for other roles, including military work. Equipment supplied by United States firms, in particular computers and sophisticated transport and electrical goods, have helped the regime achieve these aims. Many of the products of United States subsidiaries and affiliates in South Africa, such as oil, are of direct significance to the military effort of the white-minority regime. The linkages between nominally "civilian" United States companies in South Africa and the military are illustrated by examples below. In recent years, confronted by mounting criticism from international anti-apartheid groups as well as the increased political and economic instability of the South African regime, some major United States companies have sold a majority of the shares in their South African affiliates to local firms. Typically, however, the United States company continues to provide managerial and technological assistance, and to ship in the necessary parts and equipment.

Given the intimate integration of United States companies in South Africa's military-industrial complex, the only way to end United States corporate support for the regime's army and police is to force them to withdraw entirely from South Africa.

Transnational corporations based in the United States have invested heavily in the most technologically advanced sectors in South Africa. They have used that country as a base from which to export throughout the region. In many cases, they have developed raw materials sources in other southern African countries in cooperation with South African state and private interests. Consortia formed by United States and other foreign

Table 12: United States Investment in South Africa and Namibia, by Sector, 1976

Sector	$ millions	Percent of investment in total Africa
Mining and Smelting	(D)	(D)
Petroleum	(D)	(D)
Manufacturing—Total	705	78.2
food products	102	(E)
chemicals and allied products	95	84.3
primary and fabricated metals	48	35.8
machinery	167	97.7
transportation equipment	85(E)	
other manufacturing	210	67.1
Transportation, communication and public utilities	1	1.0
Trade	20466.7	
Finance and insurance	-12	
Other industries	66	30.7
Total, all industries	*1,665*	*37.3*

Notes: (D) concealed by source to avoid revealing individual firms

(E) data relating to Africa outside South Africa and Namibia concealed by source to avoid revealing individual firms

Source: Calculated from U.S. Department of Commerce, *Survey of Current Business*, August, 1977

firms with companies and parastatals from South Africa frequently ship crude materials from the neighboring countries to factories in South Africa for processing.[15] In building up this relationship between South Africa and its neighbors—a relationship which is typically neo-colonialist—the transnationals have strengthened the racist regime vis-a-vis the nations of independent Africa.

Given the intimate integration of United States companies in South Africa's military-industrial complex, the only way to end their economic, strategic and political support for the regime is to force them to withdraw entirely from South Africa. In the short space available here, it is possible to give only a few important examples to illustrate the role of United States corporations in South Africa.

Auto

Transnational corporations from the United States have played a vital role in the South African automobile industry, ensuring the mobility needed by a modern military force. Under South African law, foreign firms must locally produce two thirds of their automobiles' components, by weight. Transnational corporations constitute the core of this industry in South Africa. The United States government's recent ban on exports of motor vehicles to South Africa because of their potential military use is rendered almost meaningless by the extent of production in South Africa itself by the United States affiliates.[16]

The "Big Three" United States auto firms—General Motors (G.M.), Ford and Chrysler—all have major holdings in South Africa. Together, they supply a third of the South African market for motor vehicles, having established extensive productive capacity there. They export throughout the southern African region from their plants in South Africa; but in independent Africa, they have established only assembly and distribution operations.

General Motors, the largest manufacturing company in the world, initiated operations in South Africa after World War I.[17] It now has several plants for assembly and manufacturing in Port Elizabeth, and an engine manufacturing plant just outside that city. It produces several G.M. models, manufacturing locally components such as radiators, engines, batteries, spark plugs, springs and sheet metal parts. G.M.'s "Ranger" model was designed in South Africa and is sold both inside and outside the country. It sells almost all its locomotive output and a substantial share of its truck output to the South African government.[18] As the South African motor vehicle market grew overcrowded in the 1970s, G.M. was reported to be shipping components made in South Africa to its plants in Europe.

The author of the "Sullivan Principles," which have been advanced allegedly to improve the status of black workers in South Africa, is a G.M. board member. But G.M.'s role in strengthening the white minority's oppressive military rule far outweighs the questionable contribution which implementation of those principles might make.[19]

G.M.'s South African Chevrolet dealers boasted in its in-house organ, the *G.M. Bowtie*, of their contribution of R30,000 directly to the South African "Defense Fund" in 1976.[20] But G.M. is even more directly and fundamentally involved in the South African military machine. A secret memorandum sent by hand from G.M.'s South African affiliate to its Detroit headquarters, spells out the critical importance of G.M.'s South African facilities to the white minority regime.[21] First, the memorandum points out that the South African government has designated G.M.'s facilities a "National Key Point" because of its strategic importance for the continued operation of the South African military. G.M. South Africa is subject, therefore, to immediate takeover by the regime in the event of a "national emergency." The white supervisory and management personnel would be drafted into the South African armed forces. The memorandum asserts,

> Industries or services designated as National Key Points...will be accorded protection in emergencies through the medium of the Citizen Force Commando system...[white personnel] are encouraged by the authorities to join a local commando unit.

The memorandum explains the dual role of top G.M. personnel under military control:

> ...the "G.M. Commando" would assume guarding responsibility for the G.M. plants and would fall under the control of the local military authority for the duration of the emergency. It is envisaged...that plant personnel could be engaged in a composite function, i.e. part normal work and part guard duty in such situations.

This double-edged role is required for top G.M. personnel because of the relative scarcity of skilled whites:

> ...compulsory military service is applicable only to White male citizens. The concept of utilizing plant personnel in a dual function is related to the fact that key skills, technical and managerial expertise are concentrated in the same population group from which defence requirements must be drawn.

The memo makes clear G.M.'s decision to stand by the white-minority government during the freedom struggle. G.M. has chosen to believe, despite all evidence to the contrary, that a revolution is doomed to failure.*

*See the more extensive extracts from the memorandum, reprinted in the appendix to this chapter.

The South African facilities of the other major United States auto companies, as well as the many other United States firms' holdings in the technologically advanced sectors of South Africa's military-industrial complex, are also designated National Key Points. They play a similar critical role. Ford's South African operations began in 1923, and are about the same size as those of G.M. Ford owns administrative offices, assembly plants for cars, vans, tractors and trucks, an engine plant, and a parts and service depot.[22] Chrysler's operations in South Africa are about half the size of those of Ford and G.M. Recently, Chrysler sold a majority share to South African interests, although the parent firm continues to provide key technology and parts.[23]

Electrical Equipment and Electronics

The South African electrical equipment and appliance industry also contributes to the self-sufficiency of South Africa's military-industrial economy. Here too, United States transnationals play a critical role. This may be illustrated by the case of International Telephone and Telegraph, General Electric, Sperry Rand and Motorola.

International Telephone and Telegraph (ITT), the ninth largest firm in the United States, has extensive investments in South Africa. An ITT affiliate, Standard Telephone and Cables (STC), is one of South Africa's largest electrical manufacturing concerns, producing a wide range of technologically complex electrical equipment. It supplied communications equipment for the police and Simonstown Naval Base, and recruited engineers to operate the Simonstown equipment. In 1976, 70 percent of its sales were made to the South African government.[24] Although ITT recently sold a majority of its shares in STC to South African partners, it continues to provide advanced technological inputs and managerial assistance when necessary.

South African General Electric (SAGE), a subsidiary of the United States company, General Electric, produces a wide range of basic equipment. These products—industrial controls, capacitators, locomotives, and so on—have important military applications. SAGE is a leading supplier of the government-owned electricity utility, ESCOM,[25] which is responsible for building and maintaining a national electricity grid, including nuclear power plants, to facilitate the use of the most sophisticated technologies in all sectors of the economy. General Electric holds 15 per cent of a large FRG firm, AEG-Telefunken, which has become another of South Africa's major manufacturers of electrical equipment and appliances. AEG-Telefunken is heavily involved in providing components for Project Advocaat, an advanced military communications system that is part of the military build-up on the Cape route.[26]

Sperry Rand has a South African subsidiary which sells R7.5 million worth of aerospace, communications and farm equipment a year.[27] Clearly, much of this equipment can be used for military as well as civilian purposes. The parent company produces a range of flight systems for the United States Air Force, including altitude and heading reference systems, cockpit instruments, gyro systems, computers and ground-based equipment. Sperry Rand reports that research on and production of some of these items have led to their extensive use by civilian airlines.[28] How many of them are produced in its South African plant or sold to the regime, however, is not known.

Motorola assembles and sells a wide range of electronic equipment in South Africa, including basic components such as automobile regulators, alternators and electronic ignition systems; and two-way mobile radios and fixed transmitters. In 1977, approximately 15 percent of its South African sales were to agencies of the South African government. In 1977, its sales to the regime's "security forces" totalled $500,000. It has sold two-way radios, which are important for counter-insurgency operations, to both the military and police. Motorola has agreed to conform to Commerce Department regulations on the 1977 embargo, ending direct sales to the army and police. But it has refused to end all sales in South Africa of equipment which may serve military ends, if it is bought for nominally peaceful purposes by either the regime or private companies.* The significance of such sales is indicated by the fact that Motorola has advertised its sales of electronic components in the South African military journal, *Paratus*. Such components are required

* See Chapter 11 below.

by other companies to produce and service military equipment.[29]

International Business Machines (IBM), the giant electronics firm, and the British company ICLEF dominate the South African computers market. A third of IBM's South African sales are to the government. IBM has supplied the regime's police and Defence Department, and its nuclear power program.[30] Computerization plays a vital role in South Africa, above and beyond its direct military uses, by enabling the white minority to maintain a tight grip on management and supervisory jobs, despite a shortage of white top-level personnel, without upgrading blacks. In this way, every computer IBM sells in South Africa contributes to the regime's strength.

Nuclear Power

The growing involvement of United States transnational corporations in South Africa's manufacturing sector laid the foundation for South Africa's acquisition of the technology needed to transform its extensive uranium deposits into nuclear power and weapons. Many United States transnational firms which were already producing electrical machinery and other equipment in South Africa contributed to the development of this, the most technologically sophisticated sector of the South African military-industrial complex. There is, of course, no such thing as a solely peaceful nuclear technology.[31]

Several countries have expressed concern over an installation in the Kalahari Desert in Namibia, observed by satellite reconnaissance, which resembles a testing facility for nuclear explosives. The government of South Africa has denied that it plans to produce nuclear bombs; but it has refused to sign the Non-Proliferation Treaty, and has also denied that it promised the United States government not to produce nuclear weapons.*[32]

South Africa bought its first nuclear reactor, Safari I, from the United States in the early 1960s, under the "Atoms for Peace" program. It was installed with the aid of the United States corporation, Allis-Chalmers. South African nuclear scientists were trained at the United States Atomic Energy Commission

---

*See Chapter Nine for further discussion of the United States contribution to South Africa's nuclear weapon capability.

laboratory in Oak Ridge, Tennessee.

In 1974, the U.S. Nuclear Corporation, based in Oak Ridge, exported 45 kilogrammes of enriched uranium to a research reactor (Pelindaba) in South Africa, after the Nuclear Regulatory Commission, the United States body which grants licenses for export of nuclear material, obtained South Africa's agreement not to divert the uranium out of the research reactor. The United States also provided enriched uranium to South Africa in 1975 and 1976, and pledged to sell more to the French-United States nuclear power plants which are to be built in South Africa by 1984. In all, the United States has sold or is committed to sell 300 pounds of weapons-grade uranium—from which 15 atomic bombs could be produced—to the South African government.[33]

The Foxboro Corporation sold Pelindaba two computers in 1973. These computers are essential to the plant's operation, and probably could not have been obtained elsewhere. IBM has also supplied computers to the regime's Atomic Energy Board.[34]

The growth of international competition in the reactor market was illustrated by the recent application of three consortia to sell reactors to South Africa for the Koeberg power station. The consortia were made up of, first, General Electric (U.S.), Rijn Schelde Verolme, Vereinigde Bedrijven Bredero, and Ingenieursbureau Comprimo (Netherlands), and Brown Boveri International (Switzerland); second, Kraftwerkunion, a joint venture of the FRG firms, Siemens and AEG-Telefunken; and third, the French companies, Framatome, Spie-Batignolles and Alsthom. Framatome is owned by the French Creusot-Loire group and the United States firm, Westinghouse. Until 1977, Westinghouse owned 45 percent of Framatome. Under French government pressure, this share has been reduced to 15 percent.[35] Framatome continues to operate, however, largely on the basis of long-term licenses from Westinghouse. South Africa eventually awarded the deal to the French consortium, reportedly because France had been an important source of military assistance to the regime.[36] Framatome is to supply the nuclear technology for the power station; much of this technology was originally developed by Westinghouse.

Oil

Oil is yet another strategic sector where transnational corporate involvement has been of primary importance. No modern military machine can survive without access to adequate supplies of oil. South Africa, which must import 90 percent of its oil, has had to rely heavily on the collaboration of transnational oil companies to keep its international pipeline open.

Only about a tenth of South Africa's oil requirements are produced locally by Sasol, the South African government-owned oil-from-coal project built with United States and FRG transnational corporate assistance. Sasol plans to build a second oil-from-coal plant for an estimated $2.2 billion, making it the biggest single project in the country.[37] It has been convincingly argued that the contract price for this plant is grossly overvalued. The reported contract price is two or three times the estimated cost of an oil-from-coal plant of the announced size.[38] The plant, which is being built in strictest secrecy, may well involve, in reality, the further development of nuclear or other military-related technology. (In particular, it may be a nuclear-enrichment plant.) United States, French and West German firms constructing the project have all participated in projects elsewhere which have utilized nuclear technology.

Three United States firms are deeply involved in the Sasol II project. Fluor is the main contractor. Raytheon's wholly-owned subsidiary, the Badger Company, is subcontracted for at least $350 million to manage aspects of construction. Honeywell is to provide much of the necessary electrical equipment.

Sasol cannot, however, replace all South Africa's oil imports. United States firms make several valuable contributions in this area. United States, British and French companies are prospecting for oil in South Africa, as well as refining and marketing oil imports. United States transnationals are leaders in this activity.

By 1973, United States investment in petroleum in South Africa totalled 12 percent of all United States investment in petroleum in Africa, despite the fact that South Africa, unlike several independent African countries, has no known petroleum deposits. Petroleum had already become the second most important area of United States investment in South Africa, next to manufacturing.[39] Since 1973, official United States data conceal the specific amounts United States firms have invested in petroleum to "avoid disclosure of data of individual reporters."

Almost all the largest United States transnational oil firms, encouraged by South African officials, have been involved in exploring for oil in southern Africa. The companies include: Amoco, Mobil, Chevron-Regent, Esso Exploration, Placid Oil, Gulf Oil, Syracuse Oil, and the Superior Oil Company of Houston.

A number of United States corporations have invested heavily in refining and distributing oil throughout southern Africa, basing their operations on their South African refineries. They import crude oil from their wells elsewhere in the world, and refine it in South Africa. From there they market it directly or through affiliates in neighboring countries, including Rhodesia.

There are eight major oil companies in South Africa, of which six are completely foreign owned, and one is largely foreign owned. The eighth is the parastatal, Sasol. Most of the refineries are held by consortia of these companies. Iran supplies most of the crude oil, which is an important tie between the two countries.[40] Iran's government owns 18 percent of the South African state-owned refinery.

Together, Mobil, Exxon and Caltex, which is owned by Standard Oil of California and Texaco, control almost half the South African market for petroleum products. Mobil and Caltex each own a refinery in South Africa.

In 1976, Mobil refined almost 90 percent of all the oil it refined in Africa in South Africa.[41] Mobil produces oil in several independent African countries; but it has invested far more heavily in refining in South Africa, which has no known oil reserves. In 1976, Mobil incorporated its Namibian operations, previously run directly from South Africa, as a separate company. The new corporation's assets were valued at about $6 million.[42] There is also evidence that Mobil has been shipping oil to Rhodesia, in violation of U.N. sanctions which are legally binding on United States companies.[43]

Caltex began to expand its South African refinery in 1975, expecting to increase output from 58,000 to 100,000 barrels daily by 1978. Caltex also owns 23.8 percent of Mobil's lubricating oil refinery in Durban.

The Role of the Transnational Banks

Transnational banks and financial institutions have helped build up South Africa's military capacity in two ways. First, they have helped mobilize domestic and international capital to assist South African and transnational corporations to finance their rapidly growing investments in South Africa's military-industrial complex. Second, especially in the economic crisis of the 1970s, transnational banks have come to the rescue of the South African government by furnishing huge international loans to the government, parastatal and private sectors.

It is more difficult to obtain precise data on the nature and extent of international banks' financial activities than on those of other transnational corporations in southern Africa. The confidentiality of relations between banks and their clients is compounded in this case by the desire to avoid criticism from anti-apartheid groups.[44] In addition, money is a fungible commodity. A loan made to the South African government, a parastatal or a private corporation for a stated purpose releases other funds to be used for another use connected more directly with military expenditures. Transfers of funds between a transnational bank and its South African affiliate cannot be monitored with any precision.

Transnational banks hold about 60 percent of the assets of the 20 largest banks in South Africa. The two largest, Barclays and Standard, are both British. The three top banks in the United States—the Bank of America, Citicorp and Chase Manhattan—also have substantial South African shares.

The United States bank, Citibank, is the fourth largest transnational bank in terms of assets in South Africa, although it ranks only 19th among the 20 largest banks there. Citibank (then the First National City Bank of New York) established its first South African branch in 1958. It now has about five branches, located in major industrial centers. Citibank admits that it holds South African government bonds, in compliance with South African law—in effect, making a loan to the white-minority regime.[45] In 1963, Citibank acquired 16 2/3 shares of the British merchant bank,* M. Samuels.[46] This interest has given Citibank an additional channel for its South African business through the Hill Samuel group's extensive holdings in South Africa and Rhodesia. Citibank also owns 49 percent of the British bank, Grindlays, and Grindlays's chairman sits on Citicorp's board. Grindlays has major holdings in Rhodesia, including one of the four largest commercial banks there.[47]

The Chase Manhattan Bank initially established a branch bank in South Africa in 1959. By 1965 it had three branches there. In that year, it purchased a 15 percent stake in the British bank, Standard, giving it access to Standard's large southern African network. In 1975, however, the United States Federal Trade Commission required Chase to divest itself of its Standard holdings, because Standard had begun to operate in the United States, which rendered the connection a violation of anti-trust laws. Chase re-established its own representative office in South Africa in 1975, continuing to work closely with Standard's South African personnel. Chase now operates essentially as a "wholesale" bank in South Africa; it concentrates on provision of major credits and international linkages for large corporate investors and the regime.**[48]

The Bank of America, the largest bank in the world, has a number of close ties with Kleinwort Benson Lonsdale and its subsidiary, Kleinwort Benson Ltd., both based in London. The Bank of America's London subsidiary, the Bank of America Ltd., shares three directors with Kleinwort Benson Lonsdale and/or Kleinwort Benson. One of these directors is chairman of the New York and London subsidiaries of Kleinwort Benson which deals in gold bullion. Another is director of the consortium bank, Midland and International Banks, Ltd. This consortium includes the Midland Bank and Standard, both of which have

---

* A merchant bank is essentially an investment bank. Under British and South African law, it may hold shares in other enterprises.
**In 1977, Chase Manhattan announced it would not make loans to the South African regime. Its South African representative, however, said it planned to expand its business there normally, nonetheless.

major South African holdings.[49] Kleinwort Benson helped the South African government establish the Accepting Bank for Industry, a merchant bank, in South Africa, and holds shares in that bank, for which it provides international linkages. Kleinwort Benson Lonsdale holds a 33-percent interest in J.L. Clark and Company, an industrial holding company in South Africa.

Although their South African affiliates are relatively small, these United States banks have extensive direct contact with the South African economic community. Their linkages enable them to provide advice and contacts to transnational corporate clients who seek to expand their South African operations, adding their contribution to South Africa's military-industrial growth.

In addition, United States transnational banks' South African affiliates mobilize individuals' savings for investment in the apartheid economy. The importance of this role is highlighted by the regime's pressure on transnational banks to buy bonds in order to finance its military build-up. Barclays South Africa publicized its purchase of $12 million in South African government defense bonds. Other transnational banks have been less explicit about their holdings, although Citicorp recently revealed that it holds some "public sector assets" in South Africa.[50]

United States transnational banks have played a leading role in mobilizing foreign capital to finance South Africa's requirements in the current military and economic crisis. In the last few years, South Africa's overseas debt has multiplied rapidly to cover the costs of its oil and military purchases, and economic development programs designed to make its white-minority government more self-sufficient. South Africa's overall debt at the end of 1976 was estimated at about $9 billion, and probably more.[51]

Loans, whatever their ostensible purpose, contribute to a country's ability to expand its military establishment. "It is statistically impossible to break down the debt services of developing countries into 'civil' and 'military' components," Locke and Wulf declare.[52]

In all, some 46 transnational financial institutions served as managers of public bond issues to South Africa from 1972 to '76.[53] Thirty-six banking groups were involved in Eurocurrency credits. These include most of the major financial institutions of the international capital market. Since the Soweto uprising in June 1976, United States banks have played a leading role in supplying capital to the South African regime. This service has become increasingly important to the maintenance of apartheid as there has been an outflow of capital since the uprising. In 1977, it was estimated that the South African regime and its parastatals owed United States transnational banks about $2.2 billion, or a third of the regime's total foreign debt.[54] This figure may well be understated. In the same year, the Bank of America, reporting its outstanding credit to South Africa at $188 million, said that over half represented short-term credit to commercial banks, and over a quarter of the remainder was loans to public and private corporations. The largest recipient of the remainder was the South African regime.[55] If this breakdown is typical for other lenders, the total value of credits from United States banks to South Africa was higher than the published figure, which includes few private sector loans and none to commercial banks.

Table 13: United States Transnational Banks and Affiliates With Major Commitments to South Africa, 1974-'76

Country	Institution (U.S. affiliate)	Number of known commitments in which participated
U.S.	Citibank	10
	Manufacturers Hanover	8
	Kidder Peabody	8
	Chase Manhattan	3
U.K.	White Weld Securities (White Weld)	10
	Hill Samuel (Citibank)	9
France	Credit Commerciale de France (Continental Illinois—4%)	15

Source: Calculated from, U.S. Senate, Subcommittee on African Affairs, Hearings on "United States Corporate Interests in South Africa" (Washington, D.C.: Government Printing Office, 1977).

The United States government has assisted banks and corporations to make loans to South Africa by providing insurance and guarantees for loans to finance exports to that country. The United States Export-Import (Ex-Im) Bank, which is government owned, insured or guaranteed trade with South Africa worth $691 million in 1972-'76. In the first quarter of 1977, loans covered by Ex-Im Bank agreements included funds for turbo-commander aircraft, as well as essential capital and equipment for the military-industrial sector.[56]

Summary and Conclusion

In short, United States corporations have played a major role in building up and supplying the South African military-industrial complex. Without the continuing contribution made by United States transnational companies, it seems unlikely that the white-minority regime in South Africa could continue to maintain and expand its modern military establishment.

By concentrating their African manufacturing investments in South Africa, United States transnational corporations have transformed that country's political economy into a regional sub-imperialist center. South Africa has not thereby disengaged itself from its dependence on transnational corporations. Rather, the transnational corporations have viewed South Africa's oppressive state-capitalist regime as a profitable base from which to intensify their penetration of the entire southern African region.

The facts presented in this article underline the further reality that, far from contributing to economic development which might in some way benefit the African majority, transnational corporate investments have helped build up the white-minority regime's military capacity to perpetuate its exploitative rule in the face of mounting protest.

References

1.   For a fuller discussion of United States transnationals in South Africa, see, Ann and Neva Seidman, *South Africa and U.S. Multinatinal Corporations* (Westport, Conn.: Lawrence Hill, 1978); and Neva Makgetla and Ann Seidman, *Activities of Transnational Corporations in South Africa* (New York: U.N. Centre Against Apartheid, 1978)

2.   Locke, Peter, and Wulfe, Herbert, *Register of Arms Production in Developing Countries* (Hamburg: Arbeitsgruppe "Rustung und Unterentwicklung," March 1977)

3. *Ibid.*
4. *Ibid*
5. *Ibid*
6. Institute for Strategic Studies, *Survival* (London), June-July 1972
7. South African Ministry of Information, *South African Digest* (Pretoria),
September 30, 1977
8. *Survival, op.cit.*
9. *International Defense* (Washington, D.C.), IV.6 (December 1972)
10. *Survival, op.cit.*
11. *The Guardian,* December 5, 1973
12. *Ibid.*
13. June, 1973
14. *The Washington Post,* November 11, 1976
15. For a more detailed discussion of this relationship, see Seidman, *op.cit.*
16. *The Boston Globe,* February 18, 1978
17. Corporate Information Center (CIC), National Council of Churches,
Church Investments, Corporations and South Africa (New York: 1973), pp. 95
ff.
18. G.M. report to stockholders, 1977
19. For a fuller critique, see Seidman, Ann and Neva, "The Political Economy of
Southern Africa," in *Southern Africa: Economy, Society and Liberation*
(Michigan: Michigan State University and African Studies Center, forthcoming)
20. *G.M. Bowtie,* November 1976
21. General Motors South Africa (Pty.) Ltd., Inter-Office Memo; published by
Interfaith Center on Corporate Responsibility, National Council of Churches,
May 1978.
22. Corporate Information Center, *op.cit.*
23. Makgetla and Seidman, *op.cit.*
24. ITT, "ITT in South Africa" (May 1976)
25. Makgetla and Seidman, *op.cit.*
26. *Sechaba,* Special Issue, IX.11/12 (November-December 1975)
27. Dunn and Bradstreet, *Principal International Business, 1975/76—The
World Marketing Directory* (New York: 1977)
28. Sperry Rand, *Annual Report, 1975*
29. Investor Responsibility Research Center, "Corporate Activity in South
Africa: Motorola Inc.," 1978 Analysis J, Supplement 4 (Washington, D.C.:
April 7, 1978)
30. U.S. Senate, Subcommittee on African Affairs, Hearings on "United States
Corporate Interests in South Africa," September 1976 (Washington: D.C.: U.S.
Government Printing Office, 1977)
31. Vayrynen, Raimo, "South Africa: A Coming Nuclear Power?" in *Instant
Research on Peace and Violence,* VII.1 (1977)
32. *The New York Times,* October 25, 1977
33. Vayrynen, *op.cit.,* p. 34
34. *Ibid.*
35. Westinghouse, *Annual Report 1976*

36. South African Ministry of Information, *South African Digest*, June 24, 1976; July 30, 1975

37. Fluor Corp. (Los Angeles), *Annual Report, 1976*

38. See, *Informationsdienst suedliches afrika* (Bonn), December 1976, re FRG firms; Fluor Corp. annual reports (Los Angeles); Raytheon annual reports (Boston); in addition, Alsthom and Spie-Batignolles, which are building the Koeberg nuclear plant, are involved in Sasol II's construction.

39. U.S. Department of Commerce, *Survey of Current Business,* August 1974

40. Mobil presentation to U.S. Senate Subcommittee on African Affairs, hearings on "U.S.Corporate Interests in South Africa," September 1976

41. Mobil, *Annual Report*, 1977

42. Mobil presentation to Senate Subcommittee on African Affairs, *op. cit.*

43. Corporate Information Center, *The Oil Conspiracy* (New York: World Council of Churches, 1976)

44. A number of organizations, including anti-apartheid movements, churches, student groups and trade unions, have organized campaigns against bank loans to South Africa made by companies in the United States, Britain, the FRG, the Netherlands and elsewhere.

45. Letter to Timothy Smith, Interfaith Center on Corporate Responsibility, from C.W. Desch, Secretary of Citicorp, dated February 8, 1978

46. First National City Bank of New York, *Annual Report, 1963*

47. Makgetla and Seidman, *op.cit.*

48. *Ibid.*

49. *Ibid.*

50. Letter to Timothy Smith from C.W. Desch, *op.cit.*

51. These estimates have been derived from that given by the Bank of International Settiements, *Annual Report, 1976*, with the addition of almost $2 billion known to have been committed to South Africa by private commercial banks but not yet disbursed (Campbell and Chiles, "New Data on LDC Debt," in *The Financial Times* (London), June 17 1977, p. 32. Data in the South African Reserve Bank, *Quarterly Bulletin* (December 1976, pp. 564-5) suggest that the international debt had already reached $9 billion by the end of 1975, which indicates that the publicly known debt may be understated because of the secrecy attendant on loans, especially to the private sector.

52. Locke and Wulfe, *op. cit.*

53. The information on publicly issued bonds and credits has been collected in United States Senate, Subcommittee on African Affairs, hearings on "United States Corporate Interests in South Africa," September 1976 (Washington, D.C.: Government Printing Office, 1977)

54. *Ibid.*

55. Letter from Mark C. Hennessey, Research Officer, International Bank of America, San Francisco Headquarters (Social Policy No. 3761) to Timothy Smith, Interfaith Center on Corporate Reponsibility, dated August 8, 1977.

56. United States House of Representatives, Committee on International Relations, Hearings on "Resource Development in South Africa," 94th Congress, 2nd Session (Washington, D.C.: U.S. Government Printing Office, 1976), p. 383, Table 11, and p. 384, Table 12; and U.S. Export-Import Bank, Discount Loan Statement as of April 1977.

Chapter 11

U.S. Observation of
The Arms Embargo

Robert Sylvester

Despite the fact that the United States government pledged to implement the voluntary arms embargo against South Africa in 1963, and the mandatory embargo in 1977, successive administrations have failed to put teeth into the enforcement machinery. Government rhetoric seems designed to conceal a complex, sometimes contradictory set of procedures which have not stopped the continued flow of arms to South Africa. Even after institution of the mandatory embargo, administrative agencies apparently arranged the shipment of "grey area" items, such as airplanes, so as to avoid public scrutiny.

There are several significant reasons to question whether the arms embargo on South Africa, instituted as unilateral United States policy in 1963, has been effectively applied. The embargo is the single most prominent expression of United States disagreement with South Africa. Citizens can judge the relative commitment of individuals and political parties to this important policy from presidency to presidency. They can also draw wider conclusions about our African policy. Furthermore, since the mandatory embargo instituted on November 4, 1977, imposes a concrete legal obligation on all U.N. member states, observers may now scrutinize the enforcement of machinery for legal, as well as moral and political, reasons.[1]

A review of the machinery designed to enforce both the voluntary embargo of 1963 and the mandatory embargo of 1977 indicates that it is complex and in some cases functions at cross purposes. This is especially true in the case of "dual purpose" civilian goods—that is, commercial items such as radios and airplanes which are normally used by civilians for civilian activities, but which can be used for military or police purposes. Continued export of these items seems to provide an important form of external support for South Africa's military build-up.

An effective embargo would halt all military-related contact between the United States and South Africa. Such contacts are not ended by the simple pronouncement that exports of military equipment will be prohibited. Analysis of the machinery designed to implement the embargo helps deepen understanding of the implications of continued trade with South Africa. When the terms of the embargo are narrowly construed, the need for further trade or commercial restraint is probably small.*

Finally, a close look at the institution, application and enforcement of this particular embargo helps each American assess the degree to which he or she must accept responsibility for the excesses of a foreign government whose actions are often aided by, if not dependent upon, equipment supplied by the United States.

Initiation of the Arms Embargo by the United States

The document purporting to institute a voluntary United States arms embargo against South Africa in 1963 did not fully lay out the lines of responsibility, detail the decision process, or enunciate criteria for judging the export of "dual purpose" goods. Furthermore, an escape clause was provided. Then-Ambassador

---

* This writer opposes the imposition of a trade embargo against South Africa but does, at present, favor fairly strict and vigorous application of the terms of the arms embargo, prohibiting United States export of civilian aircraft and parts, and those technological items that can reasonably be expected to serve a military end. The rationale is simple: absent compelling economic considerations posed by any of the affected industry, our African policy can be enhanced by a display of commitment to a tough-minded embargo position.

to the United Nations Adlai E. Stevenson stated that,

> ...The United States...reserves the right in the future to interpret this policy in the light of requirements for assuring the maintenance of international peace and security.

The embargo was instituted by internal directives which were classified until January 7, 1976—twelve years from the date of issuance. Earlier publication of the embargo's terms would have opened them to scrutiny by interested parties, including Congressional policymakers.

An unnumbered, confidential memorandum dated January 7, 1964, distributed within the executive branch, identified items which could no longer be exported to South Africa. These included: (1) goods on the U.S. Munitions List;* (2) arms, ammunition and military vehicles, as designated in the Security Council resolution; (3) equipment and materials for the production and maintenance of arms and munitions, as identified in a December 4, 1963, Security Council resolution; (4) "other items of significant use in combat or in training for the armed, police and paramilitary forces"; and (5) items especially designated by the Department of State. Aside from the reference to the Munitions List, the memorandum does not itemize goods or illustrate decisions which would satisfy the objective of not exporting "items of significant use..in training..paramilitary forces." Much is left to the discretion of the decision maker. Previously contracted strategic defense items could still be exported. Spare parts for military transport aircraft, for example, were exported long after 1963.

Items of "dual utility for civilian use" (i.e. of a "distinct non-military utility") could also be exported, if ordered by and for civilian non-governmental users. This exception is the most perplexing. How can one judge "dual utility"? If an exported good had to be "distinct non-military," then many "dual" items, like civilian aircraft, would not be exported. This designation would also seem to bar export of most of the technological and "gray area" items still being exported in 1978.

---

* The Munitions List covers items used by the Department of State's Office of Munitions Control in its control of weapons exports. 222 C.F.R., Part 121

The applications for export of "dual" or "gray area" items were to be examined on a case-by-case basis by representatives of the State Department's Office of Legal Advisor, Office of Munitions Control, Bureau of Political-Military Affairs, Bureau of African Affairs, the Office of Military Affairs in the Economic Bureau, and personnel from the United Nations section of the Bureau for International Organizations. If this group was unable to agree, the case would be referred to the under-secretary level in the State Department. This group was not required to keep records of its decisions or maintain information for public use. No other agencies were included in the team. Then as now, the State Department carried much of the weight in making "dual purpose" or "gray area" decisions.

A subsequent classified memorandum issued by then-Under Secretary of State Nicholas Katzenbach, expanded the exceptions to the embargo by stating that U.S. components in items manufactured in third countries could be shipped to South Africa unless the components or end articles were arms or articles of a weapons nature.[2] Katzenbach also expanded the group passing on "gray area" cases to include personnel from the State Department's Office of East-West Trade and the Secretary of Defense's Office of International Security Affairs. Again, neither the Commerce Department nor the Arms Control Disarmament Agency was included in this "gray zone" group.

Nothing in these memoranda provided adequate assurance that the embargo would be enforced. The material was, *en masse*, rather unimpressive as a guide for consultation, enforcement and definition of the embargo.*

Legislative Authority for the Embargo

The actual machinery for enforcing the embargo is complex, and conducted under several laws and by various agencies which

---

* One State Department official observed during investigatory conversations in 1977 that the embargo seemed to be guided by internal directives that were, over the course of the 14 years, "contradictory." Certainly, in addition to the problems created by the secrecy of government actions, the vague internal directives left ample room for bureaucratic inconsistency in passing on the "gray area" items.

do not always act in concert. In everyday practice, two government bodies have jurisdiction: the Office of Munitions Control, in the State Department, and the Office of Export Administration in the Commerce Department. Although the State Department seems to have the most weight in reaching decisions on the embargo's operation, the Office of Export Administration issues licenses on "gray area" items.* Both bodies are concerned with the non-governmental commercial transfer of military-like items, and divide their jurisdiction on the basis of how the items are classified.[3]

An examination of the legislation governing each office,[4] plus an analysis of the legislative authority controlling governmental transfers of military goods and technology,[5] can provide some understanding of the depth of the United States government's commitment to enforcement of the embargo.

The legislative authority for the Secretary of State's control of arms exports arises from the Mutual Security Act of 1954.[6] It authorizes the president, in furtherance of world peace, security, and United States foreign policy interests, to control the flow of arms and implements of war, including technical data, by non-governmental parties.[7] This act, through regulations made by the executive, controls those engaged in the manufacture, export or import of arms and related technical data.[8] Anyone who wilfully violates it is subject to a maximum fine of $25,000, imprisonment of up to two years, or both.[9] The act also calls for the Senate Foreign Affairs Committee and the House International Relations Committee to be notified of the issuance of licenses for the export of goods valued in excess of $100,000.[10] The report must include the name and address of the consignee and the ultimate user of the potential export.

The Secretary of Commerce shares responsibility with the Secretary of State for export of military-related goods by private

---

* It might be concluded that this is not the preferred way to institute an embargo, since the body sensitive to the political character of the policy is not the body that issues export licenses. The exporting agency is at least equipped to recognize and respond to the sensitive nature of the political judgments represented in "gray area" exports. In addition, the Commerce Department aims to promote free trade, and should not be expected to exercise restraints on it.

agencies.[11] Such exports "may have an important bearing upon fulfillment" of United States foreign policy objectives, and affect national security.[12] The legislation does not refer to the effect of "dual purpose" exports on the foreign policy or security objectives of the recipient nation. No reference is made to the obligation to institute an embargo as required by U.N. action.

The provisions of the Export Administration Act that delineate the authority of the Secretary of Commerce do not refer to obligations requiring a restraint of trade. On the contrary, they seek to enable the Secretary to promote trade. Although regulations may be used to halt exports on the basis of national policy concerns, there is no mention made of the Secretary's authority to enforce an embargo against South Africa or any other nation.[13] Furthermore, the agency designated to oversee exports is not required to consult with the State Department on the imposition of export controls. On the other hand, the act requires that the Secretary of Agriculture grant approval before export controls can be placed on agricultural commodities.*

The Office of Export Administration must consult other departments concerned with domestic and foreign policy issues and the president must seek advice from industry representatives when making most export decisions.[16] Upon the request of a substantial segment of any industry whose products are being considered for export controls, the Secretary of Commerce must appoint a technical advisory committee to consider difficult evaluative questions related to export decisions.[17] No such consultative body, governmental or non-governmental, need be established to aid the Secretary in implementing the arms embargo against South Africa.

An individual who knowingly violates regulations promulgated under the act is subject to a maximum punishment of

* The Secretary of Defense has the authority to review the export of goods and technology that may affect the military capacity of the recipient only in the case of socialist countries. He may recommend disapproval of the export if he determines the item will significantly increase the military capability of the recipient country.[14] If the recommendation of the Secretary to disapprove is overruled by the president, the latter is required by law to submit a statement to Congress explaining his position and the recommendation of the Secretary of Defense.[15]

$10,000 fine and imprisonment for up to one year.[18] For a subsequent offense, the violator is subject to a fine of up to $20,000, imprisonment for up to five years, or both. The act does not distinguish between violations of an embargo policy and contraventions of other foreign policy objectives.* The act also allows for imposition of a civil penalty of up to $1000 for each violation.[20] The Export Administration Office may inspect books and subpoena persons to pursue its investigations.[21] Its subpoena power is fortified by the contempt power of the federal courts.

President Nixon[22] established an Export Administration Review Board by Executive Order. Comprised of the Secretaries of Commerce, State and Defense, it reviews difficult questions concerning national security and "other major issues" relating to exports which the Secretary of Commerce refers to it.[23] Apparently, however, the board has not considered any issues affecting the South African embargo.

The Export Administration Act provides no restraint on exports to nations whose governments deny the growth of fundamental rights or social progress. The export of "dual purpose" goods and technology to an embargoed country like South Africa is thus permitted, even if the exports further the denial of rights or social progress.

The sale and export of military arms and equipment by the United States government or its agencies comes under a different set of controls promulgated by the Arms Export Control Act.[24] This act is more explicit about the aims of arms sales than either the Mutual Security or Export Administration Acts. It also provides for greater Congressional supervision of government arms sales. It asserts[25] that the ultimate goal of the United States is a world free of war, in which the use of force is subordinated to the rule of law, and in which change is achieved peacefully. It

---

* This is important since a violation that contravenes an embargo policy allows the violator to rise above the powers of government to conduct foreign affairs. In contrast, the penalties for willfully exporting an item in violation of the act with knowledge that the item will be used to benefit a "Communist" country gives on first offense a fine of up to $20,000 and the prospect of up to five years in jail.[19]

stipulates to whom sales can be made and that sales must accord with the purposes and principles of the United Nations Charter. No sales are to be made "where they would have the effect of arming military dictators who are denying the growth of fundamental rights or social progress to their own people," unless the president waives the limitations because of the sale's importance to national security.

The Secretary of State is responsible, at the president's direction, for the continuous supervision and general direction of governmental arms exports.[26] Sales are to be "to friendly countries for solely internal security, for legitimate self-defense arrangements or measures consistent with the Charter of the United Nations," or for aiding the military of a less developed country in public works and economic and social development.[27]

The Arms Export Control Act requires the president to submit a quarterly report to the Speaker of the House and the chairman of the Senate Foreign Relations Committee containing details relating to the sale and export of military supplies by government agencies.[28] The act requires notification of the Speaker of the House and the chairman of the Senate Foreign Relations Committee before an offer may be made to sell military articles or services exceeding $25 million in value, or a major defense system for $7 million or more.[29] If requested by either the House International Relations Committee or the Senate Foreign Relations Committee, the president must submit information, including a description of the capabilities of the defense articles to be furnished and a justification for sale.[30] The act enables Congress to stop the sale by adopting a concurrent resolution disapproving the offer. This Congressional veto may be overcome if the president certifies that an emergency exists which requires the sale to safeguard national security. The Export Administration Act governing private sales does not require similar reporting, nor does it allow for a Congressional veto. The Arms Export Control Act also requires the director of the United States Arms Control and Disarmament Agency to comment specifically on the effect of a proposed arms export on the arms race and any increased possibility of conflict.[31]

The act calls for a penalty of up to $100,000 and two years

imprisonment for those who wilfully make any untrue statement in registration or licensing.[32] Neither the Mutual Security Act nor the Export Administration Act, controlling non-governmental exports, have this extensive penal power.

"Dual Purpose" Exports

In the 15 years since the voluntary embargo was imposed, some important changes have been made in the regulations governing the export of military and police goods to South Africa.[33] On December 9, 1963, the Commerce Department authorized denial of export to South Africa of: (1) military automotive vehicles; (2) military transport aircraft; and (3) rifles and pistols (.22 caliber and under), component parts and ammunition (if intended for a consignee other than "an apparently legitimate private buyer") and bayonets. The basis for judging the "legitimacy" of a private buyer was not explained. On June 1, 1964, the list of prohibited exports was expanded to include non-military shotguns and ammunition.[34]

On January 20, 1964, the department's Bureau of International Commerce authorized denial of export to South Africa of items primarily used in the manufacture of arms, ammunition and implements of war. The directive allowed, however, for consideration of applications to export shotguns, rifles and pistols of .22 caliber and under, and component parts and ammunition to "legitimate" firms in South Africa.* Although it gives no definition or criteria of "legitimacy," the directive did list items used primarily in manufacturing arms which could not be exported.**

On January 4, 1966—some two years, five months after the Security Council embargoed the export of military goods to South Africa—the Bureau of International Commerce auth-

* The presumption of denial of export was attached to non-military shotguns and ammunition on June 1, 1964. After the initial U.N. Security Council Resolution on August 7, 1963, ten months elapsed during which a policy of restraint existed without actual institution within the federal bureaucracy.
**Indeed, the U.N. Security Council resolution of December 4, 1963, called for the ban of exports to South Africa of this type of "implements of war manufacturing" material.

orized denial action against civilian aircraft for either direct or *indirect* military use, if the Departments of State, Commerce and Defense (in certain cases) concur.* The directive also authorized denial of exports of, first, airborne electrical and electronic equipment, and, second, certain teflon items especially fabricated for aircraft propellors, engines, landing gear and aircraft. Nevertheless, the export of aircraft, helicopter parts and accessories continued, exceeding $202 million in 1975 alone. The nonpublic process of tracking these exports means that no easily available record exists of any items in these categories that were denied export.

On September 17, 1970, the policy of allowing denial of aircraft exports suffered a setback. David Newsom, then Secretary of State for African Affairs, announced the United States government would consider licenses for limited numbers of unarmed executive aircraft for use by the South African Air Force.[35] This act itself suggested that the embargo was not being rigorously enforced.** Newsom argued that other nations freely sold these items, and that they would not strengthen South Africa's military or internal security capacity. He did not comment on the effect of the action on perceptions of United States African policy.

In early 1977, as a result of Congressional concern that shotguns and police equipment were still being exported to South Africa, the Commerce Department authorized removal from the general license list of all such items in transit through the United States for a South African or Namibian destination. Shotguns and all crime-control detection equipment destined for South Africa required special, "validated" licenses (which are more difficult to obtain than "general" ones). It became official policy to deny applications to export or re-export commodities to South Africa or Namibia when there was a likelihood of military,

---

* Presumably the concurrence of all three Secretaries was required for denial.
**It has been reported by the Commerce Department that no such licenses were issued until March 1975. Newsom himself asserted that the embargo was vigorously enforced. See Chapter 7.

Items on the Commodity Control List require a validated, not a general, license, and as a result are more difficult to export.

police or other use contrary to United States policy. Despite this new regulation, United States exports to South Africa of shotguns, police equipment, aircraft, helicopters and the like did not cease.

Finally, on February 16, 1978, in light of growing criticism of the South African government and United States exports of "dual purpose" goods, the Commerce Department authorized denial of exports of any goods of technical data destined to *and* for the use of or by the South African military or police. The announced desire was to strengthen United States implementation of the various U.N. Security Council resolutions.

It is too early to know if the new regulations controlling the export of technical data will in fact limit South African access to computer goods. A South African subsidiary of Motorola has told its local customers that it will not accept new orders on certain equipment for fear the goods will end up in police or military hands.[36] Kodak has turned down two orders since the new regulations were introduced.[37] Yet IBM South Africa—one of the two largest electronics firms in South Africa*—will continue to service the South African military and police.[38] Non-U.S. sources may continue to supply South Africa with IBM computer parts, despite the ban, although the February 1978 regulations include a requirement that foreign recipients using the special licensing procedures must certify that the commodities received will not be used or sold contrary to the embargo.

This review of changes in the regulations governing export of military-related material to South Africa shows that the implementation of the arms embargo obligations of the United States has been exceedingly cautious. The regulations seem to continue to permit the export of "dual purpose" goods, such as aircraft and helicopters, and the export of police equipment, so long as the items appear to be exported to or for civilians.

Inadequate Enforcement

United States enforcement of the arms embargo raises doubt as to whether the government has adequately executed its obliga-

---

* See Chapter 10 for information on the role of Motorola and IBM in South Africa.

tions. Several cases illustrate this point.

Despite the voluntary arms embargo of 1963, the Department of Commerce licensed for export to South Africa in 1976 over $300,279 worth of items classified as "non-military weapons," including $157,929 worth of shotguns, and $142,350 worth of police devices.[39] South Africa was wracked with internal protest, and these items would be very useful to the police. The department was at a loss to explain the 238-percent increase in shotguns exported to the embargoed countries from 1975 to 1976.[40] Nor was there an adequate explanation of the rise in exports of foreign-manufactured shotguns from 654 to 3000 (a jump of 359 percent) between 1975 and 1976.* The export of police equipment—including shotguns, tear gas, truncheons and "captive bolt humane killers"**—increased 25 percent in the same period, from $115,023 to $143,265.

The most disturbing aspect of this case, perhaps, is the realization that no one at Commerce or State monitored these transactions. Recently, two reporters, Jim Watson of a Chicago newspaper and Ann Williams of the Associated Press, confirmed that officials in Commerce were not only unaware of the increases from 1975 to '76, but still did not know Commerce had to issue licenses for shotguns and other police-like material.

As a result of this discovery, a March 1977 House resolution[41] called on the president to undertake immediately a review of United States policies and practices with respect to shipments of weapons and related items to South Africa, and take appropriate steps to ensure United States actions were consistent with obligations under the 1963 U.N. Security Council embargo. The resolution requested that the United States prevent shipment or transshipment to South Africa of any weapon or related item which aids the maintenance of apartheid directly or indirectly. In addition, the resolution mandated the president to report on the review to Congress, and explain the licensing of "non-military

---

* This sort of trade makes vigorous prosecution of violating companies critical. There is no other way to discover the network of agents and transshipment points needed to circumvent the embargo.
**See reference 40 for a more detailed listing of the categories of exports.

weapons" that occurred between 1975 and 1976. This report should set forth steps to ensure that the arms embargo against South Africa will be strictly and rigorously enforced.

A series of hearings before the House Subcommittee on Africa followed. They prompted the Commerce Department to announce that it had placed shotguns, shells and parts under validated license control when shipped to Botswana, Lesotho and Swaziland.* It also required validated licenses for all shipments to South Africa or Namibia which were transited through the United States. The department testified that crime control and detection equipment would be the subject of a significantly increased level of control.

Stanley J. Marcus, Deputy Assistant Secretary of Commerce, wrote Congresswoman Cardiss Collins on June 10, 1977, that "the controls established by this Department, upon the advice of the Department of State, to restrict the shipment of arms to South Africa comply fully, we believe, with the spirit of the U.N. Security Council Resolution of 1963." Despite such statements by Carter Administration officials, Department of Commerce figures show that direct exports of police equipment to South Africa rose 9 percent in 1976-'77, to $156,822. Of the two shotgun categories,[43] one showed direct exports to South Africa worth $61,890, a modest decrease from 1976 levels of $83,419. Swaziland, however, imported shotguns in this category worth over $114,000.** Thus an initial review of 1977 figures reveals no marked reversal of policy.

Obligations Arising from a Mandatory U.N. Embargo

United States responsibilities to enforce the arms embargo became obligatory in 1977, when the United Nations Security Council passed a resolution imposing a mandatory arms embargo.[44] The resolution ordered a worldwide mandatory embargo on the supply to South Africa of "arms and related material of

---

* It is suspicious that Botswana imported in excess of $108,000 of one recorded kind of shotgun, while Swaziland imported over $100,000 worth of the same class of shotgun from the United States in 1976.[42]
**On Schedule "B," this category is "Shotguns, Military, $75 and over," No. 894.3025.

all types," including "paramilitary police equipment" and spare parts for weapons and military and paramilitary equipment.[45] The text declairs that the existing arms embargo needs strengthening and universal application without reservation, and so decidedly firmer embargo measures by all U.N. member states are necessary. The United States, Great Britain, and France, which vetoed complete economic sanctions, have a special responsibility to institute vigorous arms and material sanctions, to show their commitment to an effective arms embargo.

The U.N. vote on November 4, 1977, classified the situation in South Africa as a "threat to peace." Indeed, although Ambassador Andrew Young erroneously characterized past United States actions as adhering to a "comprehensive arms embargo,"[47] the November action is distinguished, not simply because it upgrades United States obligations from voluntary to mandatory, but because it requires comprehensiveness.* Young himself had called for Security Council action to "close up the loopholes that have existed in the arms embargo" in his comments before the Council on October 31, 1977.[48]

The mandatory resolution of November 1977, if violated, can lead to suspension of the violating state from the United Nations. The resolution can be enforced under United States law in domestic courts, since it is based on Article 41 of the U.N. Charter, which results in a self-executing legal obligation.** The Congressional comments surrounding the adoption of the U.N.

---

* Although President Carter, according to press reports,[46] said the prohibition of arms would extend to items not considered essentially military, the export of civilian aircraft and helicopters continues. It would be devastating to U.S. African policy if the scope of the voluntary obligations were not expanded upon significantly. Reluctance to increase the scope of the United States embargo would not serve U.S. interests in Africa, the U.N. or the world. This is why banning prominent military-like items, such as helicopters and other aircraft, is such a critical issue.

**By virtue of the "supremacy clause" of the U.S. Constitution, the U.N. Charter, as a ratified international treaty, is the supreme law of the land. The relevant provision of Article 41 differs from Article 43 of the Charter, which governs Security Council directives controlling the commitment of armed forces to U.N. actions by member states, and also from Article 41's portion concerning directives to member states to alter their diplomatic relations in furtherance of a U.N. objective. The U.S. Congress chose not to alter the

Participation Act show that both the executive and legislative branches considered Article 41's economic sanction portions to be binding once the Security Council acted.[50] To strengthen the case for self-execution, the Participation Act includes a penalty provision making violators of orders issued pursuant to Article 41 economic sanctions subject to five years imprisonment or $10,000 fine, or both.

As Chapter Eight shows,[51] in the 15 years since the initiation of the embargo, the United States has continued to export aircraft, helicopters and spare parts and accessories for these craft to South Africa. This practice apparently continues despite the U.N. mandatory embargo and the efforts of some members of Congress.

Reportedly, President Carter intended a directive banning the sale to South Africa of "gray area" items that could easily be converted to military or police use.[52] It was widely anticipated that this would mean that civilian aircraft, electronic equipment, helicopters and civilian spare parts and engines for flying craft would no longer be granted export licenses.

The State Department announced on December 15, 1977, however—the day Congress adjourned for the holiday season—that it would not block the licensing by the Commerce Department of six Cessna light aircraft for export to South Africa.[53] The aircraft were identified as crop-dusting planes. But their value, stated as approximately $500,000, did not reflect the cost of aircraft advertised for that use by the exporting company.* The Carter Administration approved the export of the planes just 56 days after the mass arrests and bannings in South Africa in

requirement for United States action pursuant to Article 41 economic sanctions directed by the Security Council. Specifically, Congress, in acting to tailor the U.S. commitment to the Charter in light of pre-existing requirements of the U.S. Constitution[49] determined that Article 43 actions necessitated Congressional action. Article 41 economic sanction resolutions, however, were construed to be obligatory with no added government action. They require no further action by the president or Congress before obligations arise and rights afix.

* Consultation with the Cessna sales catalogue indicates that no crop-dusting craft could be purchased for a cost of about $83,000 apiece.

October 1977; a mere 45 days after Congress condemned apartheid for the first time in history;[54] and 41 days after the mandatory arms embargo was adopted by the U.N. Security Council. The rationale was the shaky proposition that it is to whom a sale is made, rather than the nature of the good, that determines whether it is a "gray area" transfer.

The aircraft cleared for export in December 1977 are reported to be Cessna Model 172s (Skyhawks), which are deployed by the airforces of several countries, including Ecuador, Honduras, Peru and the United States. They can serve counter-insurgency objectives. A very similar model, the F-172, is produced by Reims Aviation of France, and access to parts and fittings for military support use is a direct possibility.[55] The International Institute for Strategic Studies reported in its 1977/78 edition of *The Military Balance* that Cessna Model 185s (Skywagons) are used by the South African military forces. In 1974, the South African military journal, *Paratus*, reported that "without these aircraft... problems of supply and communications would be insurmountable." Obviously, a civilian craft can be used by civilians to advance military ends.*

Public pronouncements by United States officials raised the expectation that the embargo would be sternly enforced. For example, Secretary of State Cyrus Vance announced on November 2, 1977, that the United States, in addition to supporting a mandatory arms embargo vote in the Security Council, was prepared to "prohibit the export of items for police and military in South Africa." He added that there would be "no more exports of spares and maintenance shipments for items whose export would be prohibited."[56]

In response to a Congressional telegram protesting the decision to export the Cessnas, the State Department argued in a letter dated December 29, 1977, that exports of this type had

---

* See also Chapters 7 and 8. Furthermore, on November 10, 1977, the South African government activated an emergency law, last invoked in World War II, which allowed it to seize, without compensation, the goods of any private citizen. The law could also force foreign foreign companies located within South Africa to turn their efforts to the production of war materiel.[55]

occurred for some time, and that it had no evidence the civilian aircraft had been diverted to the use of the South African military. In effect, it discounted the fact that the aircraft could be so used. This placed Congress and the public in the untenable position of having to show that the specific exports were to be "diverted" to police or military use.*

Members of the House *Ad Hoc* Monitoring Group on South Africa responded that the civilian aircraft were of military significance. As a consequence, the exports violated expressed United States policy of eliminating "gray area" sales, and indeed the sales may have violated the arms embargo. Their letter stressed that "it is the type of commodity—given the reasonable likelihood of its eventual assignment to use under military circumstances—which should be the decisive issue." The *Ad Hoc* Group concluded that continuation of these exports would result in a policy of rhetoric that falls short of practical results.

Congresswoman Collins, along with Congressmen Edward Markey and Tom Downey, introduced a bill on February 2, 1978, to amend the Export Administration Act to bar the export of aircraft, helicopters, spare parts and accessories for both, flight equipment, and non-military arms.[57] The bill would also establish a monitoring process which would require the Commerce Department to notify Congress at least 30 days before granting a validated license for a good to be exported to South Africa. The bill would allow the Congress, in a one-House veto, to disapprove of the license by passing a resolution within 30 days after the granting of the license.

---

* The department stated it would expand "end-use" monitoring; but this would require placing numerous personnel in South Africa. The State Department also argued that the craft would not be sold to an agency of the South African government, that all aircraft companies would have to submit a quarterly report of ownership of their craft, and that the distributor receiving these aircraft agreed to sell only to customers who agreed to the original license. The terms of the license required that: (1) resale and registry are limited to South Africa and South West Africa (Namibia), for normal civilian or commercial uses only; (2) that sale, lease or charter to any entity of the South African government requires separate and specific authorization of the U.S. Commerce Department; and (3) that the aircraft is not to be used in Rhodesia or by a Rhodesian party. There was no prohibition against *use*, by a private citizen, for military purposes; nor against government *use* for this purpose.

On March 23, 1978—again the day Congress was prepared to adjourn for a recess period—the General Aircraft Manufacturers' Association announced that the export of up to 80 light aircraft had been approved.* The warnings of the American Committee on Africa that the export of civilian aircraft would be viewed by African states as "another instance of American duplicity and hypocrisy" ring clearer every day.[58]

Even in the very rare case where a violator of the embargo was brought to court, the outcome did not suggest the government was prepared to conduct vigorous, effective enforcement. The *Wall Street Journal* of October 21, 1976, reported that the Justice Department was conducting a "broad scale" grand jury investigation into illegal transshipments of arms and ammunition to South Africa. Among the United States companies reported under investigation were Colt Industries and the Winchester Group of Olin Corporation. The *New Haven Advocate* detailed the nature of the companies' violations of the embargo.[59] These were said to involve a network of agents working in foreign transshipment points. As a result of the grand jury investigation, a Colt employee entered a guilty plea in July 1976, and was sentenced.[60] The federal judge in the case reluctantly accepted the defendant's plea, noting that at least 33 separate shipments were involved, which suggested the complicity of other individuals. The *Advocate* reported that initial comments by Olin-Winchester pointed to a similar phenomenon of several mid-level management employees independently engaged in gunrunning activities.

The judge in the Colt case had good reason to doubt that one employee alone was responsible. The use of transshipment points is probable whenever exports to a country which is not embargoed jump dramatically. For example, the *Advocate* noted that Winchester's sales of arms and ammunition to the Canary Islands

* Piper and Cessna are among the companies which will export as a result of this decision. Neither State nor Commerce made the announcement—they are not required by law to do so! It has been reported to the author that the export decision was made on March 9, 1978. In all likelihood, the craft were in transit to South Africa, or had already arrived there, by the time the public and Congress learned of their export.

had climbed from $52,000 to $406,000 in 1973-'74.[61] The *Advocate* also published Winchester documents citing exports of arms and ammunition to South Africa planned for 1975 worth $357,000.[62]

Since the Colt employees pleaded guilty and accepted an indictment on information, thus avoiding a grand jury indictment, the defendant and others who might have been involved escaped a federal trial, in which a public record on the process of transshipment could have been established.

Olin is not the only company whose practices cast doubt on United States enforcement of the arms embargo. Nonetheless, in March 1978 that company appeared in the news again, when it was indicted on 21 counts of falsifying records to hide the shipment of over 3200 rifles and 20 million rounds of ammunition to South Africa in violation of the United States embargo. This indictment stemmed from the 1976 events which had already resulted in the imprisonment of one Colt employee. Olin contended its employees carried out the actions without knowledge of senior management.

As in the Colt employee's case, the Olin Corporation was allowed to enter a plea of no contest to this indictment, covering illegal arms shipments to South Africa from 1971 through 1975.[63] The same federal judge who presided on the 1976 Colt employee's guilty plea also accepted this arrangement, over the protest of the United States Attorney for Connecticut. A chance to build a public record on the operation of gunrunning schemes to South Africa was thus effectively eliminated. Olin was eventually fined $510,000, a small price compared to the profits it must have made in four years of illegal activity which circumvented United States foreign policy commitments.

It is essential, given the past reluctance of United States policymakers to construe obligations under the arms embargo broadly, to prosecute suspected violators vigorously. Anything short of aggressive enforcement, given the narrow definition of goods affected, leaves serious doubt about United States commitment to an arms embargo against South Africa.

Conclusion

By almost any objective measure, the United States arms embargo against South Africa can be characterized as self-righteous public acknowledgement of our commitment without actually ending the flow of arms and military-like equipment to South Africa. When the embargo was first applied, Ambassador Adlai Stevenson proclaimed that self-righteousness is no substitute for practical results. If this standard is applied to the conduct of the United States government during the 15-year embargo period, it must be concluded that the United States has failed to institute an embargo with the desire to induce the government of South Africa "to remove the evil business of apartheid."[64]

Many changes are required of the United States if an effective embargo policy is to be achieved.

- A presidential review should be made of the manner in which the arms embargo has been implemented within the executive branch. Responsibility and authority for the embargo ought to rest clearly with one agency or department. The embargo policy should be coordinated with other departments.
- Decisions on the embargo ought to be subject to both Congressional and public scrutiny.
- Implementation of the embargo must apply to goods and technology, not just arms, which can aid the embargoed country's military establishment. "Dual purpose" goods should be banned from export, particularly in the absence of evidence that the prohibition would result in economic hardship for an industry or locale in the United States.
- Congress must be formally and regularly informed of the nature of all exports to the embargoed country.
- The present executive branch fiction that it is the recipient, not the nature of the good, which determines the character and purpose of a "dual purpose" item must be eliminated. Similarly, the executive branch notion that the "end-use" of "dual purpose" items can be successfully monitored once they are exported must be laid to rest.
- Penalties for violation of the embargo must be severe, enforcement reliable, and prosecution swift and public.

Of a more general nature, but with reference to the effective enforcement of an embargo, the United States must turn attention to the flow of conventional arms to the developing nations of the world. Serious attention must be given to curbing the unrestrained licensing and co-production arrangements that allow for horizontal proliferation of conventional arms manufacturers. The United States should place the issue of horizontal proliferation through licensing and co-production agreements and enforcement of the arms embargo against South Africa on its diplomatic agenda with fellow Western states. The United States must itself hinder use of its ports as transshipment points in the international sale of arms and equipment to embargoed states.

It would make good sense for the United States to avoid the mode and style of the past, which saw the government narrowly construing its obligations under the embargo. A forceful application of the terms of the embargo would clearly benefit United States policy in Africa.

References

1.   U.N. Security Council Resolution 418
2.   January 15, 1968
3.   For the Office of Munitions Control, see 22 C.F.R. 121-128; for the Office of Export Administration, see 15 C.F.R. 368-399
4.   Mutual Security Act of 1954, 22 U.S. 1750-1965, governs the office of Munitions Control, while the Export Administration Act of 1949, 83 Stat. 841, governs the Office of Export Administration.
5.   The control of government transfers of military items is found in the Arms Export Control Act, 82 Stat. 1320
6.   22 U.S.C. 1934
7.   Section 414, 22 U.S.C. 1934 (a). The enumeration is found in the Munitions Control List, 22 C.F.R. 121-28
8.   22 U.S.C. 1934 (b)
9.   22 U.S.C. 1934 (c)
10. 22 U.S.C. 1934 (e), added on December 17, 1973
11. The Export Administration Act of 1949 as amended, 50 U.S.C.A. 2401-2413.
12. Section (2)(1) of the act.
13. See Section 4 (b) (1)
14. Section 4h (2) (A)

15. Section 4(h)(3)
16. Section 5(a)
17. Section 5(c)(1)
18. Section 6(a)
19. Section 6(b)
20. Section 6(c)
21. Section 7(a)
22. Executive Order Number 11533, issued on June 4, 1970
23. *Ibid.*, Section 3. The chairman of the East-West Foreign Trade Board was added by Executive Order No. 11907, March 1, 1976
24. Formally known as the Foreign Military Sales Act, this can be found in 22 U.S.C. 2751
25. Chapter 1, Section 1
26. Chapter 1, Section 2(a)
27. Chapter 1, Section 4
28. Chapter 3, Section 36(a)
29. Chapter 3, Section 36(b)(1)
30. *Ibid.*
31. Chapter 3, Section 38(a)(2)
32. Chapter 3, Section 38(c)
33. Regulations of the Office of Export Administration at the U.S. Department of Commerce, 15 C.R.S. 368-399
34. Presumably military shotguns came under the jurisdiction of the Office of Munitions Control at the Department of State
35. Taken from an address by David D. Newsom, Assistant Secretary of State for African Affairs, before the Chicago Committee, Chicago, Illinois, September 17, 1970
36. African American Institute, *Update*, March 29, 1978
37. *Ibid.*
38. *The Star* (Johannesburg), weekly edition, March 18, 1978
39. In the arcane recording lingo of the department, a good portion of this police equipment is found on Export Schedule "B" document as "spare parts" (Schedule "B" item No. 894.3040
40. In 1975, the United States exported 786 shotguns to South Africa, while in 1976 the exports rose to 2603. The total increase in "non-military arms"— Schedule "B" numbers: 894.3011 (rifles), 894.3012 (rifles), 894.3021 (shotguns), 894.3025 (shotguns), 894.3030 (blackjacks, police billies, shock-batons, rifle-shotgun combinations, spring guns, tear gas guns, truncheons and "captive bolt humane killers," etc.), 894.3040 (adaptors, barrels, butt olates, magazines, rifle stocks, shotgun parts, silencers, etc.)—was 68 per cent.
41. H.J. Res. 338, 2nd Session, 94th Congress, March 22, 1977 (drafted by author)
42. See Table 2, Commodity Schedule "B," December 1976, U.S. Department of Commerce
43. On Schedule "B" this category is "Shotguns, Military, $75 and over," No. 894.3025

44. Security Council Resolution 418, adopted by consensus, November 4, 1977 (see Appendix B)
45. Operational Paragraph Two, Security Council Resolution 418
46. See *The New York Times*, November 5, 1977; and *The Washington Post*, October 28, 1977
47. *Department of State Bulletin* (Washington, D.C.) December 12, 1977, p. 860
48. *Ibid.*, p. 864
49. See Congressional Consideration of the U.N. Participation Act of 1945, in H.R. Rept. No. 1383, 79th Congress, 1st Session (1945)
50. 22 U.S.C. 287c (1970)
51. See also, hearings of the House Subcommittee on Africa, March 20, 22, and April 26, 93rd Congress, 1st Session, including documents furnished by the Office of Export Administration of the Department of Commerce; and El-Khawas, M.A., and Cohen, Barry, eds., *The Kissinger Study of Southern Africa* (Westport, Conn.: Lawrence Hill, 1975), p. 37
52. *The Washington Post*, October 28, 1977
53. *Ibid.*, December 15, 1977
54. The House of Representatives voted 347 to 54 to adopt the Collins resolution (H.Con.Res.388) of condemnation on October 31, 1977
55. *The Washington Post*, November 11, 1977
56. Department of State, "Press Memo," November 2, 1977, No. 497; see also Department of State, "Press Briefing Paper," December 14, 1977, and *The Washington Post*, October 28, 1977
57. H.R. 10722
58. Originally made concerning the November, 1977, exports. *The New York Times*, December 1, 1977
59. October 20 and 27, 1976
60. This marked the first sentencing under the Mutual Security Act since its passage in 1954.
61. The pre-sentence hearing in the Colt case also referred to the Canary Islands as a transshipment point.
62. A public statement issued by Olin-Winchester in October 1976 stated that illegal munitions sales to South Africa averaged $310,000 per year from 1972 to 1975. Internal Winchester documents cited in the *New Haven Advocate* show sales to South Africa for the first months of 1975 totalled $501,784 ($299,528 shipped, $202,256 awaiting shipment); October 20 and 27, 1976
63. This marked the first indictment of a United States corporation for a violation of the arms embargo since its inception in 1963
64. Cited in *Department of State Bulletin* (Washington, D.C.), August 20, 1973, p. 335.

Chapter 12

Postscript:
What Needs to Be Done?

As the preceding chapters show, military support—both direct and indirect—has been an important feature of United States relations with South Africa, helping the minority regime maintain its threatening, powerful role in the southern third of the continent. United States military involvement in southern Africa has several aspects.

First, the sale of arms to the region has been profitable for the United States transnational corporations involved. These companies have filtered arms shipments to South Africa through several channels in order to avoid the U.N. arms embargo. They have been officially permitted to send dual-purpose goods, allegedly for civilian use. They have made sales through foreign subsidiaries and affiliates operating with licenses provided by the U.S. parent company. South African affiliates of United States firms have been integrated directly into the military-industrial complex. They produce a wide range of dual-purpose and military goods within the country itself, in direct cooperation with the South African government and its parastatals. In many instances, the United States government has turned a blind eye to these activities. It has interpreted both the 1963 (voluntary) and the 1977 (mandatory) embargoes loosely, facilitating the continued shipment of all but the most obvious army weapons to

South Africa. Only rarely have violators of the embargo been prosecuted.

Beyond the immediate profitable business of arms sales, United States military involvement in southern Africa fits a larger pattern of foreign policy aims. The government has tended to adopt the transnational corporations' definition of United States interests. It has sought to protect cheap sources of raw materials and markets for United States firms, disregarding the question of whether such a policy benefits either the peoples of the countries involved or the people of the United States. It has resisted efforts to attain political-economic change which might direct resource development more equitably to raise the living standards of local populations. As a result, the United States has become notorious for supporting the most repressive and corrupt governments in Africa, as well as Asia and Latin America. In this, the United States has been able to count, ultimately, on the support of the Western European countries and Japan. International competition has generated occasional conflicts of interest between these countries over spheres of interest; but their perception of their larger strategic interests appears to have persuaded them to unite to prop up the racist *status quo* wherever possible.

In endeavoring to advance the interests of transnational corporations, the United States and other Western powers have tended to focus on regional subcenters in Africa, Asia and Latin America as the key to the stability of entire regional systems. South Africa, like Brazil, Iran, Israel and others, is expected to act as a proxy for Western interests in political and military matters, as well as economically. United States transnationals, as well as those of Western Europe, have invested heavily in the advanced industrial sectors of such subcenters as a springboard for penetrating the neighboring countries. United States spokesmen have repeatedly emphasized that they hope to use United States involvement in South Africa as a lever for promoting "moderate" governments in Namibia and Zimbabwe, in order to forestall more fundamental structural change.

Naturally, United States spokesmen seldom publicly state these underlying goals. In the U.N. and other international forums, United States diplomats have taken an appropriately horrified stance with respect to apartheid and white-minority rule in southern Africa. Similarly, they have condemned human rights violations in Brazil and Iran. But United States actions in southern Africa—as elsewhere—speak louder than words. United States transnational corporations continue to shape U.S. policy in the region through the kinds of investments they make and the goods they sell, as well as through their influence on policymakers. United States government corporate strategic and outright military support, although increasingly camouflaged, has also continued.

The practice of strengthening the South African subcenter militarily, economically and politically runs counter to the long-term interests of the majority of Americans. Most obviously, it increases the possibility of spreading the war now being waged in several countries in the region. The apartheid regime has insisted that all of sub-Saharan Africa falls within its zone of defense. It still holds Namibia as a colony; has kidnapped opponents from Botswana, Lesotho and Swaziland; and has periodically invaded independent Angola. South Africa remains the primary supporter of the illegal Rhodesian regime, which has repeatedly raided Mozambique, Zambia and Botswana.

The continued provision of nuclear technology to South Africa by the United States and France has frightening implications. It is not at all beyond the realm of possibility that the white-minority regime will use this weapon in a genocidal attempt to stay in power. This possibility appears even more likely if South Africa gains access to the neutron bomb with its potential for local focus on urban uprisings in black townships.

There is an alternative to viewing the interests in southern Africa of the people of the United States as identical with those of the transnational corporations which invest and sell their wares there. If the regional economy could be restructured to raise the standards of living and spread productive employment opportunities to the masses of the people, a more balanced and equitable pattern of trade could be developed, to the benefit of both Americans and southern Africans. An increasingly industrialized economy, geared to meeting the needs of the tens of millions of people who live in the region, could provide a far larger market for United States exports, while supplying materials needed in the United States, including, more and more, manufactured goods. One need only compare the more positive consequences for the United States economy of the relatively extensive trade with Europe to the current minimal trade with Africa. If conditions in the United States were changed to cooperate with, rather than hinder, such developments, this alternative kind of solution could in the long-term help alleviate the conditions of oversupply in important industries like steel, auto and chemicals. It could clearly benefit, not only the peoples of southern Africa, but the majority of Americans as well.

This type of solution would require that the people of Africa gain, not only political freedom, but also full control over the basic industry, financial institutions and trade of their nations. In the long run, they would need to acquire social ownership of the region's agricultural and mineral riches.

United States transnational corporations have helped shape and profited from the current oppressive situation in southern Africa. The United States government has preferred to depend on repressive regimes to block the wheels of change, not only in southern Africa but throughout the developing world.

The evidence compiled in this book reveals in some measure the continued funneling of United States military support, despite government rhetoric, to bolster the white-minority regimes of southern Africa. More research is necessary to illuminate all aspects of the on-going ties between the United States and the southern African minority regimes, as well as to explore alternative possible relationships. Research alone, however, will not change the behavior of the government or transnational corporations. Rather, the united action of all Americans must prevent the United States from becoming further involved in a new Vietnam in southern Africa, an involvement still carried on, perhaps covertly and through proxies— mercenaries, undercover agents and corporate affiliates—but nonetheless with disastrous consequences.

Much is already being done. Students on many campuses have organized campaigns to press university administrations to sell stock in companies with South African investments. Church, union and university groups have mobilized to withdraw pension and other funds from banks which continue to lend money to South Africa.

But more is needed. Pressure must be exerted on the administration and Congress to enforce strict observation of the mandatory U.N. embargo. This would require an end to all exports of dual-purpose goods to South Africa, and withdrawal of all licenses for production of such goods within that country. Moreover, the evidence shows that as long as transnational corporations are free to invest in and trade with South Africa, effective enforcement of the embargo is almost impossible. Furthermore, it convinces the South African minority that the United States will ultimately take its side. Only a complete boycott, like that proposed by the U.N. resolutions vetoed by the United States and other Western powers, can halt continued strategic and military support for the apartheid regime.

Still more fundamentally, as Americans we must seek to understand government and transnational corporate relationships to other countries—the developing world and Europe—and how those relationships affect our lives, as well as those of other peoples. Continued government overt or covert military support of the South African and other such "moderate" Third World regimes contains grave dangers in the current crisis. Mobilization against the Vietnam war proved the United States citizens can help stop United States military involvement to support the repression of the people of another nation. We must now unite, again, this time to demand an end to all corporate and government support for the exploitative white-minority regimes of southern Africa.

Appendix A

An Outline for Further Research

During the Amherst conference, the participants made a number of recommendations about possible areas of further research. These suggestions are outlined here in hopes that interested individuals or groups will pursue them.*

I. Western Strategy:

A. What is South Africa's military importance to the West?

B. How valid are the arguments that South African raw materials are strategically critical?

1. What alternative technologies could be developed in lieu of buying South African raw materials?

2. Are South African deposits not unique, but merely more profitable because of forced labor?

3. What are available stockpiles in the United States of the relevant raw materials?

II. Western military presence in the Indian and Atlantic Oceans:

A. How important are the sea lanes around South Africa?

B. What naval and other shipping links does South Africa have with other countries?

C. What NATO ties does South Africa have in relation to the Simonstown naval base and/or other facilities?

D. What ties has South Africa established with Latin American nations such as Brazil, Chile and Argentina?

III. Covert operations:

A. Comparative study of covert activities by foreign countries in southern Africa, and the extent of cooperation between them.

* Compiled by Ingrid Babbs. Scholars who wish to contact others regarding research relating to specific topics may contact the co-chairpersons of the research committee of the Association of Concerned African Scholars: Professors Asa Davis (History Department, Amherst College) and Ann Seidman (Sociology Department, Brown University); or Professor Philip O'Keefe (Geography Department, Clark University).

B. Further analysis of United States and other foreign countries' covert activities in other parts of Africa.

IV. Loopholes in United States enforcement of the U.N. mandatory arms embargo:

A. To what extent have United States corporations licensed European or other affiliates to sell military-related hardware to South Africa?

B. The sale of spare parts to South Africa:

1. The sale of spare parts as a technique used by transnational firms to evade the arms embargo, and the identification of violating firms.

2. Do initial sales and exports have a contractual relationship for spare parts or for engineering or managerial personnel ("white collar" mercenaries) to maintain the system?

3. How do United States firms use technicians and spare parts to control the policies of purchasing countries?

4. Probability that military equipment is being shipped in components to South Africa.

C. The function of markets in second-hand conventional weaponry:

1. Conversion of military equipment such as cars, trucks and planes into military vehicles.

2. Refurbishing and standardization of old arms into new weaponry.

3. Investigation of customs records of exports to expose such sales.

D. Look into sales of military equipment under different classifications—i.e., "gray area" and "dual purpose" sales, such as communications systems and private airplanes—and the possibility and extent of use of such items for military purposes.

V. The transfer of military technology:

A. Its use as a bargaining tool by South Africa.

B. Implications for warfare in southern Africa and the world.

C. The implications of explicitly excluding trade and cooperation in nuclear technology from the U.N. mandatory arms embargo.

D. The importance of uranium in South Africa's policy planning for immediate and long-term markets and external relationships.

E. South Africa's uranium enrichment program.
1. Implications for South Africa's export potential.
2. Implications of the use of lasar-technology in enriching uranium;
3. Whether SASOL II is in fact related to the nuclear enrichment program, as has been widely alleged.
VI. Potential Congressional policies:
A. Requirements of export licensing.
1. How do other nations control licenses?
2. What does the application of licensing to technology exports mean to the United States economy, and to the economies of the importing countries?
B. Possibilities of extending United States law to overseas activities of U.S. individuals and/or firms.
1. What are the limits on United States anti-trust laws, affirmative action legislation, etc.?
2. How can Congress strengthen laws to end violations by United States citizens abroad (e.g. mercenaries, breaking the U.N. embargo, etc.)?
VII. United States transnational corporations:
A. The extent of the white-minority regime's reliance on United States corporate personnel accompanying technical transfer packages.
B. How many technicians come into the United States for training by U.S. corporations?
C. Case studies of the role of United States affiliates in helping to build up South Africa's military capability.
D. Impact of United States corporations' investments in South Africa on employment and working conditions in the United States and South Africa.
1. Impact on the standard of living of United States workers, including effects in terms of unemployment and nature of employment.
2. Impact on South African workers, including role of capital-intensive technology.
VIII. The function of relations to other sub-imperialist states such as Brazil, Iran and Israel:
A. Their role in providing assembly points and conduits for arms to South Africa.

B. State relations based on clientelism and trade flows.

C. The transfer of United States military technology to South Africa.

IX. The implications of trilateralism for South Africa.

X. South Africa's militarized political economy:

A. Military and counter-insurgency strategies adopted by the white minority.

1. Analysis of South African government's evolutionary strategic thinking and politics of military doctrine.

2. Transfer of military strategy from other countries, e.g. Israel's counter-insurgency experience; United States theories about urban riots and counter-insurgency strategies developed in Vietnam.

3. Relationship between South African military doctrine and equipment (purchased and deployed).

B. Types of warfare.

1. The change in theory and strategy of counter-insurgency warfare, and its implications for the white-minority regimes' strategy.

2. To what extent does the white-minority regime have a stake in turning insurgency into conventional war in order to employ its capital-intensive military capabilities?

3. Assessment of United States equipment shipped to South Africa in terms of counter-insurgency strategy.

C. Historical analysis of South Africa's capacity to produce military goods.

1. What is meant by "war" production?

2. What inputs would South Africa require to produce given quantities of specific military equipment?

D. Aspects of South Africa's internal political economy in relation to its military stability and strategy.

1. Further data on the unviability of the Bantustans.

2. What is the (conscious and unconscious) role of United States transnational corporations in attempting to create a black middle class in South Africa?

3. What is the role of "non-political" trade unions, as encouraged by the AFL-CIO in South Africa?

Appendix B

The U.N. Embargo Resolutions

The following resolution, adopted by the U.N. Security Council on August 7, 1963, established the voluntary arms embargo on South Africa:

The Security Council,

Having considered the question of race conflict in South Africa resulting from the policies of *apartheid* of the Government of the Republic of South Africa, as submitted by the thirty-two African Member States,

Recalling the Security Council resolution of 1 April 1960,

Noting with appreciation the interim reports adopted on 6 May and 16 July 1963 by the Special Committee on the Policies of *Apartheid* of the Government of the Republic of South Africa,

Noting with concern the recent arms build-up by the Government of South Africa, some of which arms are being used in furtherance of that Government's racial policies,

Regretting that some States are indirectly providing encouragement in various ways to the Government of South Africa to perpetuate, by force, its policy of *apartheid*,

Regretting the failure of the Government of South Africa to accept the invitation of the Security Council to delegate a representative to appear before it,

Being convinced that the situation in South Africa is seriously disturbing international peace and security,

1. *Strongly deprecates* the policies of South Africa in its perpetuation of racial discrimination as being inconsistent with the principles contained in the Charter of the United Nations and contrary to its obligations as a Member State of the United Nations;

2. *Calls upon* the Government of South Africa to abandon the policies of *apartheid* and discrimination as called for in the Security Council resolution of 1 April 1960, and to liberate all persons imprisoned, interned or subjected to other restrictions for having opposed the policy of *apartheid*;

3. *Solemnly calls upon* all States to cease forthwith the sale and shipment of arms, ammunition of all types and military vehicles to South Africa;

4. *Requests* the Secretary-General to keep the situation in South Africa under observation and to report to the Security Council by 30 October 1963.

The following resolution, passed by the U.N. Security Concil on November 4, 1977, established the mandatory arms embargo against South Africa:

The Security Council,

Recalling its resolution 392 (1976) strongly condemning the South African Government for its resort to massive violence against and killings of the African people, including schoolchildren and students and others opposing racial discrimination, and calling upon that Government urgently to end violence against the African people and take urgent steps to eliminate *apartheid* and racial discrimination,

Recognizing that the military build-up and persistent acts of aggression by South Africa against the neighbouring States seriously disturb the security of those States,

Further recognizing that the existing arms embargo must be strengthened and universally applied, without any reservations or qualifications whatsoever, in order to prevent a further aggravation of the grave situation in South Africa,

Taking note of the Lagos Declaration for Action against *Apartheid* (S/12426),

Gravely concerned that South Africa is at the threshold of producing nuclear weapons,

Strongly condemning the South African Government for its acts of repression, its defiant continuance of the system of *apartheid* and its attacks against neighboring independent States,

Considering that the policies and acts of the South African Government are fraught with danger to international peace and security,

Recalling its resolution 181 (1963) and other resolutions concerning a voluntary arms embargo against South Africa,

Convinced that a mandatory arms embargo needs to be universally applied against South Africa in the first instance,

Acting therefore under Chapter VII of the Charter of the United Nations,

1. *Determines*, having regard to the policies and acts of the South African Government, that the acquisition by South Africa of arms and related materiel constitutes a threat to the maintenance of international peace and security;

2. *Decides* that all States shall cease forthwith any provision to South Africa of arms and related materiel of all types, including the sale or transfer of weapons and ammunition, military vehicles and equipment, paramilitary police equipment, and spare parts for the aforementioned, and shall cease as well the provision of all types of equipment and supplies, and grants of licensing arrangements for the manufacture or maintenance of the aforementioned;

3. *Calls* on all States to review, having regard to the objectives of this resolution, all existing contractual arrangements with and licences granted to South Africa relating to the manufacture and maintenance of arms, ammunition of all types and military equipment and vehicles, with a view to terminating them;

4. *Further decides* that all States shall refrain from any co-operation with South Africa in the manufacture and development of nuclear weapons;

5. *Calls upon* all States, including States non-members of the United Nations, to act strictly in accordance with the provisions of this resolution;

6. *Requests* the Secretary-General to report to the Council on the progress of the implementation of this resolution, the first report to be submitted not later than 1 May 1978;

7. *Decides* to keep this item on its agenda for further action, as appropriate, in the light of developments.

Appendix C

Letter from the Chairpersons of the Association of Concerned African Scholars to President Carter

June 15, 1978

Dear Mr. President,

The Association of Concerned African Scholars is dismayed by increasing United States intervention in opposition to popular forces in southern Africa, and takes issue with the rhetoric used to justify such intervention, which in our view directs attention away from the real issues of African liberation and human rights.

The recent events in Shaba (Zaire) as well as the continuing guerrilla warfare in Zimbabwe and Namibia, are part of a single picture, which is the struggle to establish democratic, popular governments throughout southern Africa, a struggle which entered its accelerated phase in 1974 with the overthrow of Portugal's fascist regime. This struggle was launched by Africans and has been conducted by Africans. Non-African countries— whether they be the United States, the USSR, France or Cuba— are judged in Africa by the position they take on this struggle.

To make the Cubans a bogeyman deflects American public opinion from seeing that the primary problem is the continuing oppression of the Black majority of the population in South Africa, Zimbabwe, Namibia—and in Zaire. The question is rather whether the United States, Cuba, or any other particular state is ready to support the African liberation movements or is instead trying to stymie their efforts, and support their opponents.

The United States government is not well placed to complain about presumed Cuban indirect support for the FNLC in Zaire, when the United States government supported coups by Mobutu against legally constituted regimes in 1960 and 1965—ten years before Cuban soldiers were invited into Angola. In any case, thus far, the U.S. government has declined to make available to the public its evidence for the Cuban involvement in Shaba, and members of the Senate Foreign Relations Committee who have seen the "evidence" evince skepticism as to its worth. What is not in doubt is that the U.S. has been sending Mobutu weapons, flying in troops from other countries to aid him, and coordinating efforts of various Western powers to support the Mobutu government.

Similarly, the United States government is not well-placed to complain about an Angolan foreign policy geared primarily to the liberation of southern Africa. The United States government persistently opposed the MPLA in Angola since 1961—supporting both the Portuguese colonial regime and its political rivals within Angola. Recent evidence, offered by the former head of the CIA team in Angola, John Stockwell, has demonstrated that the U.S. appropriated large sums of money to oust the MPLA *before* there were any Cuban troops. The U.S. encouraged South African and Zairian troops to invade Angola to overthrow its government, and alone among the major powers of the world does not have diplomatic relations with Angola.

We further take issue with the racist way in which our policy is formulated. We note that Europeans were killed in Kolwezi but not Africans (and neglect to point out that the Zairian army rather than the FNLC did much of this killing). We encourage rescue missions for whites but when, two weeks earlier, South African forces invaded Angola and killed 604 Namibians (including women and children) we did not speak of rescue missions. We organized along with the former colonial powers a meeting in Paris to decide issues such as the formation of an African military force and invited not one African state to that meeting.

The real problem in southern Africa is the existence of undemocratic regimes in these areas—starting with South Africa —and those external forces which sustain them. The real danger is that the United States has started once again on a path of involvement in economic, political and military aid to anti-popular, anti-democratic forces.

The interests of the American people do not lie in such involvement. This is the path of war, not peace; of oppression and repression (abroad and at home) and not of human rights and liberty; of U.S. government expenditures leading to hyperinflation and not economic revitalization; of antagonism to popular forces throughout Africa rather than friendship with them.

African peoples are kindred to a substantial portion of the U.S. population just as much as they are to the Cuban population. These historic social ties should create a genuine understanding of and support for liberation forces in Africa. Cuba's rising prestige throughout Africa results from its support for such forces. The foreign policy of the United States is now instead being linked to minority privilege in the South.

We call on the American people, through your leadership, Mr. President, to join *with* popular forces in southern Africa. Their struggle for liberty is our struggle for liberty. To support them is to fulfill our ideals and to advance the long-term interests of our citizens.

Sincerely yours,

Prof. James F. Turner   *Prof. Immanuel Wallerstein*
(Cornell University)   *(SUNY/Binghamton)*
Co-chairpersons, Association of Concerned African Scholars

Appendix D

The following extract from a 28-page Contingency Planning Report by General Motors South Africa excerpts the most relevant sections. More extensive extracts from the memo were reprinted in *Southern Africa* in June, 1978.

Emphasis is added, throughout.

General Motors South Africa (Pty.) Limited
Inter-Office Memorandum

To: Mr. D. Martin, Jr.
From: L.H. Wilking
Date: 20 July, 1977
Subject: *Contingency Planning—GM South Africa*

...We have summarised the potential situations which might arise and the proposed action by the plant, without of course the benefit of any experience of such conditions.

No doubt the type of civil unrest experienced in the U.S. comes to mind in this context, but as you are well aware, the free mobility of dissidents and the ability to organise large number of non-whites and generate action is not the same in South Africa as in the U.S....law enforcement action is pretty fast and aims at confining disturbances to residential areas.

To minimise detrimental effect on employee morale and to avoid giving the impression that we expect these things to happen, all preparatory work has been carried out quietly and discreetly.

L.H. Wilking

Related Assumptions

It is assumed that almost 100% of White employment at GMSA would not be party to creating or stimulating civil unrest and that the population groups involved would be African and Coloured...

Comments

Under normal conditions, the motor manufacturing and assembly industry is one of the largest in the country with considerable economic weight. The recent downswing has clearly indicated the extent to which it is affected by declining market demand. While there is little indication as yet that the Government may prescribe some course of action to the industry, it is almost certain that should economic conditions decline sufficiently far, there could be a directive issued on model build by various companies—first to preserve the capability of building vehicles and secondly, *to ensure sources of supply in the case of greater emergency requirements...*

Thus, through a series of events, not necessarily affecting the economy in the short term, GMSA could find itself obliged to cease doing business and obtaining supplies, know-how and other forms of assistance from its U.S. based parent corporation. Options open at such a time would be to either close the Plant down and "mothball" it or dispose of the assets to a local buyer.

Action by the local Government in terms of any or all of a series of possibilities arising from conditions of social unrest or further economic decline can be seen broadly as follows:

(a) on the basis of National key point status, assume responsibility for guarding premises, training plant personnel for military type duties and upgrading of security facilities to a specified level.

(b) exercise a measure of control over facilities to be used to meet imposed requirements, e.g. trucks and other commercial vehicles, passenger or modified passenger cars and possibly other wheeled, non-fighting vehicles such as trailers and supply or medical units.

(c) assume responsibility for assigning scarce categories of manpower and possibly crash training of lesser skilled trades.

(d) impose requirements with regard to security rating of employees, with particular reference to foreign nationals employed in the industry.

(e) screening of employees to eliminate possibility of sabotage. These conditions would amount to virtually having the South African Goverment as a partner and poses the question as to whether this situation would be acceptable to the Corporation and/or international community.

It is possible that such a situation might be seen from the Government viewpoint as an opportunity for the Industrial

Development Corporation [a parastatal] to be used to cover this "joint venture" approach.

Based on the philosophy of the central government of developing, since the early 1960's, the local motor vehicle manufacturing and assembly capability through the introduction of the local content programme, it would be fair to assume that *under conditions of National emergency the major elements of this industry would be taken over by an arm of the Ministry of Defense (Armscor?)* which would completely regulate output and co-ordinate it within the entire industrial effort.

***

In assessing the potential effects and probability of serious civil unrest developing in the Port Elizabeth area and formulating contingency plans, the following factors have been taken into consideration...

2. Assessment of the in-plant situation indicates that the risk of open unrest among employees on the premises is low. *The White employee group would not be party to such action and could be relied upon to take action to contain it and/or isolate any outbreak* pending arrival of law enforcement authorities...

Deterioration of Business Conditions

Because of the wide geographic spread of principal centres in South Africa, it is unlikely that successful co-ordination of civil unrest could be achieved to the point where it coud cripple business on a short term or predetermined timing basis. The cumulative effect of such action, however, could in time severely depress the economy.

The more likely pattern of events might be:

(a) Gradual enforced reduction in economic activity through trade recession and financial stringency affecting ability to maintain job opportunities.

Business could and in many cases would reach a point of non-viability, at which time the only options would be to cease operation, disperse material and human resources and mothball facilities or go into liquidation.

(b) There is a possibility in the interim period that U.S. based companies might incure the "annoyance" of the South African Government by apparently failing to meet their (the government's) view of support from local enterprises.

GM South African has, for example, *been requested to supply vehicles such as the K25, K31, 4x4 LUV for Defence Force purposes, and refusal to offer such might be interpreted as reflecting doubt on the motive of the Company.*

Such interpretation or a variation thereof could lead to direct loss of other government business and seriously affect GM South African's share of the vehicle market and very likely threaten its viability.

Alternatively, should international political issues compound the situation postulated, it is within the bonds [*sic*] of possibility that the Government might request the GM South African be shut down.

Declared National Emergency:

In the event that a National emergency is declared, there is little doubt that control of GM South African's facilities, already designated a National key Point industry, *would be taken over by an arm of the Ministry of Defence, and its production capabilities integrated into the national industrial effort. It is highly likely that in a developing situation affecting the national stability and maintenance of law and order, some measure of government direction be introduced ahead of time.*

At the time of declaration of a national emergency (state of war), if not before, the question of continuing American participation in South African business may well have been resolved and operating control of the GM South African facility may be vested in South African nationals.

At the point when government takes action in terms of the Civil Defence Act No. 39 of 1966, such as in the form of placing a military presence on the property, it is understood at this time that all aspects of security will fall under their control. Plant management and personnel will have specific requirements to meet and there will undoubtedly be additional security facilities requested.

The full implications of this eventuality cannot be assessed at this time.

Bibliography

Background on South Africa:

Benson, Mary, *The Struggle for a Birthright* (Harmondsworth: Penguin, 1966). History of the ANC (S.A.).

Bunting, Brian, *Rise of the South African Reich* (Harmondsworth: Penguin, 1970). Details the development of apartheid.

Davenport, T.R.H., *South Africa, A Modern History* (Cambridge: Cambridge University Press, 1977). A scholarly history of South Africa over the past 200 years.

Davidson, B., Slovo, J., and Wilkinson, A., *Southern Africa: The New Politics of Revolution* (Harmondworth: Penguin, 1976). Articles on Angola, South Africa and Zimbabwe today.

Desmond, Father C., *The Discarded People* (Harmondsworth: Penguin, 1971). An eyewitness account of the effects of the Bantustan system.

First, R., Gurney, C., and Steele, J., *The South African Connection, Western Investment in Apartheid* (London: Maurice Temple Smith, 1973).

Houghton, D.H., *The South African Economy* (Cape Town: Oxford University Press, 1973). A traditional economic overview.

Palmer, R., and Parsons, Q.N., eds., *Roots of Rural Poverty in Southern Africa* (Berkeley: University of California, 1977). Histories of southern-central Africa; the effects of colonialism on African society.

Johnstone, Frederick A., *Class, Race and Gold* (London: Routledge and Kegan Paul, 1976). The relationship between the need for a labor force on the gold mines and the development of apartheid.

Kaplan, I., et. al., *Area Handbook for the Republic of South Africa* (Washington, D.C.: U.S. Government Printing Office, 1973). A traditional survey of the country's resources, history and politics.

Makgetla, Neva, and Seidman, Ann, *Activity of Transnational Corporations in South Africa* (New York: U.N. Unit Against Apartheid, 1978).

Mandela, Nelson, *No Easy Walk to Freedom* (London: Heinemann African Writers Series, 1965). A collection by the president of the African National Congress of South Africa, who is presently in jail on Robben Island.

Nolutshungu, S.C., *South Africa in Africa* (Manchester: Manchester University Press, 1974). Discusses the economic and political relationships between South Africa and independent Africa.

Seidman, Ann, "Post-World War II Imperialism in Africa: A Marxist Perspective," in *Journal of Southern African Studies* (Maryland), II.4 (October 1977). The role of the United States, Japanese and Western European transnational corporations in South Africa in the context of Africa as a whole.

Seidman, Ann, and Seidman, Neva, *South Africa and U.S. Multinational Corporations* (Westport, Conn.: Lawrence Hill, 1978, and Dar-es-Salaam: Tanzanian Publishing House, 1977). The support of transnational corporations based in the U.S. for South Africa and South African imperialism in southern Africa.

Seidman, Judy A., *Ba Ye Zwa* (Boston: South End, 1977). The history, culture and struggle for freedom in South Africa, portrayed with text, poetry and pictures.

Simons, H.J. and R.E., *Class and Colour in South Africa, 1850-1950* (Harmondsworth: Penguin, 1970). The origins of apartheid and resistance in South Africa.

U.N. Unit Against Apartheid, *Notes and Documents* (New York: United Nations). A series of in-depth articles about various aspects of apartheid, including foreign investment, treatment of workers and political prisoners, the Bantustans, etc.

U.S. Senate, Committee on Foreign Relations, Subcommittee on African Affairs, Report on U.S. Corporate Investment in South Africa (Washington, D.C.: U.S. Government Printers, 1977). Includes a report on U.S. banks' activities in South Africa and results of a survey on the behavior of U.S. transnational corporations in that country.

——Hearings on "U.S. corporate investment in South Africa," October 1976 (Washington, D.C.: U.S. Government Printing Office, 1976). Testimony by corporations and individuals on the role of U.S. investors in South Africa.

Periodicals

Financial Mail (Johannesburg). South Africa's leading financial journal; weekly

African Communist (London). Marxist analysis, focusing on South Africa. Journal of the SACP; quarterly.

Anti-Apartheid News (London) Digest of southern African news, emphasis on resistance. Journal of the Anti-Apartheid Movement; monthly.

Informationsdienst sudliches afrika (Bonn) Articles on FRG involvement in southern Africa. Journal of Informationstelle sudliches afrika; monthly

Journal of Southern African Studies (Maryland). Scholarly articles on southern Africa. Journal of Southern African Research Association quarterly.

Sechaba (Tanzania). Articles on South Africa, international opposition to apartheid, and news digest. Journal of the ANC (S.A.); quarterly.

South African Digest (Pretoria) News digest put out by the white-minority regime. Published by South African Department of Information; weekly.

Southern Africa (New York). Comprehensive review of current events in South Africa, with longer articles on articles of especial interest, especially to the United States.

General Military Background

Aviation Advisory Services, *International Military Aircraft and Aviation Directory* (Essex: 1970 and 1976)

Booth, R., *The Armed Forces of African States* (London: IISS, 1970)

Burchett, W., and Roebuck, D., *The Whores of War: Mercenaries Today* (New York: Penguin Books, 1976)

Cline, R.S., *World Power Assessment* (Boulder, Colo.: Westview Press, 1975)

Cohen, B., and El-Khawas, M., eds., *The Kissinger Study of Southern Africa: NSSM 39* (Connecticut: Lawrence Hill, 1975)

Defense and Foreign Affairs Handbook, 1976-'77 (Washington, D.C., and London, 1977)

Defense Marketing Service, "South African Force Structure," in *Foreign Military Markets* (Conn.: 1976)

Enloe, C., *Police, Military and Ethnicity* (New Jersey: Transaction Books, forthcoming)

Grundy, K.W., *Defense Legislation and Communal Politics* (Ohio: Ohio University Center for International Studies, 1978)

International Institute for Strategic Studies, *The Military Balance, 1977-'78* (London: IISS, 1977)

Investor Responsibility Research Center, *Foreign Arms Sales* (Washington, D.C.: 1978)

Jane's All the World's Ships (London)

Jane's Weapon's Systems (London)

T.N. Duprey and Associates, *Almanac of World Military Power* (New York: 1974)

Wolfe, P. and Locke, H., *Register of Arms Production in Developing Countries* (Hamburg: Arbeitsgruppe "Rustung und Unterentwicklung," March 1977)

Periodicals

Armed Forces Journal International (Washington, D.C.) Information about U.S. and overseas military, also major arms sales

International Defense (Washington, D.C.) Information on United States and overseas military; also on military technology and defense industry news

Paratus (Pretoria) South African military magazine; published by the South African Defense Force.

Survival (London) Miscellaneous military and strategic analyses. Journal of the International Institute for Strategic Studies

Foreign Military and Strategic Support For Apartheid

African National Congress of South Africa, *Conspiracy to Arm Apartheid Continues: FRG-SA Collaboration* (Bonn: Progress Dritte-Welt, 1977)

Ahmad, B., *South Africa's Military Establishment* (New York: U.N. Unit on Apartheid, December 1972)

Baker, P.H., "South Africa's Strategic Vulnerabilities: The 'Citadel Assumption' Revisited," in *African Studies Review*, XX.2 (September 1977)

Corporate Information Center, World Council of Churches, *The Oil Conspiracy* (New York: 1977)

Gervasi, S., "What Arms Embargo?" in *Southern Africa* (New York) X.6 (August 1977)

Groesbeck, W.A., "The Transkei—Key to U.S. Naval Strategy in the Indian Ocean," in *Military Review* (Washington), June 1976

Halliday, F., "British Mercenaries and Counter-Insurgency," in *Race and Class* (London), XIX.2 (Autumn, 1977)

Lake, A., *The 'Tar Baby' Option: American Policy Toward Southern Rhodesia* (New York: Columbia University Press, 1976)

Minty, A.S., *South Africa's Defense Strategy* (London: Anti-Apartheid Movement, 1969)

Murapa, R., "A Global Perspective of the Political Economy of U.S. Policy Towards Southern Africa," in *Journal of Southern African Affairs* (Maryland), II.1 (January 1977)

Republic of South Africa, Department of Defense, *White Paper on Defense, 1977* (Pretoria: government Printer, 1977)

Royal United Service Institute for Defense Studies, *The Security of the Southern Oceans—Southern Africa the Key: Report of a Seminar, 16 February, 1972* (London: The Institute, 1972)

Spence, J.E., "Nuclear Weapons and South Africa," in Laros, J., and Lawrence, R.M., eds., *Nuclear Proliferation: Stage II* (forthcoming)

——*The Strategic Significance of Southern Africa* (London: Royal United Services Institute, 1970)

Stockwell, J., *In Search of Enemies—A CIA Story* (New York: Norton, 1978)

U.N. Committee Against Apartheid, Proceedings of Seminar on Effectiveness of the U.N. Embargo on Arms Sales to South Africa, May 30, 1978; to be published.

U.S. House of Representatives, Committee on Foreign Affairs, Subcommittee on Africa, Hearings on "Implementation of the U.S. Arms Embargo (Against Portugal and South Africa) and Related Issues" (Washington, D.C.: Government Printing Office, 1973)

Index

A

ACAS, see Association of Concerned African Scholars.
ACDA, see Arms Control and Disarmament Agency
Aden, 61
Ad Hoc Monitoring Group on South Africa, 242
Adoula, Cyrille, 94-5
advanced technology and the South African military market, 200-201
advertisers for mercenaries, 126-7
Advocaat, see Project Advocaat
AEG-Telefunken, 209, 182-3, 211
Aermacchi, 163
Africa, U.S. investment in, 212-3; French in, 68-9; importance to U.S., 45; Kissinger in, 45; response to Carter Administration, 48-9
African American Labour Center, 92
African states' conference in Paris, 68
African National Congress of South Africa, 23ff., 33fn., 180; revelations about FRG role in South Africa, 174, 182-3
Africans in Rhodesian military, 114, 117-8
Agusta, 167
Air Commandos (South Africa), 164
aircraft sales: after mandatory embargo, 234fn.; as dual-purpose good, 229-33; capabilities of, 160-1; Carter Administration and, 168-70; "civilian" aircraft, 159-61, 163-6; Department of State on, 159-60, 160; as dual purpose export, 229-33; Nixon Administration and, 160; to Portugal, 43, 92; to South Africa, 156, 158ff., 230, 231, 235, 237; South African Air Force and, 143, 144, 146, 158-9
Allis Chalmers, 188, 210
Alouette helicopters, 156
Alsthom, 211, 220
American Committee on Africa, 244
Amoco, 212
Angleton, James, 91
Anglo-American proposals on Rhodesia/Zimbabwe, 50-1, 52, 116
Anglo-Boer War, 21
Angola, 5, 8, 18, 41-2, 201, 257; Carter Administration and, 52, 55, 257, and Andrew Young on, 47-9; CIA and, 82, 83, 84, 87, 90, 91, 96, 109-113, 135; Ford Administration and, 44; mercenaries in, 112; Nixon Administration and, 41-2; South African attacks on, 136, 246, and U.S. aircraft, 160, 161; and Saudi Arabia, 52. See also, Frontline States.
anti-Sovietism, 11-2, 52, 55ff., 66, 256ff.
anti-Vietnam War movement, 9
apartheid, 22; and Namibia, 33
Argentina, 81, 82, 249
Armed Forces Journal International, 203
Armed Forces of the World, 134
arms control, 64ff.
Arms Control and Disarmament Administration (ACDA), 64, 65-6, 224, 228
Arms embargo on South Africa, 4, 157-8, 223; and nuclear technology, 4, 178; U.S. enforcement of, 134ff., 217ff., 231-5, 240-1. See also, mandatory arms embargo; voluntary arms embargo.
Arms Export Control Act, 228-9
Arms sales to South Africa, 41-2, 136-7, 142, 244-5. See also aircraft, shotguns, ARMSCOR, 203
Arsenal of Democracy, 134
Association of Concerned African Scholars (ACAS), 249, 256-8
Atlas Aircraft, 162-3
Atomic Energy Board (South Africa), 180-181fn., 210, 211
Atomic Energy Commission (U.S.), 210-1
auto industry, 200, 204, 206ff.
Azores agreement, 42-3

B

Badger Company, 212
Baker-nun optical tracking station, 176
Banes, Howard T., 98
banks, see transnational banks
Bank of America, 214, 215-6; British affiliate, 215-6; and South Africa's foreign debt, 217
Bantu Education, 22
Bantustans, 22
Barclays, 216
Barnaby, Frank, 181-2
Becker, Erwin, 174
Beckman Instruments, 188

267

Bedrijven Bredero, 217
Belgium, and Zaire, 53-4, 58-9, 95. See also, France, NATO, Shaba and Zaire.
Bell, 167
Berbera (Somalia), 73
Biko, Steve, 3-4, 178
Binza group, 93-5
Bissell, Richard, 85
Botha, R.F., 173, 175
Botswana, 8, 18, 231, 246
Bravia, 154
Brazil, 7, 78, 245-6, 249, 251; and SATO, 78
Britain, see Great Britain
British South Africa Company, 26, 27ff.
Brown, Harold, 10fn., 60, 65
Brown, Maj. Robert K., 126-7
Brown Boveri and Company, 211
Brzezinski, Zbigniew, 10fn., 54-5, 83, 191-2
Bureau of African Affairs, 224
Bureau for International Organizations, 224
Bureau of Political-Military Affairs, 224
Bureau of State Security (BOSS), 89, 90, 100
Burchett, Wilfred, 112
Burundi, 92
Byrd Amendment, 42, 45, 50

C

Cactus missile system, 181-2
Cadillac Gage, 154
Caltex, 213-4. See also, oil, Standard Oil of California, Texaco
campaigns against loans to South Africa, 220
capabilities of U.S. planes in SAAF, 160-1, 162-3, 164-5, 167-8, 223
Carter, President James, 10fn., 65, 66, 158, 175, 176, 192; on U.S. investment, 48, 198
Carter Administration, 233; anti-Soviet-ism of, 52ff.; Indian Ocean and, 65ff., 74-5; and Namibia, 51-2; and Rhodesia/ Zimbabwe, 49-51; and South African nuclear capability, 180ff.; and southern Africa, 47ff.; and strike force, 74-5; and trilateralism, 10ff. See also, Departments of State, Commerce and Justice; U.S. Government; Cyrus Vance; Andrew Young.

Central African Federation, 29
Central Intelligence Agency (CIA), 45, 82-104; decision-making structure, 84-88; links with other intelligence agencies, 88-92; and Africa Division, 88-9; low-level covert operations, 92-3; and Angola, 44, 82, 83, 84, 87, 90-103, 125, 257; and Con-go (Zaire), 82, 83, 84, 93-7, 101, 103, 257; and Ghana, 82, 84, 96, 97-8; Diego Garcia, 63-4; and mercenary recruit-ment, 128
Cessna, 161, 236, 238 fn.; sale to Rhodesia, 167-8; sale to South Africa, 165-6, 235-6
Chad, 68
Chase Manhattan Bank, 214, 215, 217 (table)
cheap labor system: in Namibia, 23; in Rhodesia, 27ff.; in South Africa, 22ff.
chemicals industry, 204
Chevron-Regent, 212
Chile, 87
chrome, 10 fn., 42, 48
Chrysler, 206, 208; see also auto industry
Church, Senator Frank, 65
civilian aircraft sales, see aircraft sales
Citibank (formerly First National City Bank of New York), 214-5, 216
Collins, Congresswoman Cardiss, 233, 237
Collins Bill, 159, 237
Colt Industries, 154, 238-9
Commerce Department, see Department of Commerce
computers, 189, 210, 211
Congo (Kinshasa), see Zaire
Congressional Black Caucus, 190, 191; Brzezinski letter to, 191-2
corporate involvement in South Africa, see transnational corporations and individu-al companies
covert activities, 82-104; see also Central Intelligence Agency
Creusot Loire Group, 211
crisis in West, 10-11
Cuba, 8, 11, 45, 118, 256ff.; and Carter Administration, 52, 55ff., 66, 85, 256ff.; CIA activities in relation to, 85, 87, 88; and Angola, 103

Cunene Dam, 177

D

Davis, Jennifer, 164
Defense and Foreign Affairs Handbook,
1976-'77, 134
Defense Department, see Department of
Defense
definition of mercenarization, 111
Department of Agriculture, 222-3
Department of Commerce, 225, 227, 231,
243; and dual purpose exports, 229-30;
and Export Administration Act, 226-7,
231, 237; and export of shotguns to South
Africa, 240; and Mutual Security Act,
225-6. See also, Carter Administration,
Nixon Administration, U.S. government.
Department of Defense, 61-2, 63, 65, 86-7,
226 fn., 227, 230
Department of Justice, 238
Department of State, 65, 225-6, 227, 228;
and aircraft sales, 159-60, 162, 165, 169,
230, 237; and mandatory embargo, 235,
236-7; and mercenaries, 127; and private
corporations' violations, 168; and voluntary embargo, 133-4, 139, 154, 223, 220.
See also Carter, Ford or Nixon Administration; U.S. government.
Devlin, Lawrence, 93
Diego Garcia, 61-4, 65, 66
Direccao Geral de Seguranca (DGS), 90-1,
99, 100
Distribution of petroleum in southern Africa, 213; see also oil and individual companies.
Downey, Congressman Thomas, 237
draft: in Rhodesia, 118; in South Africa,
121-2; see manpower shortage, white-
collar mercenaries.
dual-purpose goods, 198, 223, 222-3, 226,
231. See also gray area goods.
dual-utility goods, 223. See also gray-area
goods.
Dutch East India Company, 20
Dutch settlement of South Africa, 20

E

EEC, see European Economic Community
economic sanctions: on South Africa, 197-
8, 230; on Rhodesia, 8, 51, 213

Ecuador, CIA in, 84-5
Edlow International, 188
education in South Africa, 22
electrical equipment, 204, 208; see also
individual companies
electronics, 200, 208; see also computers,
individual companies
embargo enforcement machinery, 223
emigration from Rhodesia, 117
Energy Research and Development Administration (U.S.), 188-9
England, see Great Britain
enriched uranium, 174, 188, 189-90, 211.
See also, uranium enrichment process.
escape clause in voluntary embargo, 139,
228-9
ESCOM, 189-90, 208-9
Esselen Park radio tracking station, 176
Esso, 212. See also Exxon.
Ethiopia, 92
Ethiopian-Somali war, 54-5
ethnic divisions among whites in South Africa, 119
Eurodollar market, 6
Europe, 6, 8; see also EEC, Western gov-
ernments, NATO, and individual coun-
tries.
European Economic Community, 193
Ex-Im Bank, see Export-Import Bank
Export Administration Act, 226-7, 229
Export-Import Bank (Ex-Im Bank), 43,
164-5, 218
export licenses for Namibia and South Af-
rica, 230-1
export of aircraft, see aircraft
export of shotguns, see shotguns
extension of draft in Rhodesia, 118; in
South Africa, 120-1
Exxon, 212, 213

F

Federal Republic of Germany (FRG), 6-7,
181-2, 183; and South African nuclear
power, 172-3, 174; transnational corporations from, 6-7, 121-2, 161, 181, 212. See
also, AEG-Telefunken, Projekt Advocaat, Siemens, NATO.
First National City Bank of New York, see
Citibank

Fluor Corporation, 212

FMC Corporation, 154, 167

FNLA, 44, 87, 100, 103, 256ff. See also Holden Roberto.

Ford Administration, 41, 44. See also Kissinger, Department of State

Ford Corporation, 206, 208. See also auto industry.

Foreign Affairs Committee, U.S. Senate, 225, 228

Foreign debt of South Africa, 214, 216-8; estimates of, 220-1

foreign investment, 7, 9, 245-7; in Shaba, 54; in South Africa, 7, 10, 200, 204

foreign mercenaries in Rhodesia, 116-8; see also manpower shortages, white-collar mercenaries

Forty Committee, see National Security Council

Foxboro Corporation, 201

Framatome, 174, 211. See also Westinghouse.

France, 6-7, 8 fn., 80, 137, 141ff., 145-7, 181-2, 197, 212, 234; and independent Africa, 52, 53-4, 58-9, 68-9, 256; and South African nuclear power, 172, 173-4, 180, 181-2, 211, 246; intelligence agency (SDECE) in Africa, 10, 15, 99, 102. See also Cactus missile system, Europe, Framatome and other companies, NATO.

FRG, see Federal Republic of Germany

Front for the Liberation of Angola, see FNLA

Front for the Liberation of the Enclave of Cabinda (FLEC), 99

Frontline States, 18, 47, 51. See also Angola, Botswana, Mozambique, Tanzania, Zambia.

Further research, 16-7; Chapter 12.

G

G.E., see General Electric

General Aircraft Manufacturers Association, 235

General Electric, 43, 208-9; and Koeberg nuclear station, 188, 211; and AEG-Telefunken, 209. See also electrical industry.

General Motors, 206-7; secret memorandum, 207, 259ff.

German colonization of Namibia, 31-2

Germany, Federal Republic of, see Federal Republic of Germany

Gervasi, Sean, testimony on violations of embargo, 136ff.

Ghana and the CIA, 82, 84, 97-8

Glen, Senator John, 190

"gray area" sales, 224, 225, 235, 236

Great Britain, 6-7, 61, 79-81, 141ff., 145-7, 197, 212, 234; and CIA, 88-92; and the Indian Ocean, 61, 68, 80, 81, 82; and South African nuclear program, 164-5, 172; and southern African history, 20ff.; and United States corporations affiliates, 6, 214-6. See Europe, NATO, Western governments.

Green Berets, 97

Great Trek, 21

Grindlays Bank, 214-5

gulf General Atomic, 188

Guatemala and the CIA, 85

Guevara, Che, in Africa, 96

Guinea, 98

Gulf General Atomic, 188

Gulf Oil, 49, 188, 212

H

Halperin, Morton, 88

helicopter sales to South Africa, 227; see also aircraft

Helms, Richard, 89

Hill Samuels, 214

Holden Roberto, 44, 91, 99, 100, 102

Honeywell, 212

Humphrey, Senator Hubert, 65

I

IAEA, see International Atomic Energy Association

IBM, 189-90, 210, 211, 231

ICLEF, 210

illegal arms sales in southern Africa, 166-7. See also Colt, Olin, Winchester, aircraft, shotguns.

Imports and South Africa's military build-up, 140-1. See also nuclear power.

Indian Ocean, 61ff.; arms control and,

64-6; Soviet presence in, 70ff.; U.S. allies in, 61ff., 66-9; U.S. presence in, 61ff., 64, 74-5; and U.S. strike force, 74-5
Indochina War, 111. See also Vietnam.
INFA, see International Nuclear Fuel Authority.
Ingenieursbureau Comprimo, 211
"internal settlement," so-called, 8, 51, 52, 117-8
International Atomic Energy Association, 191
International Business Machines, see IBM
International Institute for Strategic Studies (IISS), 142ff., 158-9, 202, 236. See The Military Balance.
International Nuclear Fuel Authority (INFA), 190
International Relations Committee, 225, 226
International Telephone and Telegraph, see ITT
Iran, 7, 68, 85, 251; relations with South Africa, 8, 78, 80, 199, 213, 245-6
Iscor, 8
Israel, 7, 64, 70, 245-6, 251; and mandatory embargo, 184; and South Africa, 8, 182, 199; intelligence service in Africa, 91-2; in Congo (Kinshasa), 96
Italy, 145-7
ITT, 208

J

Jane's Weapons Systems, 134
Japan, 6-7, 8
Jericho missile system, 182, 184
J.L. Clarke, 216
Johnson, President Lyndon Baines, 91

K

Kalahari Desert nuclear testing station, 176, 185-6, 210. See also South African nuclear program.
Katzenbach, Nicholas, 220
Kennedy, President John, 91
Kennedy, Senator Edward, 65
Kenya, 64
Kerr-McGee, 188
Khoi-Khoi, 20
Kissinger, Henry, 39, 41, 44-5; initiative on

Rhodesia, 49-50; strategy in southern Africa, 45-7; and the CIA, 101, 102
Kleinwort Benson, 215-6
Kleinwort Benson Lonsdale, 215-6
Kodak, 231
Koeberg nuclear station, 177, 188, 199-200, 211
Koor Group (Israel), 8
Kraftwerkunion, 211

L

Lagos conference on apartheid, 178
Lamprecht, Maj. Nick, 127
land reservation: in Namibia, 31, 32; in Rhodesia, 28; in South Africa, 22. See also apartheid, Bantustans, cheap labor system.
Laos, 101-2
League of Nations, 32-3
legal obligations under mandatory embargo, 234-5 fn.
Lesotho, 233, 246
Lewis, William H., 133-4
Lindau and Harz Group, 181
loans to South Africa, 214, 216-7; participation by bank (table), 217. See also Export-Import Bank, transnational banks, foreign debt.
Lobengula, Chief, 26
Locke and Wulfe, 198-200
Lockheed, 160, 163, 167
Lumumba, Patrice, 93, 94, 95-6
Lycoming aircraft engines, 162; see also aircraft

M

Machel, President Samora, 47
machinery industry, 204
major weapons systems in use in South Africa, 143-4 (table); 153-4
Malan, Prime Minister, 20
Malawi, 29
manpower shortage of minority regimes, 112ff., 118-9, 204, 210. See also mercenarization; white-collar mercenaries.
Mansfield, Senator Michael, 174
mandatory embargo (1977), 135, 197, 233-4, 244-5; Carter Administration and, 4, 158; nuclear technology and, 4; obliga-

tions under, 217-8, 230-1 fn.; U.N. resolution, 254-5; transnational corporations and, 197ff., 200-10, 227. See also arms embargo, Carter Administration, Department of State, voluntary embargo.

Marcus, Stanley J., 233

Marder, Murray, 173

Markey, Congressman Edward, 237

Martin, Sir Richard, 27

McHenry, Donald, 134-5

mercenaries, 109ff.; foreign, 116-8, 125ff.; U.S. government and, 125, 127, 128; in Congo (Kinshasa)/Zaire, 95, 97, 101. See also mercenarization.

mercenarization, 110ff., 111-3, 113-4; and foreign policy, 113-4; in Rhodesia, 110, 114-8; in South Africa, 110, 118-22; and third party states, 111; and transnational corporations, 112-3, 251, 204, 210; and U.S. government, 111-2, 123; white-collar, 112-3, 251

merchant banks, 215

MIDEASTFOR, 61ff.

Midland Bank, 215-6

Midland and International Banks, 215-6

Midlink-74 naval exercises, 68, 80

Military Balance, The, 134, 148-9, 158-9, 236

military capability of South Africa, 140ff.; and manufacturing, 140, 201-2

military expenditures: by South Africa, 140, 200-1; Western, 9

military intervention theories, 59-61

Mobil Oil, 8; and southern Africa, 212-3, 214

Mobutu, 68, 93-4, 96, 97

Morocco, 68, 78

Mossad, see Israeli intelligence service

Motorola, 208, 209, 231

Mozambique, 5, 8, 18, 41-2, 201; Rhodesian aggression against, 147-8, 246; Andrew Young on, 47-8; and covert activities, 91, 100

MPLA, 52, 96, 100, 102, 103

M. Samuels, 214-5

Mugabe, Robert, 52

Munitions List, 219

Mutual Security Act of 1954, 229

N

Namibia (South-West Africa), 5, 8, 54-5, 161, 193, 213, 226-7, 229, 242, 256; history, 31, 32ff.; and South African nuclear program, 174-5, 176, 188; SWAPO, 33, 52; Western strategy and, 33-4, 51-2, 245-6. See also Kalahari station.

Nairobi, Kenya, 64

NASA, 195

national liberation movements, 5, 7, 8, 10, 16-7, 193; and transnational corporate investments, 10; and Western strategy, 8 fn., 40, 43-4, 136. See also African National Congress of South Africa, MPLA, Patriotic Front, SWAPO of Namibia.

National Key Point Status, 207-8, 259ff.

National Security Council, 86, 87, 89, 93; the 40 Committee, 86-7, 98, 100, 102

National Security Study Memorandum, see NSSM

Nationalist Party, 22

NATO, 41-2, 67, 69, 70, 74, 249; see also Western governments, individual countries.

Natref, 8

Ndebele, 26

Netro, President Agostinho, 47

New Haven Advocate, 238

Newsom, David, 140, 230

Nigeria, 40

Nixon Administration, 40ff., 43, 59-60, 64-5, 89, 160, 227; and NSSM 39, 39, 150; and South Africa, 42, 43, 160. See also Departments of State and Commerce, Kissinger, Western governments.

Nixon Doctrine, 59-60

Nkomo, Joshua, 51

Nkrumah, Kwame, 97-8

North Atlantic Treaty Organization, see NATO

"North-South" relations, 10-11

NSSM 39, 41, 47, 91, 160

NSSM 104, 64

Nuclear Non-Proliferation Act, 184ff., 185-7

Nuclear Non-Proliferation Treaty, 189-90, 210

nuclear program of South Africa, 78, 174-5, 176ff., 188, 192-3; capability, 173, 178-71; Israel and, 182-4; France and, 172,

173-4, 180; Federal Republic of Germany and, 172-3, 174; France and, 172-3, 174, 180, 181-2; Namibia and, 174-5, 188; trade and, 42, 174, 178, 182, 187-8, 193-4, 246; transnational corporations and, 174, 188, 200, 210; United States and, 4, 42, 175, 176, 177-8, 187-94, 246; and uranium reserves, 79, 187-8, 193-4; and uranium enrichment plans, 174, 180-1, 210, 212
Nyerere, President Julius K., 55

O

OAU, see Organization of African Unity
Oberdorfer, Don, 173
October 1977 crackdown in South Africa, 178
Office of East-West Trade, 224
Office of Export Administration, 225, 226-7
Office of International Security Affairs, 224
Office of Legal Advisor, 224
Office of Munitions Control, 154, 224, 225
Oil, 67, 212ff.; U.S. investment in, 204, 212-3. See also individual companies.
oil from coal, 188, 212, 213
Olin, 166, 168, 238-9
OPEC, 9
Organization of African Unity, 178, 182
Oto Melara, 154, 167
OTRAG, 54

P

PAIGC, 111
Panama, 158
pass laws, 22ff.
pan-African military force, 68
Paratus, 161, 209-10, 232
Patriotic Front, 40, 52, 115
Pelindaba, 211
Persian Gulf, 113
Phoenix Associates of U.S. Marines, 126
Piaggio, 152
Picker International, 188
Piper, 238 fn.
Placid Oil, 212
Plowman, Walter S., 168
Polaris communications net, 61
population (chart), 116
Portugal, 40, 41, 79, 80; and covert activi-

ties, 90-1, 99, 101, 102
Procurement Act, 163, 203, 236
Projekt Advocaat, 181-2, 208
Project Syncom, 170
provisions of mandatory embargo, 233-4
Puma helicopters, 156

R

radio tracking station, 176
Rapid Reaction Strike Force, 171-2; see also, U.S. strike force
Raytheon Co., 212
recruitment of mercenaries, 126-7, U.S. laws against, 125
Reims, 167-8
Republic of South Africa, see South Africa
Resistance: in Namibia, 33; in South Africa, 23; in Rhodesia/Zimbabwe, 29. See also African National Congress of South Africa, national liberation movements, Patriotic Front, SWAPO of Namibia.
Rhodes, Cecil, 21, 24, 27
Rhodesia/Zimbabwe, 5, 8, 24ff., 54-5, 246, 256; secret arms sales to, 166, 167-8; so-called "internal settlement," 8, 50-1, 52, 116-7; and covert activities, 89, 95, 96, 97, 100; and Congo (Kinshasa), 95, 96, 97; transnational corporations and, 7-8, 42, 213, 214-5; U.S. policy and, 45ff., 49-51, 245
Rijn Schelde, 211
Rockefeller, Nelson, 10 fn.
Roebuck, 112
Rossing, 174-5
Rwanda, 92

S

Safari I, 188, 210
SAGE, see General Electric
San, 20
Sasol, 182, 212, 213
Sasol II, 212, 251
satellite tracking, 176
SATO, 79-81
Saudi Arabia, 52
Savimbi, Jonas, 112
secret arms trade, 135, 142ff., 145-6, 166
Senate Intelligence Committee, 94
Senegal, 68-9
Service de Documentation Exterieure et

Contre Espionage (SDECE), see France

Shaba, Zaire, 53-4, 58-9, 66-7, 256ff. See also Zaire.

Sharpeville massacre, 24

shotguns, export of, 230-4

Siemens, 211

Silvermine, 67, 69

Simonstown, 67, 69, 79, 80, 81, 208

Smith, Ian, 8

Soares, Mario, 101

Soldier of Fortune, 116-7, 126-7

Somalia, 66, 92

sources reporting on South African weapons systems, 234

South Africa, see under specific issue.

South African General Electric, see General Electric.

South Atlantic Treaty Organization, see SATO

Southeast Asia, 82-3, 97. See also Vietnam, Laos.

Southern Rhodesia, see Rhodesia/ Zimbabwe

South-West Africa, see Namibia

Soviet Union, see USSR

Soweto revolt, 24, 134-5

Special Coordinating Committee, see National Security Council, Central Intelligence Agency

Sperry Rand, 208, 209

Spinola, 99

Spie Batignolles, 211, 220

Standard Oil of California, 8, 214

STEAG, 164

Stevenson, Adlai, 139, 222-6

Stockwell, John, 83, 88, 90, 92, 94, 96, 104

Strijdom, 22

strike force, see U.S. strike force, 60-1, 74-5

Subcommittee on Africa, 188-9, 233

sub-imperialist powers, 7, 8, 241-3; South Africa and, 5, 7-8, 204-5

Sullivan principles, 206

Superior Oil Company, 212

Survival, 202

SWAPO of Namibia, 33, 40, 52, 190 fn.

Swaziland, 8, 233

Syracuse Oil, 212

T

Tanzania, 19, 92; see also Nyerere

Texaco, 8, 213-4

Texas Nuclear, 188

third country transshipment points, 154-5, 166-8, 238-9

third-party states and mercenarization, 111

Third World, 5, 7, 8

Toure, President Sekou, 98

trade unions, 22ff.

training of South African scientists in the U.S., 42, 189-90

transnational banks, 6, 7; in South Africa, 214-8; and South African government bonds, 216. See also Bank of America, Chase Manhattan, Citibank, loans to South Africa, and transnational corporations.

transnational corporations, 6; in southern Africa, 10, 245-7; in South Africa, 197ff.; and arms embargo, 231, 250. See also individual companies, transnational banks, nuclear program.

Tshombe, Moise, 95

U

Union Carbide, 8 fn.

Union of South Africa, 21; see South Africa

Union of Soviet Socialist Republics, see USSR

UNITA, 55, 87

United Kingdom, see Great Britain

United Nations, 64, 208, 222, 234-5; and Namibia, 33; arms embargo on South Africa, see arms embargo, mandatory embargo, voluntary embargo.

United Nations Participation Act, 234-5

United States, see under specific topics.

U.N. resolutions establishing arms embargoes, 253-5

U.S. Air Force, 209

U.S. attempts to split Patriotic Front, 52

U.S. Congress, 45, 63, 86

U.S. laws against mercenaries, 124

U.S. House of Representatives, 232-3; see also specific subcommittees

U.S. investment in South Africa, 48, 198ff.; by sector (table), 205

U.S. marines, 126

U.S. mercenaries in southern Africa, 124ff.; number, 125

U.S. Navy, 61, 63-5

U.S. Nuclear, 188, 211
U.S. Nuclear Regulatory Commission, 211
U.S. Senate, 65; see also specific subcom-
   mittees
U.S.-South Africa Agreement for Nuclear
   Cooperation, 185-6
U.S. Steel, 188
U.S. veto of economic sanctions on South
   Africa, 197-8, 234
USSR, 11, 64ff., 66, 70, 256ff.; Andrew
   Young on, 48-9; and CIA, 89, 98. See also
   anti-Sovietism in Carter Administration.
uranium enrichment program of South Af-
   rica, 78, 174, 180-1, 210, 212, 251
Valindaba, 180-1
Vance, Cyrus, 236
Vernon Craggs, 188
Verolme Vereinigde, 211
Verwoerd, 22
Vietnam, 8, 9, 10, 82-3, 97
Vorster, 22, 192
Voluntary embargo, 133-4, 136ff., 154,
   156ff., 220, 223, 236-9; U.N. resolution,
   253-4
Walvis Bay, 52
Warnke, Paul, 66-7

Watson, Jim, 232
Western governments, 5, 7, 10, 56, 58, 61ff.,
   123-4, 175; proposal on Namibia, 51-2
Westinghouse, 174 fn., 211; see Framatome
white-collar mercenarization, 112-3, 207,
   251

U
V
W
Y
Young, Andrew, 10 fn., 47-9, 191, 234

Z
Zaire, 53-4, 58-9, 66-7, 68, 78, 82, 84, 102,
   256ff.; and Binza group, 93-4; CIA in, 88,
   93-7, 101, 103; aid to FNLA, 103; rebel-
   lions in, 83, 92; Rhodesian and South Afri-
   can covert activities in, 95, 96, 97
Zambia, 29
ZANU (Patriotic Front), 52
ZAPU (Patriotic Front), 52
Zimbabwe, see Rhodesia/Zimbabwe
Zimbabwe Development Fund, 45, 47, 50
Zirconium of America, 188

The Contributors

Dovi Afesi, a Ghanaian, is assistant professor of History in the African American Studies Department of the University of Massachusetts at Amherst. He has taught and conducted research on southern Africa.

Courtland Cox, former secretary general of the Sixth Pan African Congress, is now treasurer of TransAfrica and co-director of the Emergency Fund for Southern Africa. He has extensively researched United States policy on southern Africa, including, while at the Center for National Security Studies, the Intelligence Report on covert action in Angola.

James Dingeman, a Ph.D. candidate in International Relations at Columbia University, has written articles for several military reviews, including *Strategy and Tactics,* relating to various aspects of United States military involvement in southern Africa.

Cynthia Enloe is professor of Government at Clark University. She has specialized in analyzing ethnic divisions in the military forces of various countries, and has written many articles and books, including *The Military, Police and Domestic Order: British and Third World Experiences* (London: Richardson Institute for Conflict and Peace Resolution, 1976).

Sean Gervasi is currently advisor to African delegations at the U.N. He has taught and researched at the London School of Economics, Oxford University, the University of Paris and City University of New York. He is author of a forthcoming book, *Portugal, the NATO Powers, and South Africa*, as well as other books and articles on economic and political developments on the continent.

Michael T. Klare is director of the Militarism and Disarmament Project of the Institute for Policy Studies, Washington, D.C.

Neva Seidman Makgetla is co-author of *South Africa and U.S. Multinational Corporations* (Lawrence Hill, 1977). She has written a number of articles on South Africa, and has co-authored a study on transnational corporate investment in South Africa for the U.N. Special Committee Against Apartheid, and participated in preparing reports for the U.N. Center on Transnational Corporations.

John Prados, a doctoral candidate in Political Science at Columbia University, specializes in international relations and military affairs. His interest in sealanes and the Indian Ocean was sparked by requests to expand the Diego Garcia base, and he has observed the evolution of events in that area since then with care.

Eric Prokosch is a staff member of National Action/Research on the Military-Industrial Complex (NARMIC), a project of the American Friends Service Committee, Philadelphia, Pa.

Ann Seidman, formerly visiting professor of Economics at the University of Massachusetts, is now Nancy Duke Lewis Professor of Sociology at Brown University, and co-chairs the research committee of the Association of Concerned African Scholars. She has conducted research and taught for eight years in Africa, and served as consultant to the U.N. Special Committee Against Apartheid and Center on Transnational Corporations.

Robert Sylvester is a lawyer with graduate training from Johns Hopkins University in United States foreign policy and international economics. His interest in Africa and knowledge of United States African policy results from three years of work in Congress as a legislative assistant for foreign affairs.

Ronald Walters, formerly chairman of the Department of Political Science and director of the Social Science Research Center at Howard University, is currently associate professor of Political Science there. He is a member of the board of directors of TransAfrica, and has authored over 20 articles and monographs on Africa, including *South African Nuclear Power: Military and Strategic Implications* (Social Science Research Center, Howard University).